COLLEGE OF MARIN LIBRARY
KENTFIELD, CALIFORNIA

D0908303

# THE EMERGENCE OF THE LABOUR PARTY
## 1880-1924

**HODDER AND STOUGHTON**
LONDON  SYDNEY  AUCKLAND  TORONTO

# THE EMERGENCE OF THE LABOUR PARTY
# 1880-1924
## ROGER MOORE

JN
1129
.L33

Moore, Roger
    The emergence of the Labour Party, 1880–1924
    1. Labour Party—History
    I. Title
    329.9'41      JN1129.L32

ISBN 0 340 17890 6 Boards
ISBN 0 340 17891 4 Paperback

First published 1978

Copyright © 1978 R. F. Moore

All rights reserved. No part of this publication may be
reproduced or transmitted in any form or by any means,
electronic or mechanical, including photocopy, recording,
or any information storage and retrieval system, without
permission in writing from the publisher.

Printed in Great Britain for Hodder and Stoughton Educational,
a division of Hodder and Stoughton Ltd,
Mill Road, Dunton Green, Sevenoaks, Kent,
by Hazell Watson & Viney Ltd, Aylesbury, Bucks

# Contents

# Acknowledgments

This book owes a good deal to the researches and writings of a number of scholars, in particular the work of two men, the late G. D. H. Cole and Henry Pelling, on whose findings I have freely drawn.

I would also like to thank the following for permission to make use of copyright material from the sources indicated:

EDWARD ARNOLD for the use of G. R. Smith *The Rise of the Labour Party* (1969) as a source of extracts from J. Bruce Glasier *William Morris and the Early Days of the Socialist Movement* (1921); the Annual Register of 1893; Herbert Morrison *An Autobiography* (1960); Beatrice Webb *Diaries* (1952); J. R. Clynes *Memoirs* (1937); Philip Snowden *An Autobiography* (1934); L. MacNeill Weir *The Tragedy of Ramsay MacDonald* (1938); Emanuel Shinwell *The Labour Story* (1953). B. T. BATSFORD M. Bruce *The Coming of the Welfare State* (3rd edition, 1966). ERNEST BENN E. Halevy *The Rule of Democracy 1905–14* (1961). BODLEY HEAD A. H. Marwick *The Deluge: British Society and the First World War* (1965). CAMBRIDGE UNIVERSITY PRESS J. Clapham *An Economic History of Modern Britain* (1932); M. Cowling *The Impact of Labour* (1971); A. M. McBriar *Fabian Socialism and English Politics* (1962). JONATHAN CAPE John Bowle *Politics and Opinion in the Nineteenth Century* (1954). CLARENDON PRESS Henry Pelling *The Origins of the Labour Party* (2nd edition 1965); H. A. Clegg, Alan Fox, A. F. Thompson *A History of British Trade Unions since 1889* Volume I (1964); Roy Gregory *The Miners and British Politics, 1906–14* (1968); *Dictionary of National Biography*; E. L. Woodward *The Age of Reform 1815–70* (2nd edition 1962); R. C. K. Ensor *England 1870–1914* (1936); A. J. P. Taylor *English History 1914–45* (1965). WILLIAM COLLINS Trevor Wilson *The Downfall of the Liberal Party* (1966). THE CO-OPERATIVE UNION G. J. Holyoake's pamphlet 'Rationalism' in the Holyoake Papers in the Union's library in Manchester. GRANADA PUBLISHING for MacGibbon and Kee L. J. MacFarlane *The British Communist Party: its Origins and Development until 1929* (1966). GEORGE G. HARRAP David Kirkwood *My Life of Revolt* (1935). HEINEMANN EDUCATIONAL BOOKS R. T. McKenzie *British Political Parties* (2nd edition, 1963). WILLIAM HEINEMANN M. A. Hamilton *Arthur Henderson* (1938). HISTORICAL ASSOCIATION F. C. Mather *Chartism* (1965). HUTCHINSON PUBLISHING GROUP R. K. Middlemas *The Clydesiders* (1965); J. R. Clynes *Memoirs* (1937). LABOUR PARTY Party Conference Proceedings; *The Book of the Labour Party* (1925). LONDON SCHOOL OF ECONOMICS Beatrice Webb *Diaries*. MACMILLAN Henry Pelling *A Short*

*History of the Labour Party* (1961) and *Popular Politics and Society in Late Victorian England* (1969); Frank Bealey and Henry Pelling *Labour and Politics 1900–1906* (1958); G. D. H. Cole *A History of Socialist Thought* (1952–60); A. Briggs and J. Saville *Essays in Labour History* (1960); E. H. Phelps Brown *The Growth of British Industrial Relations* (1959); D. Butler and J. Freeman *British Political Facts 1900–68* (3rd edition, 1969); S. B. Saul *The Myth of the Great Depression* (1969). METHUEN W. Ashworth *An Economic History of England 1870–1939* (1960); G. D. H. Cole and R. Postgate *The Common People* (4th edition, 1949); C. L. Mowat *Britain Between the Wars* (1956). PENGUIN BOOKS Henry Pelling *A History of British Trade Unionism* (1963, 1971). ROUTLEDGE AND KEGAN PAUL and A. M. Kelly G. D. H. Cole *A History of the Labour Party from 1914* (1948). ROUTLEDGE AND KEGAN PAUL G. D. H. Cole *British Working Class Politics 1832–1914* (1941); Royden Harrison *Before the Socialists: Studies in Labour and Politics 1861–81* (1965); Paul Thompson *Socialists, Liberals and Labour: the Struggle for London 1885–1914* (1967). TUC extracts from motions from the 1893, 1899 and 1914 Congresses. UNIVERSITY OF WALES PRESS K. O. Morgan *Wales in British Politics* (1970). WEIDENFELD AND NICOLSON E. J. Hobsbawm *Labouring Men: Studies in the History of Labour* (1964) and *Industry and Empire* (1968).

In addition to the above I have also made use of some short extracts from Philip Snowden's *Autobiography* originally published by Nicholson and Watson. It has been impossible to trace the present holder of the copyright for this material.

Most of the illustrations, including those on the cover and in the preliminary pages, are reproduced by kind permission of the Labour Party. I should like to express my thanks to the staff at Transport House, and in particular to Mrs. I. Wagner and Mrs. J. Samuel, for their invaluable assistance.

Other illustrations are reproduced by permission of Syndications International (for G.B.S. with Keir Hardie); Independent Labour Publications (formerly Independent Labour Party) for the 1895 Membership Certificate; London News Agency Photos (for the 1912 Labour Party Conference); and Barratt's Photo Press (for the Webbs with Arthur Henderson and the photograph of a group of Labour M.P.s taken after the 1922 election).

# *Part I*

## Introduction: The Roots of the Labour Party

### [1] The Traditions of the Labour Movement

In his memoirs, published in 1931, Robert Blatchford drew attention to the heterogeneous nature of the support the political Labour movement was attracting in the 1890s: 'To the ILP* came women and men from the ranks of Tories, Liberals, Radicals, Nonconformists and Marxians. . . . There were Free-Traders, Home Rulers, Local Optionists, Republicans, Roman Catholics, Salvationists, Church and Chapel-goers and believers in the cosmopolitan brotherhood of the workers.' In essence, he was stating a profound truth about the Labour Party which even today is perhaps still not fully understood not only by its more unfriendly critics but even by some of its own supporters. The Labour Party was no mere sectional pressure group simply called into being to act as the instrument or the cat's-paw of the trade union movement, although inevitably the latter played a decisive role in its inception and development. On the contrary, the party embodied and derived inspiration from a number of different sources and traditions dating back to the turn of the eighteenth and nineteenth centuries.

The earliest and perhaps the most obvious of these was that of radical secularism which first sees the light of day in the writings of Tom Paine. Paine, hated and vilified in his day as a renegade, was not a great or original thinker, deriving many of his ideas from the free-thinkers of the eighteenth-century enlightenment. Moreover, he tended to oversimplify issues and at times gives the impression of being not entirely in touch with reality, but his easily understood, often witty style was to ensure his ideas a wide circulation long after his death. The main themes in his work are twofold: an attack on Christianity coupled with a demand for democratic republicanism. Christianity he reckoned was a parody, a perversion of a religion: 'As an engine of power, it serves the purpose of despotism; and as a means of wealth, the avarice of priests; but so far as respects the good of man in general, it leads to nothing

* See Appendix I, List of Abbreviations (p. 200).

E.L.P.—I*

here or hereafter.' (*The Age of Reason*, Part 2, 1795.) And as for man's good on this earth, Paine had much to propose. Not only did he argue for a recasting of the political system with a republican form of government based on manhood suffrage, he also had plans for a large-scale social reconstruction containing suggestions that were to recur in the socialist programmes of a century later. Thus he anticipated the followers of the Henry George school that the land was part of the 'natural right' of the whole community and not the exclusive possession and privilege of a small class. Admittedly he did not suggest nationalisation, but rather compensation for the poor for the loss of those rights, partly through the poor rate and partly by payment of a lump sum of £15, accompanied by an annual pension of £10. It should further be noted that the considerable sums of money necessary for this modest exercise in redistribution were to be raised by a 10 per cent death duty on the propertied classes.

The impact of Paine's work and ideas was naturally heightened by the fact that he was writing at a time of crisis and upheaval with events across the Channel very much in people's minds and the whole situation complicated by the outbreak of a European war involving Great Britain and revolutionary France. Thus the many radical clubs and societies which sprang up in the 1790s were inspired by him and gave him publicity while often making a contribution of their own to advanced thought. In particular, their anti-clericalism was most marked as instanced by the popularity of the Republican saying: 'May the last king be strangled in the entrails of the last priest.' The most prominent of these was the London Corresponding Society, founded in 1792 by a group led by the shoemaker Thomas Hardy, and having links with similar bodies in a number of provincial centres, particularly Manchester, Stockport, Norwich and Sheffield. In addition to a demand for democracy—annual parliaments based on manhood suffrage—the society also campaigned for what might be called a moderate socialist programme. Thus the points made in its 'Address to the People' in August 1792: 'taxes diminished, the necessaries of life more within the reach of the poor, youth better educated, prisons less crowded . . . old age better provided for'. With this platform and a fairly well developed system of organisation and propaganda, some historians have argued that this was the very first truly working-class political group. But this view does not entirely command acceptance, for others have been quick to point out that only a comparatively small section of the working class, the skilled artisans, was involved, and that it had no appeal to the mass of the labourers. Nonetheless, in spite of such doubts, we can at least go along with Professor Briggs, when, writing of the society's leaders, he claims they 'pointed the way forward to the development of working-men's politics in the nineteenth century, particularly to Chartism'.

In the period after the Napoleonic war, the anti-religious tradition of Paine was publicised to an even wider audience by a number of Radical journalists, prominent amongst whom was Richard Carlile. In 1818, he published a new edition of the *Age of Reason*, together with others of Paine's writings, and secured valuable publicity by getting himself prosecuted for both blasphemy and sedition. He lost his case and finished up in gaol for six years but the stimulus to sales was undeniable: 2,000 copies of the *Age of Reason* were sold in a period of six months and the circulation of his own journal the *Republican* rocketed to some 15,000 per week. If anything, his condemnation of religion was even more forthright than Paine's; in his view, 'all religious notions in all their degrees must properly be termed a species of madness'. (*Address to Men of Science*, 1821.) Also in this period, Robert Owen was beginning to publicise his proposals for a new social order and, while we shall delay consideration of these, it is important to notice that he too was a part of this secularist tradition. Thus in a public meeting at the London Tavern in August 1817 he attacked religion—all religions in fact—as being based on errors and having 'made man the most inconsistent and most miserable being in existence'.

The imprisonment of Carlile and other journalists and the decline of the Owenite movement from the middle 1830s onwards did not mean that their tradition was lost. On the contrary it found continued expression in the writings of G. J. Holyoake and the Secularist movement. He first came into prominence with some remarks made off the cuff at a lecture at Cheltenham in 1842, which resulted in his being accused, condemned and imprisoned for six months on a charge of blasphemy. In 1845 he published a tract, *Rationalism, a Treatise for the Times* which was largely a rehash of Owen's *Book of the New Moral World* and which contained this searing indictment of religion: '. . . man, to all practical purposes, [is] a purely material being—other systems have chiefly spiritualised him. It would have been well if they had spiritualised his miseries, but they have only refined into nothings his happiness, and left his wrongs and wretchedness solid, material, and enduring.' There is, however, a paradox here. Secularist pamphlets might well proclaim that 'human nature is improvable under well understood conditions . . .

[and] that the dependence or the well-being of one depends on all', but this was not a veiled call for state intervention to improve social conditions. Rather, it was merely another manifestation of the favourite mid-Victorian doctrine of 'self-help'. In politics, Holyoake—and his more famous successor, Bradlaugh—were true Liberals who, while encouraging the idea of labour representation, stood firmly by the principles of individualism. For instance in 1856, Holyoake in a public debate on total abstinence committed himself to the view that 'the world is too much governed'. Yet having said that, the fact remains that the National Secular Society played an important part in the revival of English socialism in the 1880s. In 1884, Bradlaugh, then the president of the Secularists and at the height of his influence, met H. M. Hyndman in public debate on the motion 'Will socialism benefit the English people?' This encounter resulted in a general controversy amongst Secularists throughout the country in the mid 1880s, and many now changed their allegiance, entering the socialist movement in one way or another. Thus, John Burns who had been a regular speaker at Secularist meetings in Battersea, now joined the new Social Democratic Federation and an even more prominent catch for socialism was Annie Besant who joined the Fabians in 1885 and later involved herself in the development of the 'new unionism' in the late 1880s.

Finally, in outlining this continuous anti-religious tradition in the nineteenth-century labour movement, we should notice Robert Blatchford. One of its most colourful and perhaps rather under-estimated personalities, Blatchford, was a journalist and a propagandist of considerable effect. He edited the *Sunday Chronicle* in Manchester for a time and then in 1891 launched the *Clarion*. His criticisms of religion, and Christianity in particular, were violent and to the point: 'In such a world as this, friend Christian, a man has no business reading the Bible, singing hymns and attending divine worship. He has not time.' In short, what he and indeed all the others back to Paine were saying was this: that religion, Christianity, at best has no relevance to the real everyday world; at worst it could be a positive barrier to human progress. And these sentiments had a powerful appeal to a significant body of nineteenth-century working-class opinion.

This development of religious disillusion was detected by some contemporaries in the 1840s. Engels in 1844 commented: 'All bourgeois writers are agreed that the workers have no religion and do not go to church. Exceptions to this are the Irish, a few of the older workers, and those wage-earners who have one foot in the middle-class camp—

overlookers, foremen and so on.' The reports of other observers seem to confirm this. Thus a school inspector writing in 1846 calculated that nearly half the population of Bilston in the Black Country 'neglect the public ordinances of religion', and in the same year, the vicar of Leeds was even more pessimistic: 'Not one in a hundred attends any place of worship.' Furthermore, impressive statistical backing was provided by the census of 1851, which put non-attendance as high as 60 per cent throughout England and Wales and almost 75 per cent in London. Horace Mann, the census reporter, drew attention to the 'negative inert indifference' to religion, and how 'especially in cities and large towns it is observable how absolutely insignificant a portion of the congregation is composed of artisans'. In the second half of the century, the decline seemed to have been reversed and by 1900, numbers of church attenders had risen. But so too had the population and proportionally speaking, the churches had only just about held their own: about 25 per cent of the population overall regularly attending a place of worship. The Church of England seemed particularly affected: for example, surveys carried out in London in the last fifteen years of the century indicated a decline of 150,000 and almost all of it attributable to losses from Anglican congregations.

In the face of such facts, it may at first sight seem perverse for historians such as Eric Hobsbawm to argue that there was still a strong working-class religious tradition which contributed significantly to the modern labour movement. Yet this was indeed the case and a strong innate religious feeling could co-exist quite happily with the infidel tradition. Samuel Bamford, describing his family's part in the early radical movement, gives striking confirmation of this: 'My father . . . read . . . Paine's *Rights of Man* . . . *Age of Reason* and his other theological works, but they made not the least alteration to his religious opinions. Both he and my uncle had left the society of Methodists, but to the doctrines of John Wesley they continued adherents so long as they lived.' Moreover there is other evidence to support the theory.

For example, while the Anglican Church clearly lost touch with the working classes in the nineteenth century, the dissenting sects made some progress. These were the Wesleyan Methodists, even more the Primitive Methodists who split off from the parent church in 1810, the Unitarians, the Congregationalists and the Quakers. They were able to retain some appeal for the working class in a way that the established church did not. Their more emotionally fervent forms of service perhaps fulfilled a deep rooted need amongst people whose worlds had been turned upside down by the industrial revolution. In addition, theirs was a more democratic tradition than that of the Anglican Church which was too closely identified with the state and the existing social order which seemed intent on grinding the working classes down. In time dissent lost this advantage. It became more closely identified with the employing class, it became more 'respectable', and inevitably the working class withdrew their confidence. Keir Hardie, writing in 1894, explained the reason clearly: 'They would often find even the churches marked off in sections, one part for those who did not care to associate with the common herd. . . . They were sometimes asked why the working-man did not attend church, but was it to be wondered at?'

But while the average working-man might distrust, with good reason, formal institutionalised Christianity, further evidence of at least a residue of religious feeling is provided by that strange phenomenon that emerged alongside the Independent Labour Party in the 1890s, the Labour Church movement. In essence, this appears to have been the brainchild of a Unitarian minister born in Cambridgeshire, John Trevor. He, like many ministers, was particularly distressed by the growing evidence of what he called 'the frightful gulf between the Churches and the World' but, unlike most of his fraternity, he tried to meet the problem by an entirely fresh initiative. This involved nothing less than the creation of a network of so-called 'Labour Churches'. Trevor opened the first congregation in October 1891 and at its height there were some fifty individual bodies, mainly in the north, affiliated to the Union of Labour Churches. Admittedly these were scarcely religious organisations in the conventional sense of promoting belief in a deity; rather, as Trevor himself put it, 'the Labour Church demands no acceptance of a religious belief from its members. . . . It makes life and work the basis of union rather than a confession of faith.' It must also be pointed out that this was a mushroom growth whose life was short, reaching its peak in the middle 1890s. It had declined to virtually nothing by the opening years of the present century. Yet, having due regard to such provisos, it is difficult to deny Hobsbawm's conclusion that such a movement would have been quite impossible had not religion still counted for something in the working-class strata of society.

In practical terms, this religious tradition expressed itself in a number of ways. It has, for example, been suggested that the labour movement, on both the political and the industrial side, was profoundly affected by the organisational techniques of the Methodist Church. The 'class' meeting, the delegate conference, the travelling lecturer were all borrowed from the Methodists and adopted by the leaders of the working class throughout the nineteenth century. Also, it is often pointed out, the strong lay preaching tradition in the Methodist and other non-conformist connections was of immense value as it gave labour politicians valuable experience in the difficult art of public speaking. Nor was it just a matter of borrowing a form of organisation, for many of the pioneers of the labour movement openly admitted the influence of religion on them. This was particularly true of Keir Hardie, the founder of the ILP. In a sense there is something of the seventeenth century about Hardie with his belief that religion and politics were closely intertwined and his rejection of the materialist view that 'bread and butter were the end and the means' (*Labour Leader* January 1893). Not only was there a strong religious flavour to his oratory but, as contemporary reports make clear, he often conducted his political meetings more on the lines of an act of worship. Thus, an ILP Council report of a meeting held in South Wales in 1898: 'The meeting was of a religious character, opened by a Hymn, Lesson and Prayer and Keir preached the sermon to a large and attentive audience.' Indeed, writing in the *British Weekly* in 1894, Hardie went so far as to 'claim for Socialism that it is the embodiment of Christianity in our industrial system.' Of his leading colleagues, Philip Snowden and Fred Jowett felt similarly, the former so much so that his emotional revivalist method of appealing for ILP recruits was jocularly nicknamed 'Philip's Come to Jesus!' Moreover the influence of religion showed itself in some very curious places. Firebrands like Tom Mann and Ben Tillett, who first came to prominence as leaders of the 1889 London dock strike, were not unaffected: Mann was a frequent speaker at Labour Church meetings, while Tillett proclaimed to a Unitarian conference in 1891 that he wanted 'churches where people could get what they needed'. Even within the ranks of secularist atheists who formed the backbone of the Social Democratic Federation, it was possible to find a man like George Lansbury whose devotion to the principles of the New Testament almost verges on the saintly. One could go on and on giving examples of such men—and women—who devoted their lives to the labour movement, but one final instance will perhaps suffice to drive the point home. In 1906, following the general election which brought into the House of Commons thirty 'Labour' MPs, the distinguished journalist, W. T. Stead, took it upon himself to present each of them with a questionnaire to elicit their views and outlook. Amongst the questions were two which asked which books had influenced them most and which religious belief they professed if any. In their answers to the first, many of them mentioned the Bible (while only two claimed to have been influenced by Karl Marx); to the second question the great majority expressed allegiance to one or other of the Methodist groups with a few Congregationalists thrown in for good measure.

But this religious tradition could have even more profound effects on the labour movement as a whole and not just on individuals. It may well have contributed significantly to the formulation of the high moral tone in foreign affairs and specifically an aversion to aggression. On a number of occasions in the later nineteenth and early twentieth centuries, the working class (or at least influential sections of it), have taken a stand to condemn what seemed morally unjustifiable foreign adventures, for instance: the support for Gladstone's campaign against Disraelian imperialism in the late 1870s; the opposition to the Boer War of 1899–1902; and, perhaps less convincingly, the ILP's condemnation of British action in 1914.

Finally, it could also be argued that this religious tradition, largely dissenting in character as it was, was an important factor which delayed the emergence of the Labour Party in British politics. Dissent, after all, tended to be very much orientated towards the Liberals and thus formed a powerful link between them and the working-class movement. Trade union leaders and even fiercely independent-minded men like Hardie felt the pull of Liberalism. Lib–Labism remained a force in British politics at least until 1914. Not until 1918, when Arthur Henderson and Sidney Webb gave Labour both a new organisation and a distinctive philosophy, was the break finally and irrevocably made. And then the dissenting tradition which had held Labour back so long worked in its favour by bringing into the movement most of that which was best in the Liberal Party.

But while religion had its part to play, of more fundamental importance was the emergence of a collectivist tradition dating from the early decades of the nineteenth century. This represented a reaction against laisser-faire capitalism and expressed the feeling that positive action must be taken by the community to redress the injustices and social evils suffered by the working class as a consequence of the economic system. Ironically enough, the earliest critics of this system seem to have derived a good deal of their inspiration from a man who was pledged to its maintenance, the economist David Ricardo. In his *Principles of Political Economy*, first published in 1817, Ricardo had argued that the chief measure of an object's value was the labour that had gone into it, a point that can be more easily accepted if one realises that he equated capital with stored labour. At the same time he also propounded the theory of subsistence wages which stated that wage rates were kept down to an absolute minimum sufficient merely for the labourer to exist to do his work. These ideas had the immediate result of provoking a series of attacks on the capitalist system during the 1820s. The anti-capitalist writers and propagandists, led by Thomas Hodgskin and William Thompson, concentrated on two main lines of thought. In the first place, it seemed to follow from Ricardo's theories that labour was the only factor in production and, as wages were kept at subsistence level, the whole surplus was going into the employers' pockets and the workers were being cheated of their just reward. In addition the system, by treating labour as a commodity affected by the laws of supply and demand, inevitably led to dehumanisation and callous indifference to working-class conditions. Moreover, it was argued that the unjust system of distributing wealth was in itself a cause of economic crisis by keeping down consumption. Only allow labour its due reward and consumption would rise dramatically, thus at a stroke providing social justice and economic stability. These ideas are of particular interest and importance, coming as they do almost a generation before Karl Marx formulated his theories and something like fifty years before Marxism was generally known in England.

It is, however, difficult to judge their immediate impact. Given the restricted circulation of the tracts and the low level of working-class literacy, it would appear to have been quite small. On the other hand Hodgskin may well have reached quite a wide audience through his lectures at the London Mechanics' Institute. But there is no doubt that in the long run they provoked a continuous train of thought as to the means of remedying the situation. Unfortunately when it came to practicalities there was a considerable divergence of opinion between those who advocated revolution, those in favour of taking over the system and altering it by peaceful political means and finally the followers of Robert Owen whose utopian visions we shall consider a little later. The clash of revolutionary and non-revolutionary ideals and indeed the ultimate resolution in favour of the latter is perhaps best illustrated by the case of Bronterre O'Brien, the Chartist. He had begun his active political career in opposition to William Lovett, the moving spirit in the London Working Men's Association and the framer of the Charter. In his advocacy of a working-class rising he derived much inspiration from the French revolution, in particular the activities of

Robespierre and Babeuf. But this did not last. By the 1840s there was little left of his revolutionary fervour: in 1841 he stood for Parliament and in 1848 he completely dissociated himself from the plans for violence. Finally, in the period after the Chartist collapse, he concerned himself with an organisation called the National Reform League and this body's proposals for nationalisation, Poor Law reform and education foreshadowed the demands of the socialist groups of the 1880s.

But the indictment of laisser-faire capitalism did not rest solely on the criticisms of a handful of economists and intellectuals. The unmistakeable evidence was there for all to see increasingly in the exploding towns of early nineteenth-century England. Industrialisation meant that not only was labour cheated of its just economic reward but was also subjected to grossly overcrowded living conditions coupled with an intensification of the twin evils of poverty and disease. The extent of the problem was brought to people's attention in the 1840s by a series of government reports: in 1840, that of the Select Committee on the Health of Towns; in 1842 on the Sanitary Condition of the Labouring Population; and in 1844–5, two documents from the Commission for Inquiring into the State of Large Towns and Populous Districts. But even before this comprehensive survey, there had been more immediate evidence in the form of a series of epidemics which could almost entirely be laid at the door of overcrowding and the limitations of the public utility services: cholera in 1831; typhus in 1837 and 1839; and smallpox in successive years from 1837 to 1840. And if the point needed driving home there were further severe outbreaks of typhus in 1847 and cholera in 1849.

It was evidence such as this which inevitably forced some reconsideration of the laisser-faire ethic even in its heyday. Thus the Benthamite utilitarians as a group were followers of Adam Smith, yet Edwin Chadwick, one of the most prominent of their number, was a strong advocate of state action at least in the field of public health. But this was only tentative and the real collectivist movement did not get going until a generation later. Once again it owed much to the force of circumstances. The continued rate of urbanisation and overcrowding and the fact that this was a serious threat to the community as a whole was brought home by renewed epidemics of typhus and cholera in the 1860s. Victorian opinion prided itself on its 'practical' nature and clearly something had to be done. The state, or possibly the local government authorities, were the only organisations capable of taking on the task. In addition, though, theoretical justification could be sought in the writings of T. H. Green with his argument that the individual was dependent to a considerable degree on the community and the latter had a responsibility to ensure that he lived a 'free' life. The general economic circumstances of the country also contributed to the change in attitude. While Britain was the 'workshop of the world' in the mid-Victorian years and there was an expanding market for British exports, there was much to be said for freedom from state interference. But in the late 1870s, the tune began to change and there was less talk of 'free trade' and more of 'fair trade'. Logically if government was to be asked to intervene to protect industry then it ought to concern itself equally with the interests of the labouring classes.

So the collectivist ideal came to be accepted and governments began to consider their responsibilities in the field of social reform. Even Gladstone, dyed-in-the-wool individualist as he was, felt the pressures and responded to them with a half-hearted attempt to establish a national system of education. Disraeli seemed more committed with a veritable flood of enactments in the early stages of his second ministry. At the local level, enlightened and energetic men like Joseph Chamberlain in Birmingham, A. J. Mundella in Sheffield and Henry Fowler in Wolverhampton were exponents of what came to be called 'municipal socialism'—the provision of effective public utility services for their towns.

The increasing insistence, then, of nineteenth-century working-class politicians on the use of the state to remedy grievances was neither original, nor was it due to the influence of Marx, although his writings undoubtedly reinforced the collectivist feeling. Further fuel was added to the fire by the slowness of the rate of improvement. Certainly it remains true that the idea of collective action was generally accepted by public opinion—as the Liberal Sir William Harcourt put it in 1894: 'We are all Socialists now!' On the other hand there was a world of difference between the theory and actually putting it into practice. Bad housing conditions still remained a serious problem in 1914 particularly in the north and the rate of tackling them in some areas had slowed almost to a halt. Thus the 1891 census classified 35·1 per cent of the population of Newcastle and 32·1 per cent of Sunderland as living in overcrowded conditions; by 1911 the former had dropped by a mere 3 per cent while in Sunderland the figure had actually risen, albeit marginally. In some inner London areas, the rate was even worse: Shoreditch and Finsbury for example were not far short of 40 per cent. Finally in Scotland, the 1911 census reckoned that 45·1 per cent of the population lived in one-room houses. Nor had much been done in some areas about the concomitant problem of sanitation and public health. A government *Report on Infant and Child Mortality* in 1910 declared: 'A large part of the densely populated parts of the counties of Durham and Glamorgan and certain parts of Lancashire, Staffordshire and Yorkshire, are in a profoundly lower condition as regards sanitation than other parts of England.' This was reflected most clearly in the infant mortality figures of the time. Whereas for England and Wales overall it was 12 per cent and even in heavily urbanised areas like Manchester, Leeds and Liverpool it was only a point or two higher, in parts of the Durham coal-field it was only just under 20 per cent and in the Potteries, South Wales and some of the textile towns of Yorkshire and Lancashire, there were instances where it was over that figure.

However, appalling as this state of affairs was, it cannot be assumed that the whole of the working class was necessarily enthusiastically in favour of state action as a solution. For a start, as has been pointed out both by nineteenth-century writers like Charles Booth and modern historians like Paul Thompson, economic hardship and social misery did not of themselves make for increased political awareness. Poverty has a stunting effect on the mind as well as the body and there is plenty of evidence that those in the worst conditions in Victorian England were often too apathetic to attempt any action. But apart from that, there was almost as much innate suspicion of collectivism amongst the working class as there was amongst committed laissez-faire individualists. After all, state action did not often bring much immediate benefit to those it was theoretically supposed to benefit. Compulsory education was resented as a restriction on a working-class family's capacity for earning. The much-vaunted slum clearance schemes under Disraeli's Act of 1875 certainly got rid of sub-standard housing but either did not replace the old with new houses, or if they did, at rents which the inhabitants could hardly afford. But most of all, there bulked large in the working-class mind the harsh intolerance, if not to say downright inhumanity, of the system of poor relief under the Poor Law Amendment Act of 1834. If this was the meaning of collectivism, then the working class was rightly unenthusiastic. Instead, the keenest advocates of social reform were found in the ranks of the socialist societies which emerged in the 1880s and 1890s, the Social Democratic Federation, the Fabian Society and the ILP. Significantly enough, the first two certainly, and even the latter to some degree, were dominated by middle-class converts to the cause of labour. Nonetheless, in spite of this important proviso, the collectivist ideal was an important feature of nineteenth-century working-class politics.

The final tradition that can be traced with a fair measure of continuity is a strong element of what can be described best as romantic idealism. In some cases, this tended to be rather backward looking, casting fond lingering glances at a golden age which had never really existed. This was particularly true of William Cobbett in the earlier part of the nineteenth century. Through the columns of his *Political Register*, he hammered away passionately at the obvious evils of industrialism. Echoing Paine, he argued that the poor had been robbed of their rights by the upper classes and he consistently paraded the stability and other virtues of the pre-industrial society. He was, in short, one of nature's 'conservatives' and, had it not been for the blindly repressive policies pursued by Tory governments after 1815, he could quite happily have lined up with them against the selfish Whig-based manufacturing interests.

But not everybody was looking backwards in despair. Robert Owen, for example, was looking very much to the future. A successful industrialist himself, he had high hopes that industry could solve the social problems provided that human needs were not subordinated to it. The answer was to organise communities which were not too big and which, while depending mainly for their living on industrial production, were not to be entirely divorced from agriculture. He thus postulated the establishment of 'villages of cooperation' which would contain between 500 and 1,500 people and would each need between 1,000 and 1,500 acres for their support. The scheme depended for its success on Owen's belief that he could change human nature by means of a change of environment and an intensive system of education in the acceptance of cooperative and socialist principles. It goes without saying that this utopian vision never materialised. Owen himself went to the United States in the early 1820s where he set up a trial run at New Harmony in Indiana, but within three years it had failed. On his return to Britain he associated himself with a number of trade unionists in the formation of the Grand National Consolidated Trades Union in 1834 in the hopes that this might prove a more effective instrument for his views. Unfortunately this project too collapsed in ignominy within a year and all that remained of Owenism were the cooperative trading schemes such as the famous Rochdale enterprise—a development which earned his profound disgust and contempt.

Despite Owen's failure the ideal of building a new and better world was not entirely lost. Indeed, towards the end of the nineteenth century it was powerfully revived by two men, William Morris and Robert Blatchford. Morris was an artist and poet who lived in comfortable middle-class circumstances but who had been converted to socialism mainly by the appalling ugliness of industrialisation. His commitment was almost purely emotional. At a lecture in Glasgow in 1884, he was asked if he accepted Marx's theory of value. His reply revealed his philosophy in a nutshell: 'To speak quite frankly, I do not know what Marx's theory of value is, and I'm damned if I want to know . . . political economy is not in my line, and much of it appears to me to be dreary rubbish. . . . It is enough political economy for me to know that the idle class is rich and the working class is poor, and that the rich are rich because they rob the poor.' Like Cobbett, he tended to look backwards to the mythical 'golden age' which he placed in the Middle Ages, mainly, it appears, because of his respect for the tremendously high standards of craftsmanship. But, at the same time, like Owen, he looked forward to 'the establishment . . . of a system of cooperation'. A system where life and work would be happy and where 'all men would be living in equality of condition and would manage their affairs unwastefully and with full consciousness that harm to one would mean harm to all—the realisation at last of the meaning of the word Commonwealth.'

As for Blatchford, he, like Morris, was angered by the waste of industrialism and the squalor of social conditions. His suggestions were more practical than those of Morris, but even so there is more than a touch of the visionary. 'I would stop the smoke nuisance. . . . I would have the towns rebuilt with wide streets, with detached houses, with gardens and fountains and avenues. . . . I would have public parks, public theatres, music halls, gymnasiums, football and cricket fields, public halls and public gardens for recreation and music and refreshment.' And unlike Morris, whose views were largely confined to a fairly close, rather esoteric circle, these demands had a wide circulation. Blatchford's expertise as a journalist saw to that and his hopes for the future, published in 1894 in the form of the book *Merrie England*, sold three-quarters of a million copies within a year.

The labour movement then in the nineteenth century encompassed all of these long-standing traditions and all made their contribution to the emergence of the party. It is very clear that they add up to a rather peculiar combination of reason and sentiment, of awareness of the practical necessity to relieve harsh social circumstances combined with emotional appeals to the brotherhood of man. It is this sort of mixture which makes the Labour Party unique in British politics and has allowed it to grow into a great party instead of remaining the voice of a sectional pressure group. But there is one factor which must not be forgotten in the attempt to elucidate these traditions. While the writings and speeches of philosophers, publicists and journalists were important in expressing feelings and touching unsuspected chords in men's souls, there was already present in many working men and women a natural instinct that they deserved better than they were getting. Thus, W. C. Taylor, following a tour of Lancashire in 1842, reported hearing many working-men express the opinion 'that [they had] a right to a better condition inasmuch as [they] had taken a part in raising society to the condition which established a higher average of comfort than that which [they] could attain.' In short, society's failure to recognise this claim in the course of the nineteenth century is probably the most important single cause of the emergence of the British Labour Party in its last two decades.

## [2] Working-class Politics before 1880

In 1861, Richard Cobden drew attention to what he considered to be the deplorably quiescent state of working-class politics. In slightly exaggerated terms, he demanded if there was 'no Spartacus among them to head a revolt of the slave class against their political tormentors?' and he added, by way of explanation, 'I suppose it is the reaction from the follies of Chartism that keeps them so quiet.' Cobden was only partly right in his appreciation of the situation. It certainly was true that working-class political activity was limited following the collapse of the Chartists in 1848, but it was not entirely non-existent in the 1850s and moreover was to revive only a short time after Cobden had delivered his verdict. Even less justified was his dismissal of Chartism as an aberration which failed as a result of stupidity.

The significance of Chartism in nineteenth-century labour history is considerable and lies in the fact that it was the first purely working-class political movement with working-class leaders. Moreover, as far as possible, it was particularly concerned to maintain its independence from the middle class. William Lovett made the point very clearly in his autobiography: 'We were the more induced to try the experiment as the working classes had not hitherto evinced that discrimination and independent spirit in the management of their political affairs which we were desirous to see. . . . [They] were taught to look up to "great men" . . . rather than to great principles. We wished, therefore, to establish a political school of self-instruction among them, in which they should accustom themselves to examine great social and political principles, and by their publicity and free discussion help to form a sound and healthful public opinion throughout the country.' But while this was indicative of a considerable degree of class consciousness, paradoxically it did not necessarily mean class solidarity. While large sections of the working class were drawn into the Chartist ranks at one time or another in the ten years it flourished, there were marked variations in enthusiasm for the cause. Thus, those engaged in the old domestic out-working system like the handloom weavers and the framework knitters were much more radical in their feelings than the factory operatives. A similar comparison could be drawn between the craftsmen engaged in old-established industries like tailoring and shoe-making and those in the new engineering industries. Furthermore there were geographical divisions: for example, the grievances arising out of the Poor Law Amendment Act were much more marked in the north than in the south where that measure was rather more readily accepted. Yet the *Annual Register* of 1839 was not exaggerating when it described Chartism as 'an insurrection which is expressly directed against the middle classes' and when Cobden wrote of 'the follies of Chartism' he was clearly referring to its refusal to cooperate with his manufacturers' interest group, the Anti-Corn Law League. The Chartists of Sunderland probably spoke for most when they rebuffed the local Leaguers' approach in the following terms: 'You are the holders of power, participation in which you refuse us; for demanding which you persecute us. . . . We are therefore surprised that you should ask us to cooperate with you.' There was too a shrewd and justified suspicion that one of the main motives of the manufacturers in agitating for repeal was that this would provide an excuse for a general reduction of wages. In the circumstances, a certain antipathy between the two organisations was inevitable and for a time during the years 1839–41 feelings ran so high that the Chartists deliberately set out to break up their opponents' meetings.

In the final resort the collapse of Chartism was the result of a combination of innate weaknesses and unfavourable circumstances. There was, for example, a serious failure of leadership. It was not simply a case of the alleged division between the 'physical force' school and those who opposed them. More serious was the inadequacy of Lovett and the growing influence of the demagogue Feargus O'Connor whom E. L. Woodward has gone so far as to call 'the ruin of the Chartist movement'. The damage done by the latter was perhaps decisive: his blustering, wild oratory; his mistaken belief that he could bluff the government into surrender in 1848; and the abysmal failure of his land settlement schemes. On the other hand it should not be forgotten that the political deck was very much stacked against Chartism. In spite of the Reform Act of 1832, the House of Commons had not changed a great deal, and, as the events of 1839, 1842 and 1848 showed only too clearly, it was not prepared to make any concession to working-class demands. Nor, thanks to the franchise, was there any real chance of securing the return of a sufficient number of Chartist MPs to bring pressure to bear. In electoral terms, they had but one success when O'Connor won one of the seats in the two-member constituency at Nottingham in 1847. But even this proved transitory since, when O'Connor was adjudged insane, his successor, Charles Sturgeon, failed to retain it in 1852.

But what probably did as much as anything to ensure the decline and ultimate disappearance of Chartism was the improvement in the economic situation at the end of the 1840s. We have already touched on the fact that the Chartists lacked coherence due to the variability of commitment to the cause, and what above all seems to have kept the movement together was economic adversity. The decade 1836–46 was one of prolonged depression but at its end the so-called 'hungry forties' gave way to a period of rapid economic progress which brought tangible benefits to a substantial section of the working class. Real wages were going up from 1850 onwards and the general mood of well-being was only temporarily broken by the crisis of 1857. Here indeed was the real explanation of working-class political apathy rather than any reaction to the so-called 'follies of Chartism'. Even as early as 1850 it was possible for Palmerston to take rather complacent pride in 'the example of a nation in which every class in society accepts with cheerfulness the lot which Providence has assigned to it'. The improvement in living conditions had weakened the embattled class consciousness which had been one of the main driving forces of Chartism. Now, instead of joining agitation for political change, most active working-men preferred to devote their energies to the organisation of the 'new model' unions and the burgeoning cooperative movement. But this was not entirely the case. Though Chartism had appeared to die the death in 1848, some of

O'Connor's leading associates tried to keep the movement going for some years after this collapse through the medium of a body called the National Charter Association. Prominent amongst these was Ernest Jones who in both personal and doctrinal terms was very close to Karl Marx. In his view the class struggle was to be pursued through the medium of the trade unions which he regarded as the best means of inculcating class consciousness. Given the attitudes of the leaders of 'new model' unionism, it is not surprising that he found this a particularly unrewarding field of endeavour. Nor, equally unsurprisingly, was he any more successful in his electoral ventures. On two occasions, 1857 and 1859, he stood in O'Connor's old constituency, Nottingham, in vain attempts to regain the seat. Almost unrelieved failure over ten years finally had its result, and by 1860 Jones had given up the struggle and retired from active political life.

With the final extinction of Chartism an important phase in labour politics came to an end. In the twenty-five years following the passage of the First Reform Act, the predominant theme had been independence: the belief that political activity in pursuit of economic and social improvement should be carried out on an aggressively class basis. There was comparatively little enthusiasm for the idea of cooperation with the middle class in putting pressure on the landed classes who still largely monopolised political power. However when the labour movement's interest in politics began to revive in the 1860s under the stimulus of a new reform controversy, it was this idea which was to hold the field. Generally working-class politicians thought mainly in terms of cooperating with the middle-class radicals who were to form an important element in the newly emerging Liberal Party. This in effect was the origin of Lib–Labism and the clash of Lib–Labs and 'independent' Labour men was a marked and significant feature of left wing politics until the First World War.

But although the Lib–Labs might be in the ascendant in the twenty years 1860–80, this does not mean that the independent idea entirely disappeared. There were in fact two brief attempts on these lines in the early 1870s. One was the work of the positivist, Professor E. S. Beesly, who had begun to interest himself in working-class politics some ten years previously. He was particularly concerned by what he considered to be the over-close cooperation of certain figures in the trade union movement with the Liberal Party. The other arose from the activities of John Hales, a prominent figure in the English branch of Karl Marx's First International. As with Ernest Jones' efforts in the 1850s, neither of these had much likelihood of success and the only sense in which they were historically significant was the stress all three laid on the importance of basing an independent working-class party on the trade unions.

It could be argued that the true pioneers of the idea of Lib–Labism were Francis Place and Thomas Attwood, both of whom had been particularly concerned to secure working and middle-class cooperation at the time of the reform crisis of 1832. The former had also been prominent in the vain efforts to secure an understanding between the Chartists and the Anti-Corn Law League. The arguments in favour of such an alignment were deceptively compelling. In spite of the romantic theories of Tories like Disraeli, it seemed to make sound political sense for the working and middle classes to combine to secure a further extension of the franchise, and perhaps the secret ballot, thus shaking the predominance of the landed classes. Unfortunately the chances of agreement on economic and social issues were not so good. Free trade and retrenchment, the watch-words of the middle-class radical, made little appeal to those sections of the working classes who were sufficiently articulate to express an opinion. There were fears that the former would create difficulties for British industry and thus inevitably make life harder for the British workman. As for the latter, Cobden's schemes for cutting government expenditure involved amongst other things putting workers in government establishments on the much resented piece-work system and also a reduction in the armed forces which, it was feared, would flood the labour market. More serious even was the commitment of many middle-class radicals to a general laissez-faire philosophy which viewed any state interference in industry with distaste. As employers moreover this was the class most actively engaged in the exploitation of the workers. It cannot have escaped the attention of some thoughtful men that one of the bitterest opponents of the legislation to reduce factory hours in 1847 and 1850, was Cobden's closest colleague, John Bright. But, for the time being, such considerations did not seem to matter and in the 1860s and 1870s, working-class politicians generally aimed at an entente with the Liberal Party. Three distinct phases can be discerned in this period: the close cooperation in the reform agitation of the 1860s; the disagreements and tensions aroused by the issue of the labour laws; and the apparently triumphant resolution of these difficulties by the end of the 1870s.

The initiative for a new labour political movement came in the early years of the 1860s, mainly from a group of 'new model' trade union leaders who were later nicknamed the 'Junta' by Sidney and Beatrice Webb: William Allen of the Amalgamated Society of Engineers; Robert Applegarth of the Carpenters; George Odger of the Shoe-makers; Daniel Guile of the Ironfounders; and Edwin Coulson of the Bricklayers' Union. The group had been instrumental in forming the London Trades Council in 1860 with the prime objective of keeping 'watch over the general interests of labour, political and social, both in and out of Parliament'. In pursuit of their political ends, they had formed in 1862 an organisation called the Trade Union Political Union which a year later was renamed, somewhat clumsily, the Man-hood Suffrage and Vote by Ballot Association. If it did nothing else, the name certainly indicated the movement's main aims, but it was later deemed that something handier was desirable, so in 1865 it finally emerged as the National Reform League. The significant point about this organisation was that, although it was basically trade union orientated, it was open to membership of middle-class sympathisers.

The trend towards cooperation was further strengthened by the fact that for some time already other trade union and working-class leaders had cooperated with middle-class radicals in the establishment of local reform associations. One of the earliest examples was the Northern Reform Union, established in 1857, in which John Kane of the Iron-workers was a prominent member. Two years later, Benjamin Lucraft, well known in London trade union circles, became the secretary of the North London Political Union, and in 1860 a Midland Counties' Reform Association was formed with trade union participation. Eventu-ally from these and other bodies there emerged the predominantly middle-class Reform Union in which Kane and others were closely in-volved. Between them, the League and the Union applied a good deal of pressure on the government and it is not unfair to say that this made some significant contribution to the passage of the 1867 Reform Act. At this stage the League, believing its work completed, dissolved itself. The Union remained in existence as an auxiliary of the new Liberal Party in which the middle and working classes could combine against the old guard Whig aristocrats.

However, hardly had the League's decision been taken when cir-cumstances compelled the trade union leadership to reconsider the matter. Of late the unions had been coming under increasing pressure and now the situation attained something of the dimensions of a crisis. Part of the trouble was the weak legal position of the unions, the result of the unfair operation of the Master and Servant Law by which it was a criminal offence for a workman to break his contract whereas similar action by the employer only rendered him liable to civil proceedings. Now in addition, three developments seemed to threaten the very existence of British trade unionism. The first was the slump which began in the City in 1866 and rapidly spread to affect most of industry in the following year. This not only weakened the unions' bargaining position through the rise in unemployment, but also precipitated a campaign of denigration with the argument that it was the fault of demands for higher wages which made British goods less competitive abroad. The second factor was a series of incidents in the Sheffield area in which violence was offered by trade unionists to alleged 'black-legs' in the cutlery industry. This culminated in the destruction of a workman's house by dynamite in October 1866, triggering off a general anti-union campaign in the newspapers. Finally, there was the blow of the judgment handed down in the famous case of *Hornby* v *Close* in 1867. The case arose out of the embezzlement by the secretary of £24 from the funds of the Bradford branch of the Boilermakers' Society. On suing for restitution, the union found its funds were not protected by the 1855 Friendly Societies' Act and, if this were not bad enough, the court held that as organisations 'in restraint of trade', unions were illegal, though not necessarily criminal, bodies.

The disturbing nature of these events led to an immediate resumption of political activity by the trade unions. The initiative was taken not by the Junta but by an energetic working-class journalist, George Potter, who had previously attempted to build up a personal body of support in the trade union movement. Already in 1866 he had formed the London Working Men's Association 'to procure the political enfranchisement of the workers and promote the social and general interests of the industrial classes'. Now, in November 1867, the LWMA issued a manifesto, signed by twenty-four leading trade unionists, calling on all working-class organisations to work for the return of working men to Parliament. The general election of the following year allowed Potter and his friends the chance to put this policy into practice.

From the first it is clear that they had no intention of trying to form a new 'independent' party. While their programme contained demands for trade union rights, a reduction of hours and better working conditions, these merely gave the impression of being hurriedly tacked on as an afterthought. Its basis was a series of proposals all too faithfully reflecting the anti-landlord, nonconformist principles of the middle-class radicals. Further, in the election the LWMA went out of its way to

avoid a clash with the Liberal Party. The most obvious instance of this
was George Odger's withdrawal from the contest at Chelsea. Chelsea
was a two-member constituency at the time, and there was a strong
well-organised working-class element who wanted Odger to run in
harness with the popular radical candidate, Sir Charles Dilke. Unfortunately there was a Whig candidate in the field for official Liberal
backing and he refused to stand down. Accordingly a sort of conciliation board was hastily set up to deal with the matter and this body
recommended that Odger give way. In the interests of working-class/
radical unity he agreed, but the decision caused a good deal of annoyance amongst his erstwhile supporters and there were rumours that he
had been bribed. In the end only three LWMA candidates actually went
to the polls: George Howell at Aylesbury; W. H. Cramer at Warwick;
and William Newton at Tower Hamlets. None of them was successful
and the failure was quickly followed by the collapse of the organisation.

But this was not the end of the story. The members of the Junta, who
had hitherto stood aloof from Potter's scheme, were now persuaded by
the mediation of two radical barristers, R. M. Latham and F. W.
Campin, to join with him in a new venture in working-class representation. Opinion in the newly founded TUC favoured the idea and the
result was the establishment of the Labour Representation League in
1869. This body also continued the traditions of Lib–Labism insofar as
its membership was open to all and not just working-men. Its president,
until 1875, was Latham, and its general aim was to secure the adoption
of working-class candidates by the local Liberal associations. Unfortunately it soon exhibited serious weaknesses. It lacked a really clear, well
defined programme, and it was entirely London based with no following in the northern industrial districts. Worst of all, the idea of cooperation was soon subjected to considerable strain. The fact of the
matter was that middle-class constituency parties were unwilling to
accept a 'labour' candidate not just because they felt this to be socially
undesirable, but also on grounds of expense, since the LRL had insufficient funds for 'nursing' a seat. Attempts by Odger to secure the
Liberal nomination at by-elections at Stafford in 1869 and Bristol in
1870 were rebuffed, as were similar ventures by Potter at Nottingham
in 1869 and George Howell at Norwich in 1871. Admittedly Odger did
succeed in being adopted at Southwark in 1870 but although performing creditably at the poll he was beaten by 304 votes by the Conservative. Apart from this the factor which contributed most to the strain on
Lib–Lab relations was the Gladstone government's trade union legisla-

tion of 1871. This was a classic instance of giving with one hand while taking away with the other. The unions were now recognised bodies in law but the Criminal Law Amendment Act made picketing virtually impossible thus denying the only effective action open to them in an industrial dispute. This indeed was so bitterly resented that the LRL abandoned its original policy to the extent of running candidates against the official Liberals in elections. In the general election of 1874, this happened in no less than eight constituencies. It was this which provoked the veteran Bright to complain in a letter to *The Times* that the League, was 'disorganising the party'. Henry Broadhurst, for the League was quick to retort that the fault was more on the other side: whenever a working-man stood as a candidate, the mass of middle-class votes was switched to the Tories.

By the middle of the 1870s it appeared that Lib–Labism was all but dead. Yet appearances proved very deceptive, for by the end of the decade the idea was showing marked signs of revival. Partly this was due to the removal of the main bone of contention between the trade union leaders and the Liberal Party through the Disraelian legislation of 1875. This repealed Gladstone's Criminal Law Amendment Act of 1871, allowed picketing as long as it was 'peaceful' and altered the Master and Servant Law so that both parties were treated equally in a case of breach of contract. The paradox is that the Conservatives had hoped by such measures to win mass working-class support, whereas the precise reverse was the outcome. Disraeli might well have ruminated bitterly on this second instance within a space of less than ten years that there was no such thing as gratitude in politics. The other main factor explaining the continuation of Lib–Labism against all the odds was perhaps religion. We have already remarked on the importance of the nonconformist tradition in the history of the British working-class movement. Many of the trade union leaders of the 1870s were pious dissenters and as such were extremely reluctant to break their natural political links with Liberalism. Nor was this all. It was this tradition which led such men to align themselves closely with the Gladstonian foreign policy based on the moral considerations of peace and respect for other nation's rights. Consequently, since the great issues of the late 1870s proved to be Gladstone's attacks on the wickedness of Turkish misgovernment and the unnecessary 'forward' policies of the government in South Africa and India, these had a powerful effect in drawing the working class back to cooperation with the Liberals. Finally, it is questionable whether the original division was ever as deep as it seemed.

Even in 1874, with the LRL running candidates against the Liberals, two MPs, Thomas Burt and Alexander MacDonald, both working-men and trade unionists, were returned with Liberal support. More-over, in the following year, the League had issued a manifesto (the *Address to the People of Great Britain*) which repeated most of the Radical/ Liberal programme of the time and, striking a distinctly nauseous note, protested its loyalty to the Liberal cause: 'We have ever sought to be allied to the great Liberal Party to which we by conviction belong.' The declaration further drew pleasure from 'the fact that men of the highest standing in the Liberal ranks have both written and spoken in favour of the object of the League.'

But while Lib–Labism flourished in theory, in practice things were rather different. The League found it increasingly difficult to maintain an independent and effective existence. Its sole material success was the election of its secretary, Henry Broadhurst, as Liberal MP for Stoke in 1880. In 1881, on the death of MacDonald, it failed to hold his seat at Stafford and with Broadhurst becoming more and more immersed in trade union work, it simply faded out. The overall situation at this time was well summed up by Engels when he claimed that the British working class was merely 'the tail of the great Liberal Party'. Neither he, nor indeed anyone else at the time, seems to have realised that fresh developments were already under way which were to result in the emergence of the independent 'labour' party within a period of twenty years.

### PRINCIPAL EVENTS, 1789–1880

1789. Outbreak of the French revolution
1791. Publication of Tom Paine's *Rights of Man*
1792. Formation of the London Corresponding Society and the publi-cation of *The Address to the People*
1794. Trial and acquittal of the Corresponding Society's leaders
1799. Suppression of the Corresponding Societies
1802. William Cobbett began the publication of his *Register*
1816. Spa Fields Riots
1817. The 'Blanketeers' march and the Derbyshire 'Rising'
1818. Richard Carlile's edition of Paine's *Age of Reason*
1819. Peterloo and the Six Acts

1830. Formation of the Birmingham Political Union by Thomas Attwood
1831. Reform riots in Bristol and Nottingham
1832. Passage of the First Reform Act
1836. William Lovett established the London Working-men's Association
1837. Feargus O'Connor took over the *Northern Star* newspaper
1838. Publication of the *People's Charter*
1839. Failure of the first Chartist Convention and Petition
The Newport Rising
Formation of the Anti-Corn Law League
1842. Failure of the second Chartist Petition
1845. O'Connor established the Chartist Cooperative Land Society
1846. Repeal of the Corn Laws
1847. O'Connor elected MP for Nottingham
1848. Failure of the third Chartist Petition
1860. Formation of the London Trades Council by the 'Junta'
1861. George Potter established the *Beehive* newspaper
1864. Formation of the International Working-men's Association (the 'First International')
1865. National Reform League set up mainly on the initiative of the 'Junta'
1866. George Potter formed a new London Working-men's Association
1867. Second Reform Act. Royal Commission on the Trade Unions
1868. First official Trades Union Congress. Failure of LWMA candidates in the general election
1869. Formation of the Labour Representation League by Potter and the Junta
1871. Gladstone government's trade union legislation: the unions now legal bodies but actions severely restricted by the Criminal Law Amendment Act. Formation of the English (later British) Federal Council of the International
1872. Ballot Act
1874. General election: LRL intervention against the Liberals but two trade unionists, Thomas Burt and Alexander MacDonald, elected with Liberal support
1875. Disraeli's government repealed the 1871 Act and 'peaceful' picketing now legal
1880. Henry Broadhurst of the LRL elected Liberal MP for Stoke in the general election

# Part II

## New Initiatives in the 1880s

### [3] The Revival of the 'Independent' Idea

It is generally agreed by historians of the labour movement that it was the decade beginning in 1880 which saw the initiation of the process culminating twenty years later in the foundation of the modern Labour Party. However, what is less generally agreed—or rather, is often simply passed over—is the explanation of this. After all, the Chartists' attempt to establish an independent party had been an abysmal failure only a generation or less before, and subsequent working-class political leaders had apparently not seriously considered anything more ambitious than to get a handful of candidates adopted and returned on the Liberal ticket. How was it then that this comfortable basic Lib–Labism came to be challenged effectively in working-class circles at this time? The answer would appear to lie in a complex and interrelated set of economic, social and political circumstances.

According to one contemporary, the social scientist Charles Booth, 'the springs of socialism and revolution' were to be found amongst the better-off sections of the working class. These, mainly artisans living 'independent lives' in 'fairly comfortable homes', were both the most numerous and the most influential. Politically they were now becoming restless, and mainly because of certain far-reaching changes in their economic circumstances. At first sight this seems a little difficult to comprehend since economic historians have been telling us for years that working-class conditions improved quite markedly in the second half of the nineteenth century. Thus, whereas real wages in the twenty years before 1850 had been almost stationary, in the next twenty-five years, they seem to have increased by about one-third. One says 'seem to' advisedly since any statistics before 1880 are unofficial, culled from all sorts of out-of-the-way sources and therefore not entirely reliable. Nonetheless there was quite a firm rising trend and this continued throughout the last twenty-five years of the century, the period of the so-called 'great depression'. Not only were money wages rising, but there were sharp falls in prices. According to the Board of Trade price index, taking the quinquennium 1871–5 as 100, by 1886–90, some 30 points had been lopped off and it stood at 70·6. This general figure concealed a number of individual variations but it appears that many foodstuffs like sugar, tea and coffee came down significantly as did tobacco. Admittedly meat and meat products did not fall quite so much but this seems to have been due to increased demand, itself the result of higher incomes. By 1900, it has been calculated that wage rates generally were 75 per cent up on 1850. But this is not the whole story, as the economic historians themselves are the first to admit. In the first place this upward trend was not consistent, for in periods when the economy was depressed, as in the late 70s, the mid 80s and the early 90s, there was a tendency for wages to slip back if only temporarily. Some industries, in particular coal mining and some sections of the iron trade, were more affected by these fluctuations than others due to the operation of a device known as the 'sliding scale'. This worked on the principle that the men's wages varied according to the price the industry could get for its product. That this could and did cause wide variations from year to year is shown by its operation in one specific instance, the South Wales coal-field in the 1890s. Here, a scale had been introduced on the basis of prices current in December 1879. In 1892 the miners' wages were 46 per cent above the standard but four years later they had fallen to only 10 per cent above, thereafter recovering to a level of 30 per cent above by the end of the decade. The effect of this sort of thing can easily be imagined. Men had no idea what they might call on in the future to meet their responsibilities and the resultant uncertainty, if not to say insecurity, inevitably bred resentment.

But in general terms it is in the period immediately before the outbreak of the First World War when the material improvement of working-class standards was most obviously checked. From 1900 onwards wages were on a plateau with, if anything, a slight downward drift. In 1914, while it was true that they were 45 per cent higher than in 1880, the greater part of this improvement had been achieved by the late 1890s. But what was most serious in view of this was the change in the direction of prices. Their fall, associated with the 'great depression', reached its lowest point in the five years 1891–5 when the government index registered 68·3. Now, from the beginning of the present century, a marked inflationary trend set in, with food prices in particular rising by up to 10 per cent. Admittedly not all of the essentials of life were affected; for example, as far as can be ascertained, rents of houses re-

mained stable, and the cost of coal, at one point at any rate, was as
much as 20 per cent below the 1900 level. But, as a rule, the average
wage-earner in 1914 was getting little if any more money than he had
ten years previously and he found that it was not going anything like so
far.

Apart from these specific factors there was a more deep-rooted cause
of discontent. Once again, it was Charles Booth who first put his finger
on it when he talked of the artisans 'whose lot today is most aggravated
by a raised ideal'. Although wages had gone up considerably in the
second half of the nineteenth century, they were still none too generous,
particularly when compared with the large slices taken from the
national economic cake by the upper and middle classes. Paradoxically
but not surprisingly a real feeling of deprivation developed in the working-class soul and this feeling was fostered in those sufficiently intelligent
to read the works of contemporary social commentators. As early as
1867 R. Dudley Baxter in his book *National Incomes* had shown that a
mere 10 per cent of the population owned half of the country's wealth.
Twenty years later that indefatigable body of socialist researchers, the
Fabian Society, drew further illustrations on the same theme. Using
material from the official Wage Census of 1886, they argued in a
pamphlet *Facts for Socialists from the Political Economists and Statisticians*,
that the country's wage-earners secured between them only 40 per cent
of its wealth. But probably the most explosive and influential exposé
was delayed until the publication in 1905 of L. G. Chiozza Money's
book, *Riches and Poverty*. He reckoned that 12 per cent of the population
received half the national income—a calculation not very different
from Baxter's—but in addition he argued that there was an even
smaller group of scarcely one-thirtieth of the total population which
possessed one-third of the total wealth. Nor was this an inaccurate
exaggeration designed to stir up class strife. Chiozza Money was a
respectable economist and Liberal MP, albeit on his party's radical left
wing. Moreover, careful research by modern economic historians has
verified his basic figures and conclusions. But the intelligent working-
man did not have to read Baxter, the Fabians or Money to realise this,
for the evidence of his own eyes was sufficient. The rapidly rising standards of the middle and upper classes were all too apparent in late
nineteenth-century England, culminating in the ostentatious opulence
of the Edwardian era. Well might the average working man, earning,
in 1914, 30 shillings for a 54-hour week, feel deprived and, in the words
of Sidney and Beatrice Webb, lose 'faith in the necessity, let alone the

righteousness of the social arrangements to which he finds himself subjected'.

But before leaving the question of wage levels, there is another issue to consider. It has been argued that, in spite of the overall material improvement, there was a substantial minority of the working class whose conditions did not improve in absolute terms and who continued to live in the most abject poverty throughout the period up to 1914. Furthermore this is held by some to explain in part the revival of the idea of a working-class party. The evidence for the existence of a substantial measure of poverty is clear enough from the work of Booth, B. S. Rowntree and other social investigators. According to their findings almost one-third of the urban working class lived in really distressed conditions. But this mass of misery was not necessarily a spur to political action. On the contrary, detached observers like Booth drew attention to the marked lack of political interest and understanding amongst the lower sections of the working class, and working-class writers themselves agreed that this analysis was correct. One observer, writing in 1879, said of the unskilled labourer that 'force of circumstances . . . certainly tends to keep him quiescent'. Another in 1895 claimed 'the poorest workers . . . are incapable of understanding or discovering the problems which concern them more nearly than any other'. Modern research tends to substantiate these observations. Thus, in a recent survey of London working-class politics at the turn of the century, Paul Thompson has shown that it was in areas where poverty was most marked and social conditions most deplorable that Labour had the hardest job to establish itself.

Wages though were not the whole story. Of almost as much concern in working-class circles was the incidence of unemployment. The 'great depression' may have aided the rise in working-class living standards by bringing down prices but at the same time it necessarily meant that the chances of losing one's job were greater. The available statistics underline this point clearly enough. The average annual rate of unemployment for the depression years (the mid 70s to the mid 90s) was just over 7 per cent of the working population compared with 5 per cent for the preceding 20 years and nearly $5\frac{1}{2}$ per cent for the period from 1896 to 1914. The averages conceal fairly wide fluctuations. For example in the periods 1870–8, the late 80s and the last 5 years of the century it was about 2 per cent. On the other hand taking the 10 years following 1878, in 7 of those years the rate exceeded 5 per cent, being particularly high in 1879 and 1886. The middle 90s saw 4 more bad consecutive years,

1892–5. After 1900 the average rate was not unusually high but there were two sharp peaks, in 1904 (when it went to 6 per cent) and 1908–9 (when it was well on the way to 8 per cent). There were also wide discrepancies between different industries. Some workers were hardly affected, but others, particularly those engaged in the export and constructional industries, lived in constant fear of the possibility. These included a very large number of men in engineering, shipbuilding, the metal and textile trades and some of the coal-fields. The uncertainty thus created was inevitably a factor stimulating ideas of political change.

The questions of wages and employment were clearly of paramount importance in working-class eyes but the actual conditions of work were another factor breeding unrest. The last two decades of the nineteenth century saw the initiation of a number of new and unsettling trends in British industry. In the first instance, industrial concerns tended to become much larger and less personal. Whereas in early and mid-Victorian England the typical firm had been the one man (or family) business or alternatively a partnership, now the limited liability company was becoming the norm. This development, made necessary by the high capital requirements of large-scale operations, is dramatically illustrated by the fact that in 1885 there were 10,000 registered companies in the United Kingdom whereas by the end of the century this figure had trebled. Furthermore, the move towards bigger units was stimulated by a series of amalgamations mainly affecting heavy industry round about the turn of the century. These changes, it must be emphasised, did not affect all workers but they certainly influenced a significant and increasing proportion. Resentment built up for a number of reasons. First, the sheer size and impersonality of the units made industrial relations much more difficult. Whereas in the past, the owner of a firm could make immediate decisions and talk things over with his employees, now matters had to be referred to a 'faceless' board of directors whose decisions might be delayed for days or even weeks. In such circumstances, not only was there the danger of a breakdown in communication leading to serious industrial strife, but also, once begun, such disputes were much more difficult to settle. Also, the reorganisation and rationalisation which tended to follow amalgamations had a disturbing effect, and could, in certain circumstances, mean the loss of jobs. Finally, the bigger the firm, the more clear-cut was the division between workers and employers, between 'us' and 'them'. Previously, when businesses were small, in times of economic adversity, the 'boss' might suffer almost as much as his men, but now size cushioned him against such set-backs. He was clearly much more powerful and his work-people more obviously dependent on him than hitherto.

In addition to size, the increasing mechanisation of industry also significantly affected the worker. Power driven machinery was introduced where there had been none before and existing machinery was speeded up. In particular, the last vestiges of the domestic outworking system which had played a significant part in some industries, particularly boot and shoe making, now finally disappeared. In one respect this was of advantage to the worker since, generally speaking, the introduction of improved machines meant that the job could be done with far less physical effort. But, on the other hand, new machinery meant that there was more noise and the pace of the work speeded up with necessarily bad effects on men's nerves. More tangible was the fear aroused in the average employee's mind that by doing the work more speedily he was working himself out of a job. Finally, and perhaps most resented of all, was the fact that the increasing reliance on machinery tended to erode the status of the skilled craftsman for often the job could now be subdivided, needed less training and, greatest indignity of all, could be done by mere boys or even women.

In short, from about 1880 onwards, a good deal was happening to make a large and influential section of the working class increasingly discontented with things as they were. Until then they had swallowed the mid-Victorian gospel of 'self-help', accepting the existing system and trying to work within it in remedying specific grievances. In economic and social terms this meant a reliance on cooperative trading ventures and a moderate trade unionism which was more concerned to build up financial reserves for members' benefits than for aggressive industrial action. In politics it meant deferentially trailing along after the Liberal Party with the modest hope of a few working-class MPs in the Commons should the Liberals feel sufficiently magnanimous. But now the economic security on which this rested was going and in its place was a growing uncertainty. Real wages might be rising, but working-men were beginning to feel strongly that they were not getting their just reward in comparison with other sections of society. With the onset of the 'great depression' unemployment, previously more of a threat to the unskilled, now seemed a misfortune likely to befall anybody. And even if a man did have a tolerably secure job, it seemed more demanding and frustrating than previously. For these people the great Victorian dream of ever-increasing prosperity and inevitable progress was coming to seem the illusion it really was.

In social terms, this realisation implied a marked closing of the ranks of the working class, and the emergence of a real class consciousness. This did not happen overnight but it certainly began in the 1880s. Hitherto, contemporaries had always tended to speak of the working class*es* rather than the working class and this distinction pointed up particularly the great difference existing between the skilled craftsman and the unskilled labourer. Indeed, in comparison the former were much closer to the small businessmen and tradesmen, who regarded themselves as middle class. Now this state of affairs was changing and there were factors other than the economic which contributed to the process. One of these was the growth of a national elementary education system as a result of the Education Act of 1870. All working-class children now received a common education and cultural experience whereas, generally speaking, the middle and upper classes were educated separately in grammar and public schools. The education provided by the state, although limited, may have had a further profound effect by making the working class even more conscious of their grievances and more able to take in the propaganda of the new socialist groups which now made their appearance. Another social development which had a similar effect in stimulating class consciousness was the increase in separate housing areas. Housing had always been separate to a certain degree, but now it became much more so as urban development proceeded apace and the improvements in transport resulted in the construction of 'residential' suburbs in the major industrial towns and cities. Later, with the arrival of the motor car, there was even a tendency for the wealthiest of the middle class to leave the towns altogether and 'go county', although they often had difficulty in securing acceptance in the upper echelons of rural society.

But economic and social changes are not in themselves sufficient explanation of the rise of the Labour Party. There were two other elements in the situation to which due weight must be given. The first was the fact that it was only now that the political and constitutional system was altered in such a way as to make a working-class party truly feasible. The second factor was the growth of really serious doubts as to the efficacy of the Liberal Party as a means for the realisation of working-class aspirations.

The three main defects in the nineteenth-century British constitution which had hitherto made the establishment of an independent working-class party highly unlikely, were the disfranchisement of the majority of that class, the incidence of bribery and intimidation at elections, and the non-payment of MPs which effectively barred all without substantial private means. Already before 1880 something had been done on the first two counts. In 1867 the Second Reform Act had brought a significant section of the urban working class on to the electoral roll. This, together with the introduction of vote by ballot in 1872, had made elections less expensive by reducing the effectiveness of bribery. But in the '80s there followed more measures which not only affected the parliamentary but also the local government system. The most important was the extension of the household franchise to the counties by the Reform Act of 1884, chiefly because of its effect on the mining districts. The miners, heavily concentrated as they were in certain areas, were thus presented with a unique opportunity to return a significant number of their representatives to the House of Commons. Previously, there had been the Corrupt Practices Act of 1883 which virtually eliminated all bribery by restricting a parliamentary candidate's expenses. Finally, there was the long overdue democratisation of local government outside the incorporated towns by the so-called County Councils Act of 1888. This was completed by the District Councils Act of 1894 which established a two-tier system of local representative institutions in England and Wales. Only in the case of the payment of MPs was nothing done since it continued to be assumed that politics was still fundamentally the job of the gifted amateur, rather than the professional politician, or a sort of public service for an under-employed aristocracy and gentry. Until 1911, when the fault was remedied, there was only one way around this: working-class MPs had to get the financial sponsorship they needed from the trade unions.

As for the relationship of the working class with the Liberal Party some historians believe that the Liberal split and the secession of Joseph Chamberlain from the party in 1886 marks a real and momentous turning-point in the history of Labour. This is the view of R. C. K. Ensor in *England, 1870–1914*, who argues that if Chamberlain had 'succeeded Gladstone as Liberal Premier, social reform might have come in England twenty years sooner than it did. In that case, the Labour Party . . . might never have been born'. But this argument is not one that can be easily sustained. Even in the previous decade when Lib–Labism appeared to be the only possible way for working-class politicians there had been tensions and the alliance was subjected to considerable strain. Now, they had a growing doubt about its fundamental validity. Slowly, and reluctantly in many cases, they were becoming convinced that Liberalism neither would nor could do anything for them. It was all very well for Chamberlain to berate the aristocracy, to talk about 'wealth paying ransom' and to pose, in Lord Iddesleigh's words, as a new 'Jack Cade', but there were some who saw through the façade and doubted the sincerity of the protestations. Thus, according to one observer, Lloyd Jones, the local caucuses of the Chamberlainite National Liberal Federation were mere 'traps in which to shut up the working-men of the country, allowing them only such political action as their masters and managers may permit'. Further, it was becoming increasingly clear that the overwhelming majority of these local parties did not wish to cooperate, if any working-man sought adoption as a parliamentary candidate. There was, too, a basic inconsistency in the Radical programme, to which a socialist speaker, J. E. Williams, drew attention in 1885: 'The Radical today was the "Artful Dodger" who went up and down this country telling the people to take hold of the landlord thief, but to let the greater thief, the capitalist, go scot-free.' In the circumstances, the events of 1886 merely clinched the argument. For all practical purposes, Liberalism seemed to be finished and Labour must now make its own way.

## [4] The Socialist Pioneers

In view of what has just been said, it is not surprising that the first signs of the socialist revival of the 1880s should be found in the Radical/ Liberal working-men's clubs which had sprung up in London. In 1881 their newspaper, the *Radical*, had published criticisms of Liberal Party leadership and had gone so far as to call for the formation of a new and independent party. The suggestion soon produced concrete results. A conference of interested parties was held on 8 June 1881 and out of this meeting there emerged the Democratic Federation with a programme based largely on the old radical platform, but also calling for more attention to be paid to 'labour interests'. At first the leading personality was the veteran MP for Newcastle-upon-Tyne, Joseph Cowen. It was felt that Cowen was a suitable choice to head the new organisation because of a previous association with Chartism, but in fact he had by now lost most of his interest in radical policies and only played a brief and unimportant part.

But although there was much talk of independent representation, there was little that was specifically socialist about the Federation until

H. M. Hyndman began to take an active part in its affairs. Of all the men associated with the political side of the British labour movement, Henry Mayers Hyndman is in many respects the most curious. Even in the second half of the present century, when the Labour Party leadership is, almost to a man, middle-class, Hyndman would still stick out like the proverbial sore thumb. In his own day it seemed even more ludicrously inappropriate that a wealthy City stockbroker should seek to lead a working-class party based on socialist principles. Politically, his career was chequered, if not to say unstable. Originally on the radical wing of the Liberal Party, he had split with Gladstone over the Eastern question and then swung right over to the other side, standing, unsuccessfully, as a Conservative candidate in the general election of 1880. But sometime in the course of 1880 or 1881 he seems to have been converted to Marxism, having read *Das Kapital* in a French translation. He then took it upon himself to expound Marx's views in an article in the *Nineteenth Century* and later in a book called *England for All*, though in neither case did he acknowledge his debt to the original author. Not surprisingly, Marx was annoyed and his assessment of Hyndman distinctly unflattering. 'Self-satisfied and garrulous' were the words he used in a letter to his daughter, Jennie, in April 1881, and later in the same year to another correspondent he described Hyndman as 'a weak vessel'. The whole episode of the relations between the two men clearly illustrates one of Hyndman's most serious and persistent weaknesses as a politician, his failure to get on with others. He seems to have succeeded in upsetting almost everybody in the socialist movement with whom he came into contact, not only Marx and Engels but also such widely diverse characters as William Morris, John Burns and Tom Mann. His naturally imperious manner meant also that not only was he lacking in tact but his judgment was often seriously impaired. He tended, almost without thinking, to pour scorn on all who were outside his own little group and so in turn he decried the activities of the trade unions, the Independent Labour Party and finally the Labour Representation Committee. Ultimately of course, events showed that it was he rather than they who was out of step. Yet he had his good points and his political life was not entirely without achievement. Writing of him in 1911, Bernard Shaw paid tribute to his unselfish and incorruptible devotion to his cause. Moreover, it should not be forgotten that it was Hyndman who really began the socialist movement of the 1880s.

As the new Democratic Federation began its life, it soon came to be very much dominated by Hyndman. Not only was he elected president but he took it upon himself to pay the organisation's expenses out of his own pocket and very soon Cowen and the radical club politicians began to drop away and he was left supreme. His first task was to commit the Federation to the support of his own newly acquired socialist views but it took him nearly two years before this was accomplished. His ultimate success was due partly to his own persistence and the influence his wealth gave him, but of equal importance was the effect of the American land reformer Henry George who chose to make a tour of Britain at this moment. George's views were already becoming well known. He had published his most famous work *Progress and Poverty* in 1879 and this was first printed in London in 1881, running through ten editions in the next three years. In 1882, the year of his personal speaking tour, sales rose to 400,000 copies. Strictly speaking he was not a socialist but committed to the belief that all society's problems could be solved by the reform of the taxation system based on a single levy on land. This, he argued, would 'raise wages, increase the earnings of capital, extirpate pauperism, abolish poverty, give remunerative employment to whoever wishes it . . . and carry civilisation to yet nobler heights.' Both contemporary commentators like Sidney Webb, and a whole host of later historians are agreed that the tremendous enthusiasm thus aroused was an important factor in stimulating interest in socialism. The immediate and most obvious result was Hyndman's conversion of the Democratic Federation into the Social Democratic Federation, a process completed in two stages: at the 1883 conference, members accepted Hyndman's socialist policies, and the following year the change of name was confirmed.

But these moves were paradoxically matched by a change in the Federation's social composition which became more and more middle-class in character. Two new recruits who joined the party at this stage stand out particularly: William Morris and H. H. Champion. Morris, the writer and artist with his own peculiar brand of aesthetic socialism, now became the SDF treasurer, while Champion, who came from a military family, took on the secretaryship in 1884. The latter, however, was of most use to the organisation because he owned a share in a printing business and could therefore arrange the publication of the party's two journals, the monthly *Today* which began in 1883, and the weekly *Justice* the following year. By now the SDF appeared to be well established with able leaders, financial backing, two propaganda journals and a growing number of active branches in London. Moreover, in 1884, to advertise itself it was able to mount a sizeable public demonstration in the form of a procession to the recently deceased Marx's grave in Highgate cemetery.

But underneath this surface of apparent progress and gathering strength, there was trouble brewing. At root it stemmed from a personality clash between Hyndman and Morris as the latter and his associates found the president's dictatorial airs increasingly irksome. In addition there was a difference of opinion over philosophy, since Morris, more of a purist than Hyndman, accepted fully the theory of the inevitability of revolution. The trouble finally came to a head in December 1884 when the Morris group seceded to form their own organisation which they called the Socialist League. Unfortunately Morris's idealism was not matched by any practical organising ability and it never succeeded in gaining even a modest following. Hubert Bland, soon to be associated with the Fabian Society, described the League's headquarters as giving 'an impression of feebleness and want of method'. Its downfall was completed by the infiltration of a number of anarchists whose views were so extreme that Morris himself felt impelled to withdraw in November 1890 and with that it virtually ceased to exist.

But the internal dissensions of 1884, however serious, were not the only difficulties the SDF had to face, for the following year brought electoral disasters which badly undermined the party's credibility. In October candidates were put up at the London School Board elections in Marylebone, Lambeth, Clerkenwell and Tower Hamlets, but only in the last named was there anything like a respectable showing and this was mainly due to support from the local radical organisation. But worse was to follow when an attempt was made to run candidates in the November general election. Without sufficient funds to fight a campaign, the party approached Chamberlain and the NLF and when this failed, Champion, through certain personal contacts in the Conservative Party, secured £340 from its funds on the understanding that two SDF men would run in London, obviously in the hope of splitting the Liberal vote. The result was a complete fiasco. Jack Williams, who stood at Hampstead, received only 27 votes while John Fielding at Kennington did marginally better, securing 32. The fact that a third candidate, John Burns at Nottingham, managed 598 did not restore the situation. Not only had the SDF's men done remarkably badly but the revelation that they had been promoted by 'Tory gold' was even more damaging. Champion came out of the affair with a reputation so tarnished that, although he continued to busy himself in working-class politics for some years yet, he was never really trusted again. Otherwise the immediate result was another bout of feuding leading to the secession of a group who formed a short-lived Socialist Union.

Despite these blows, the SDF did not fold up. It now embarked on what was probably the most influential period of its existence, and the reason for its survival lies in the economic situation outlined above. With unemployment now reaching a peak not far short of that of the disastrous year of 1879, the party found a mass audience for its views and, for a time, it was able to command considerable influence by leading and organising agitation and unrest. Its first major effort was the mass meeting held in Trafalgar Square on 8 February 1886 to demand from the government a public works programme. The flamboyant oratory of Champion and John Burns stirred the crowd up rather more than they had intended, and the result was a rampage through the West End in the course of which the windows of several of the fashionable clubs in Pall Mall were smashed and some shops in Mayfair looted. The upshot was that the four leaders—Hyndman and Williams in addition to the other two—were indicted for conspiracy. The trial lasted four days and ended with all the defendants being acquitted. This triumph and the publicity it had received encouraged the SDF to further efforts, holding meetings, processions and church parades of the unemployed culminating in a peaceful demonstration in St Paul's Cathedral in February 1887. Inevitably perhaps the campaign reached another violent climax with the Trafalgar Square meeting of 13 November 1887. On this occasion the SDF were not alone but combined with Irish and radical critics of the Salisbury government's hard line policy in Ireland. The demonstration had been banned by the Home Secretary, but the police proved incapable of enforcing the embargo and ultimately the square was only cleared by the action of the Life Guards. For his part in this, Burns was later arrested and spent six weeks in gaol, but, although there was much long term bitterness engendered by the episode in working-class districts in London, there was no immediate political result. The SDF had secured a good deal of publicity and had seemed to be leading the working-class movement, but this proved to be merely a passing phase. With the revival of the economy beginning in 1887 and with the unemployment situation rapidly easing, its mass support gradually slipped away. Once again a set-back was to lead to internal disagreement, this time between Hyndman and Champion. The former had by now become thoroughly disillusioned with the more orthodox political action and was, somewhat unrealistically, pinning his faith on a working-class revolution bringing him to power. Champion, at the same time less pessimistic and more in touch with reality, demanded what he called 'more practical plans for reform'. By this he meant an alliance with the trade unions and, as we shall see, he was not the only one to have this idea.

Meanwhile, there was also emerging another group of pioneers who, like the SDF, were largely middle-class and London based and who called themselves the Fabian Society. First formed in 1884 the Fabians were initially a very mixed bag of Marxists, radicals and other odds and ends. Bernard Shaw, the playwright, who was one of the first to join, light-heartedly described the personnel at the earliest meetings: 'It was a silly business. They had one elderly retired workman. They had two psychical researchers, Edward Pease and Frank Podmore, for whom I slept in a haunted house at Clapham. There were Anarchists . . . who would not hear of anything Parliamentary. There were young ladies on the look-out for husbands who left when they succeeded.' In two important respects however they differed from the SDF. They never became, nor indeed intended to become, a mass party. They saw themselves rather as being a sort of intellectual power-house providing the ideas and pointing the way for the professional politicians. As a result, they were accorded, perhaps not unfairly, in some circles the faintly contemptuous accolade of 'drawing-room socialists'. The other major difference was their belief that socialism would be achieved by constitutional means. At first they had briefly flirted with the idea of revolution, for example Shaw's ringing challenge in the second of the Fabian tracts published in September 1884: 'We had rather face a civil war than another century of suffering as the present one has been.' But, thanks largely to the influence of such as Sidney Webb, Annie Besant, Hubert Bland and E. R. Pease, the majority in September 1886 declared its adhesion to constitutional action. As Mrs Besant put it: 'Society is to be reformed by a slow process of evolution, not by revolution and bloodshed.'

The predominant figure in the Fabian Society was soon to be Sidney Webb, a professional civil servant from a lower middle-class background and a close friend of Shaw. Increasingly, Webb and his group, priding themselves on their realism, were coming to the conclusion that the best way to advance the cause of socialism in England was not to go through the long and, they thought, inevitably unsuccessful process of forming a new party, but to try and take over one of the existing ones and mould it to their purpose. The Fabians believed that they could gain control of the Liberal Party by getting their members into the local caucuses and thus was born the idea of 'permeation'. True, not all were convinced of the rightness of this course and Hubert Bland in particular argued that 'a popular organisation must be created for the express purpose of working existing political machinery'. But he was in a minority and 1889 saw the seal set on Webb's philosophy by the publication of *Fabian Essays in Socialism*, a collection from various authors edited by Shaw and extolling the virtues of evolutionary change by 'permeation'. At first it seemed as if it would work. In the late 1880s Fabians and Fabian sympathisers were securing footholds in the local Liberal associations, particularly the recently established working-class Metropolitan Radical Federation and even in the more staid middle-class body, the London Liberal and Radical Union. Also links were being forged with the Liberal press. H. W. Massingham, the assistant editor of the new London newspaper, *The Star*, became a member of the society at about this time. But this was all something of an illusion and in due course it became clear that the tactic of 'permeation' had serious limitations.

Of all the initiatives taken by socialists in the 1880s, the most important was the one which created least impact at the time and which seemed to have made the least progress. This was the foundation of the Scottish Labour Party by James Keir Hardie. Hardie originally came from Lanarkshire and his background, by Victorian standards, was rather dubious. He was born in 1856, the illegitimate son of a farm servant, Mary Kerr, by a miner, William Aitken, but the mother later married a ship's carpenter, David Hardie, who agreed that the boy should take his name. This unfortunate beginning was merely a prelude to further difficulties, for his early life was extremely hard, though possibly not a great deal harder than the average for his class at the time. He received virtually no formal education, except that which he could scrape at night school, and he began work at the age of eight, first as an errand boy and then as a 'trapper' in the coal mines. The strongest influence on his formative years seems to have been the Chapel and, as we have already seen, nonconformity was to play an integral part in his politics. As a young man he soon interested himself in trade union work amongst the miners, being almost immediately sacked for his activities and having to fall back on a very precarious living as a journalist. This, however, did not prevent him from acting as agent to the Lanarkshire miners from 1879 to 1881, and also holding the secretaryship of the Ayrshire Miners' Union—which he helped establish—from 1886 to 1890. He was also at this time involved in a largely ineffective attempt to establish a Scottish Miners' Federation. Hardie's working-class and trade union background is in marked contrast to the leaders of the three London based groups.

Throughout this period of his life his political views were gradually evolving. At first he was a Liberal, which was not surprising in view of his commitment to nonconformity, but it is clear that he soon began to question the validity of Liberalism for the working class. This conversion was a process drawn out over several years, but it seems to have begun in the early 1880s, possibly triggered off by the propaganda of Henry George, but more likely as a result of his experience at the hands of the hard-faced Scottish mine-owners who, in general, were Liberal adherents. It seems very doubtful whether he was at all influenced by Marxism or its popularisers in the SDF. We know, for example, that he came into contact with that body while on a visit to London on union business in 1887, and had nothing but slightly priggish contempt for their clubs 'in which beer seemed to be the most dominant influence'. He was indeed not only a nonconformist but also a strong temperance man being convinced, with some truth, that a good deal of working-class poverty and misery was the result of alcohol. This too was a strong tie with Liberalism and it is possible that it might have proved strong enough to maintain his loyalty to the cause, had he not suffered a serious political reverse, if not to say humiliation, in the course of 1888. The occasion for this was the Mid-Lanark by-election where Hardie went forward as the miners' candidate in the hope of securing the official Liberal nomination. At first his chances looked good. He had the backing of the Labour Electoral Association which was a recently formed offshoot of the TUC for the purpose of promoting Lib–Lab candidatures. He also engaged the sympathies of Francis Schnadhorst whose position as national agent for the NLF gave him considerable influence in the choice of parliamentary candidates. Unfortunately this was not enough. Schnadhorst had no real control over the Scottish Liberals who had their own organisation outside the NLF, and the local caucus ran true to form in preferring a safe, middle-class London barrister, J. W. Phillips. Nonetheless, Hardie persisted, and since his election platform was not very different from his Liberal opponent's, it was clear that his main aim was to establish the principle of working-class political independence. In his campaign he spoke of 'the beginning of a new era' and, with emotion which was soon to become typical of his oratory, he defined his aims as 'bread for the hungry, rest for the weary and hope for the oppressed'. Moreover, he certainly made a stir outside the narrow bounds of the constituency, for offers of help came from a number of sources, in particular the Championite faction of the SDF. Champion himself came north and spent a good deal of time and money on Hardie's behalf. The money was certainly useful but otherwise his presence was something of an embarrassment. People still remembered all too clearly his dubious activities in 1885 and the Liberals could, and did, suggest that Hardie was being financed by the Conservatives for the sole purpose of splitting the Liberal vote. Champion particularly busied himself in an attempt to win over the significant Irish vote in the constituency, but this proved abortive. While Michael Davitt for the Nationalists welcomed the move, Parnell vetoed it since he did not wish to offend the Liberals at such a crucial stage in the Home Rule controversy. In the end, in spite of all the efforts of himself and his supporters, Hardie was crushingly defeated, coming bottom of the poll with a mere 617 votes compared with the Conservative candidate's 2,917 and the Liberal victor's 3,847.

The immediate result of Mid-Lanark was the foundation of the Scottish Labour Party in the summer of 1888 by Hardie in association with R. B. Cunningham-Graham. He was an eccentric Scottish laird who had been elected to Parliament as a Radical Liberal in 1885 and had then got himself involved in some of the wilder activities of the SDF. A preliminary meeting of all those interested was called in Glasgow in May and this was followed by the inaugural conference on 25 August. Graham was elected president and Hardie became the secretary. Also involved in the new body was Shaw Maxwell who was a follower of Henry George and was later to cooperate with Hardie in the foundation of the Independent Labour Party in 1893. The new party's object was stated as being 'to educate the people politically and to secure the return to Parliament and all local bodies of members pledged to its programme', which was composed of demands for further far-reaching political reform and industrial legislation, including the introduction of the eight-hour day. This was potentially a long step towards independence, but Hardie did not entirely shut the door of cooperation with the Liberals. The tactics which were to be pursued were first that pressure should be put on other parties' candidates to give assurances on labour questions and it was only where such assurances were not forthcoming that it was agreed that the new party should run its own men.

Writing of the Scottish Labour Party in his paper, *The Miner*, in September 1888, Hardie declared: 'If anyone, peasant or peer, is willing to accept the programme and work with and for the party, his help

will be gladly accepted.' Yet this apparent call for a truly national party
and not one based on mere sectional interests was perhaps rather misleading, for in a sense it ran counter to a conviction which was rapidly
growing in Hardie's mind. This was that if a new and effective party
were to emerge, then it must be based firmly in the trade union movement. The realisation of this idea of the 'Labour Alliance' was henceforth to be the dominant aim of Keir Hardie's political life and it was
to be twenty years before it was fully achieved. But, already in the late
1880s, developments were on foot in the trade union movement which
were to assist him in his cause, and it is these to which we must now
turn.


## [5] The 'New Unionism' and its Political Impact

Before 1880 the trade unions in Britain were not politically active
to any real degree. Some of their leaders had played a significant part
in the reform controversies of the '60s, and there had been the agitation
to achieve status and recognition culminating in the Disraelian legislation of 1875-6. But this action was spasmodic and, imbued with the
doctrine of 'self help' and inevitable progress, trade unionists believed
that their best course of action was quietly to build up their financial
strength and to secure improvements for their members as a result of
negotiation with their employers, by arbitration rather than by strike
action. In short they were seeking 'respectability'. But from 1880 onwards, things began to change. Increasingly, during the ten years of
consistently high unemployment after 1878, the sessions of the TUC were
dominated by demands for state intervention to solve the economic
problems and, as a necessary prelude to this, steps to increase working-
class parliamentary representation.

But this political awakening which is such a feature of the 1880s was
not only an apparent reflex action in the face of sudden economic adversity. It was also stimulated by a new development at the end of the
decade, the onset of the so-called 'new unionism'. The nature of the
'new unionism' and its relation to the 'old' is a matter of some controversy, and the most recent and detailed study (Clegg, Fox and Thompson *British Trade Unions*, Volume I 1889-1910) devotes some time to a
critical analysis of certain legends which have grown up over the years.
However, two features seem to be generally agreed. The new unions

which sprang up in the trade revival at the end of the 1880s were largely concerned with the recruitment of workers who had hitherto either been badly organised or not organised at all. The other feature was the increased militancy of their tactics in comparison with those of their predecessors. Tom Mann put the point clearly in a famous pamphlet published in 1886 *What a compulsory Eight-Hour Working Day Means to the Workers*: 'I readily grant that good work has been done in the past by the unions, but, in Heaven's name, what good purpose are they serving now? . . . The true unionist policy of aggression seems entirely lost sight of.' John Burns, in his description of the differences he noted between the two groups at the 1890 TUC drew a similar parallel between the 'old' unionists who 'looked like respectable city gentlemen' and the 'new delegates' who 'looked like workmen'.

Like the reviving socialist movement, the 'new unionism' derived a good deal of its inspiration from London. The first clear indication was the strike of the Bryant and May matchgirls in 1888 followed by the formation of a union which was largely masterminded by Annie Besant and Champion. More significant was the organisation of the gasworkers in 1889 by the efforts of Will Thorne. After a number of unsuccessful attempts he finally established the National Union of Gasworkers and General Labourers as the result of a public meeting in Canning Town in March of that year. The SDF was very closely involved in this. Thorne himself was a member and received valuable, if not to say essential, assistance from Eleanor Marx in the administration of the new body. Other prominent Socialists who were associated with the venture included Burns and Mann and, when the union spread to the Leeds and Bradford area, Alf Mattison who was later to be a stalwart of the ILP.

But, of all the manifestations of the 'new unionism', the most impressive was the organisation of the dockers. This arose out of the famous strike of 1889 for the 'dockers' tanner' when the dock labourers, led by Ben Tillett and supported by many of the skilled workers such as the stevedores, demanded an increase of 1d or so on their low rate of 4–5d per hour. Once more, as with the matchgirls and the gasworkers, a most significant feature was the assistance given by those connected with the socialist movement. Mann and Burns were particularly prominent and the latter, easily identifiable in his straw hat and extremely effective as an orator, very soon assumed the leadership. Tom Mann for his part took on the burden of much of the administrative work such as the organisation of a system of meal tickets for the strikers. Champion too was well to the fore. He worked to raise money from sympathisers for the strike fund. He was also involved in the establishment of picket lines to prevent the importation of black-leg labour by the employers. Finally, and most importantly, he took on the responsibilities of press officer and turned his paper, the *Labour Elector*, into the official organ of the dockers and gasworkers. The successful outcome of the clash was followed by the foundation of the Dock, Wharf, Riverside and General Labourers' Union with Tom Mann as its president, first in a full time capacity from 1889 to 1892 and then honorary until 1900.

From a political point of view all this was of great importance to Keir Hardie since it made his dream of the 'Labour Alliance' much more of a possibility. Hitherto the trade union movement had been dominated by leaders whose political inclinations were Liberal, now these were seriously challenged. Indeed, according to historians such as the Webbs and G. D. H. Cole, by 1890 the battle had been won, the Lib–Labs were in full retreat and the TUC, largely under the influence of socialist 'new unionists', was inevitably committed to the idea of a new independent working-class party. But close examination of the facts does not really sustain this optimistic view. The Lib–Labs were well entrenched and determined to fight back while the commitment of the 'new unions' to socialism and independent political action was not quite so strong as it sometimes seems in retrospect. Champion's own comment on the dock strike hints at this, for 'those socialists who took part . . . were welcomed not because of their socialism but in spite of it; not on account of their speculative opinions but for the sake of their personal ability to help.' Furthermore, the Lib–Lab position had been strengthened in the general election of 1885 by the return of a dozen trade union MPs, all on the Liberal ticket. Prominent amongst these were two sitting members: Henry Broadhurst, soon to hold minor office in Gladstone's third administration, and Thomas Burt, the general secretary of the Northumberland Miners' Association. Joining them for the first time were Charles Fenwick, Burt's colleague in the NMA, 'iron man' Ben Pickard of the Yorkshire Miners' Association, and Will Abraham, nicknamed 'Mabon' (the Bard), the leader of the South Wales' miners. At the same time, the then President of the TUC, T. R. Threlfall, was canvassing a project to secure increased political representation but under Liberal auspices. At the 1886 TUC he carried a resolution for the creation of a Labour Electoral Committee to work alongside the Parliamentary Committee. Soon afterwards it changed its name to the Labour Electoral Association and busied itself in the old policy of attempting to secure the adoption of its candidates by the local caucuses. In spite of the encouraging increase in trade union MPs in the 1885 returns, it proved to be no more successful than its predecessor, the Labour Representation League, but its very formation showed that most trade unionists were not yet willing to come to terms with the idea of a new party. Not only were their links with Liberalism strong but their deepest suspicions were aroused when the first man to come up with the idea was Champion. Following his quarrel with Hyndman in 1887 he left the SDF and, along with Tom Mann and John Burns, approached the newly formed Labour Electoral Association with an offer of financial assistance. His idea was that the LEA should attempt to put pressure on the candidates of the two existing parties to meet working-class demands and, where possible, such pressure could be made effective by running or threatening to run their own men. This was given practical expression in the Deptford by-election of 1888 where Champion put himself up and then withdrew having received vague assurances from the Liberals, including a sympathetic confidential letter from their chief whip, Arnold Morley. Whether this was practical politics is extremely doubtful but in fact Champion never had the opportunity to put the matter to a sustained test. In general, the trade union movement fought shy of involvement in his schemes. His known contacts with the Conservatives, and particularly the 1885 scandal, still made him so universally suspect that most would have agreed with Engels when he said, 'I cannot have full confidence in that man—he is too dodgy!'

So, when Keir Hardie appeared at the 1888 TUC with his resolution for the trade union movement's backing for independent representation, he was batting on an exceedingly sticky wicket. This he seems to have realised, hence his attempt to undermine the position and credibility of the chief Lib–Lab spokesman, Broadhurst, at the previous year's conference at Swansea. There, Hardie had mounted a fierce personal attack, virtually accusing him of 'collaborating' with the employers to the detriment of trade union interests and berating him in particular for his political connections with John Brunner of the firm of Brunner, Mond and Company, regarded by many as a 'sweatshop'. Broadhurst's position, however, was virtually impregnable. He had no difficulty in beating off Hardie's censure motion and then, the following year, led the opposition to the independent representation motion, defeating it decisively by 82 votes to 18. Nor was this all, for on his retirement as secretary of the Parliamentary Committee in 1890 he was able to hand over his duties to another tried and trusted Lib–Lab in the person of Fenwick. But the most devastating blow to Hardie's cause at this time was the sudden appearance of Lib–Lab tendencies in one of the most distinguished figures of the 'new unionism', John Burns. Despite real ability, as instanced by his handling of the dock strike, there were certain flaws in his character which now began to make their appearance. He proved to be arrogant, suspicious of possible rivals and, above all, rather too concerned with his own personal advancement. In 1889 he secured election to the newly constituted London County Council and immediately showed himself willing to cooperate with the Progressives who were in fact Liberals under an assumed name. Before long he was fraternising with Liberal politicians to such an extent that he was being invited to some of their country house week-ends. By 1890 his virtual defection may not have been entirely apparent—indeed, Hardie continued for some years yet to cherish the possibility of his leading a new labour party—but, in retrospect, it is clear that he had set his foot firmly on the road which was to take him into the Liberal cabinet of 1905.

Hardie's first attempt then at winning over the trade unions had failed decisively and it was very clear that he needed to do much more propaganda work if he was to succeed in the future. What also must have been equally clear was that his Scottish Labour Party was not really a serviceable instrument for this task. Therefore in the early 1890s he moved his operations into England and was soon busily engaged in the formation of yet another political organisation, the Independent Labour Party.

# *Part III*

## The Independent Labour Party and its Rivals 1890–1900

### [6] The Foundation of the ILP

Until the early 1890s, most of the initiatives for a new working-class party had come from London. True, there was the Scottish Labour Party but this was a very frail body and the real pacemaker had been the SDF. The Independent Labour Party, on the other hand, owed little to the forces emanating from the capital. It was almost entirely northern based and owed its emergence, in part, to a sudden awakening of political consciousness amongst the textile workers of the West Riding of Yorkshire. A number of factors contributed to this development. The activities of certain propagandists paved the way. Tom Maguire's work in and around Leeds, Joseph Burgess writing in the recently founded *Yorkshire Factory Times*, and a Fabian lecture tour of the area, all seem to have played their part in stimulating discussion on the subject of independent representation. More important and immediate in their effects were developments on the industrial side. The politically minded leadership of the 'new unionism' was soon at work in the shape of Will Thorne and Pete Curran attempting to organise the woollen operatives as an adjunct to the Gasworkers' union. Then an industrial dispute brought matters to a head. In 1890, the United States had imposed the so-called McKinley Tariff which had had an immediate depressant effect on British woollen exports. The Yorkshire millowners, led by Samuel Lister of the Manningham Mills, Bradford, decided that the only way to retain competitiveness was by cutting costs and that the most effective way of achieving this was by cutting wages. Lister's operatives naturally objected strongly, coming out on strike, to which he riposted by declaring a lock-out. Inevitably, although the strikers managed to stay out for nearly five months, they were ultimately forced to give in on the management's terms. But the bitterness engendered was tremendous. As Ben Turner, one of the participants, later put it, 'Sam Lister won. He was in consequence one of the most hated men of the period.' Moreover, this ill-feeling found expression in political terms. In May 1891, there was formed under the leadership of W. H. Drew (one of the strike leaders), the Bradford Labour Union, an organisation determined to push for independent representation. Its first essays into the electoral field were not long delayed. In November it put up two candidates at the local municipal elections and although they were defeated, it was decided to adopt Ben Tillett and Robert Blatchford as candidates for two of the city's three parliamentary constituencies.

This political activity was not confined to the Bradford area, for there were similar moves in other parts of the north. July 1891 saw the foundation of the Colne Valley Labour Union and the following month a similar body, the Labour Electoral Association, was formed in Salford. Then in May 1892, Robert Blatchford, who had strong connections in the area, was instrumental in establishing an independent labour party in Manchester. Further indications were provided by the number of working-class members joining Fabian branches in the north, and their strength was such that they compelled a Fabian conference to accept a resolution expressing satisfaction at 'the formation of an independent labour party and heartily wishes success to the movement.'

So far however there was no attempt to organise this on any national scale and the working-class movement was still very much in a state of disarray in 1892. The TUC continued to be opposed to the whole idea of 'labour' candidates. The SDF, relying as it did on Hyndman's personal generosity, was in serious financial difficulties due to that gentleman's losses on the Stock Exchange in the course of 1890 and 1891. Hardie's Scottish Labour Party was not only short of funds but was riven by internal disagreements between Hardie and the Scottish Miners' leader, Chisholm Robertson and between Hardie and Cunningham-Graham who was all for Lib–Labism. The prospects then were not very bright for those who wanted to try their luck in the 1892 general election. Yet of the eighteen or so 'independent' candidates at the polls, three managed to secure election, although only one maintained his independence afterwards.

The successful men were John Burns, who won Battersea in a straight fight with the Conservative by 1,500 votes or more; Havelock Wilson, who pulled off a remarkable *coup de main* by winning Middlesbrough in a three-cornered fight; and finally Keir Hardie who was elected at West Ham South. This, in retrospect, is an important stage in the history of independent labour representation. Hardie's success was due mainly to the large concentration of 'new unionists'—mainly dockers and gasworkers — in the constituency. There was in addition however the fact that Schnadhorst, the Liberal Party organiser, had used his influence to secure Hardie a clear run against the Conservative. Moreover Hardie himself realised this. Although he insisted on his independence he went out of his way to be conciliatory to the Liberal vote by declaring his 'agreement with the present programme of the Liberal Party as far as it goes'.

On the morrow of his victory, Hardie's first thought was to try and capitalise on this success by forming a new London-based independent labour party with the help of John Burns. This was not a new idea by any means. In May 1891, he had written to Burns urging 'Now is the time to realise your idea of a conference of those . . . who have not sold themselves to the party managers.' Unfortunately for Hardie, Burns had serious doubts as to the efficacy of an independent labour party and turned a deaf ear to the suggestion that they should sit on the opposition benches whichever government took office following the highly equivocal election results. Before long, Hardie was compelled to accept the fact that Burns was a broken reed. In spite of his former commitment to the 'new unionism' and his membership of the SDF, he was now to all intents and purposes a Lib–Lab.

In the circumstances, Hardie's hopes for a new party were inevitably centred on the north, where the enthusiasm stimulated by the events of 1891 was still running high. Indeed the 1892 election had provided Ben Tillett in Bradford with what Henry Pelling has called 'a remarkable moral victory'. Admittedly he came bottom in a three-cornered fight, but it was a desperately close-run thing with only just over 500 votes separating all three candidates. Meanwhile Burgess and Drew agitated for a new political initiative in the columns of the *Factory Times*. Clearly, in view of the similarity of their aims, it was only a matter of time before Hardie and the Bradford labour leaders teamed up. The decisive contacts were apparently made at the Glasgow meeting of the TUC in September 1892 where, with the help of a group of sympathetic trade unionists, a committee was set up to organise a conference of interested parties for the following January in Bradford. Naturally the news of a projected new working-class party did not find much favour with the other socialist groups. The SDF refused to cooperate on the grounds that the new body would be too much of a compromise. The Fabians still hoped for much from 'permeation' of the Liberal Party and no doubt agreed with Shaw's scathing denunciation: 'What can we do but laugh at your folly . . . the Independent Labour Party . . . turns out to be nothing but an attempt to begin the SDF over again.' (Letter to the *Workman's Times*, 8 October 1892.)

Despite this pessimism, delegates assembled in good heart at the Bradford Labour Institute on 13 January 1893. The meeting proved to be overwhelmingly northern in composition, no less than one-third of the 120 representatives coming from Yorkshire, while the only southerners were from London, Chatham and Plymouth. The Fabians in the end decided to send two delegates, Shaw and Pease, but such was the hostility towards them that the motion to accept them was only carried by two votes. Otherwise, under Hardie's capable chairmanship and thanks to some careful planning by a steering committee, the conference passed off very smoothly and at the end of two days the new party was in existence with a name, a constitution and a programme.

The name, Independent Labour Party (ILP), had been more or less agreed on even before the conference started, although there was a move to call it the Socialist Labour Party. This was rejected for the very good reason that not all those in favour of independent representation were necessarily in favour of socialism. The constitution which was adopted was very similar in form to that of a trade union. Supreme authority was vested in an annual conference of branch delegates who elected an executive of fifteen members, which tended to be rather unwieldy and lacked the power to take any real initiative. The programme to which the conference agreed was divided into two sections. The first contained a list of specific economic and social reforms, including the establishment of an eight-hour day with overtime and piecework abolished; the prohibition of the employment of children under fourteen; proper provision for the sick, disabled, aged, widows and orphans; and the general reform of taxation along the lines of less indirect taxation and the introduction of a properly graduated income tax. Also, ironically enough, in spite of the rejection of the name 'Socialist Labour Party', the conference accepted a motion 'to secure the collective ownership of all the means of production, distribution and exchange'. The second section originally contained in the draft form a series of specific political reforms but after some discussion it was agreed that these could be covered by a single all-embracing declaration: 'The Independent Labour Party is in favour of every proposal for extending electoral rights and democratising the system of government.'

Thus, at the beginning of 1893 there were now in existence three socialist or neo-socialist parties. On the extreme left stood the Marxist SDF with its main following in London though with some support in

Lancashire. To the right, the Fabians, numerically small but believing themselves on the verge of a break-through by 'permeation' of the Liberal ranks. Finally, somewhere in the middle, the new party, the basically reformist ILP drawing the bulk of its strength from the industrial north, particularly the West Riding. From now until the end of the century, working-class politics are dominated by two developments: first, the rivalries of these groups and secondly the ILP's pursuit of Hardie's dream of the 'Labour Alliance' with the trade union movement.

## [7] The Consolidation of the ILP

The new party had many difficulties to overcome before being firmly established. First, it had to face open hostility from the SDF, who regarded it with scorn as a body of compromisers, and also from the Lib–Lab element in the TUC. Speaking for the latter, John Burns had denounced the independent men in the roundest terms at the Belfast congress in 1893, referring to what he called 'the arrant frauds that in the name of Independent Labour and Socialism were going about the country doing everything to disintegrate labour and trade unionism.' (TUC Report 1893.) Secondly, the new party's organisation left much to be desired. It had no proper office nor administrative machinery and, in the first year when much needed to be done, the executive met only twice. Finally, it lacked cohesion, with no real control being exercised by the central body over the local branches.

Basically, it was kept alive in these circumstances by the dogged determination of Keir Hardie, whose vigorous propaganda poured forth both inside and outside Parliament. At the same time his spirited leadership was matched by the enthusiasm of the rank and file. Ramsay MacDonald, writing in 1894, drew attention to the almost unbelievable dedication of those at the grass roots: 'Nothing is too hard for the members in their virgin enthusiasm to do. They ran their little prints, they sell their stock of pamphlets, they drop their pennies into the collecting box, they buy their ILP tea and cocoa etc., as though they were members of an idealistic Communist Society.' As for the organisational defects, some of these were put right at the first annual conference at Manchester in 1894, where the executive council was cut down from fifteen to nine members and was instructed to meet more regularly in the future—at least once every three months. Also, a new secretary was appointed in the person of Tom Mann who proved more effective than the first holder of the post, Shaw Maxwell.

Electorally, the party was straining at the leash and early by-election campaigns seemed encouraging. In 1893–4, ILP candidates stood at Halifax, Attercliffe and Leicester and did reasonably well. The Attercliffe election incidentally was responsible for the conversion of Ramsay MacDonald, hitherto an upholder of Lib–Labism, but now disgusted by the continued stubborn refusals of local Liberal associations to select working-class men as parliamentary candidates. As things turned out the ILP did not have long to wait to test its muscles. Rosebery, who had succeeded Gladstone as premier, was having so much difficulty both with the House of Lords and the dissentients inside his own party that he tendered his resignation in 1895. At the ensuing general election, the ILP put up no less than twenty-eight candidates. The overwhelming bulk of these were in the north of England and Scotland. In the midlands and south only five candidates were run: Leicester (where Joseph Burgess had done so well in the previous year's by-election); Bristol East (where a Christian Socialist had done well in a by-election held earlier in 1895); West Ham South (Hardie's own seat), Fulham and Southampton. But the results of this ambitious campaign were nothing less than disastrous. Everywhere the ILP men suffered from the swing to the right and, worst of all, was the loss of Hardie's seat at West Ham. Hardie had spent too much time out of the constituency helping other candidates and the result was that his organisation was not as well-tuned as it should have been. In addition he alienated much Liberal and indeed Irish support, which had gone to him in 1892, by his perhaps over-rigid attitude of independence in the Commons. Suffice it to say, his majority of 1,232 now became a Conservative one of 775.

Contemporaries were all too ready to regard this as evidence that the party was finished. Burns called the ILP's campaign 'the most costly funeral since Napoleon'. Beatrice Webb wrote in her diary (10 July 1895): 'The ILP has completed its suicide. Its policy of abstention and deliberate wrecking has proved to be futile and absurd.' Even MacDonald, writing privately to his Liberal friend Herbert Samuel, claimed that Hardie had lost the election through his 'incapacity' and that for anyone to join the party was 'almost suicide'. But not everybody was so pessimistic. J. L. Garvin, by no means a sympathetic observer, was quite clear that the results did not mean 'the elimination of the Independent Labour Party from practical politics, but its permanence as an increasingly powerful and disturbing factor'. (*Fortnightly Review*, September 1895.) Certainly this performance was disappointing, coming as it did after the encouraging by-elections. What was now perfectly clear was that the cause of independent representation had a long way to go. Hardie's comment on it all was succinct and very much to the point: 'We must learn to fight elections.'

The immediate result was a severe setback for the party and for Keir Hardie's personal standing. To add to his troubles his paper the *Labour Leader* now ran into financial difficulties and he himself suffered from indifferent health at this time. Finally, there was a sharp clash between himself and Blatchford which weakened the party still further. Part of the trouble here was personality; there was a marked difference between the serious, if not religiously minded, Hardie and the more expansive, extroverted Blatchford, clearly a man determined to enjoy life to the full. The distrust each felt for the other was deepening and on Blatchford's side there was an element of contempt, hence his remark that the ILP was controlled by 'lily-livered Methodists'. But there was much more to it than clash of personality; there was also a difference over policy. Blatchford's answer to the 1895 debacle was closer cooperation with other socialist groups and he projected a grand alliance of the ILP with the SDF and the Fabians. Hardie, on the other hand, was opposed to cooperation with the SDF not only for reasons of personal antipathy but also because of a deeply-held feeling that they were out of touch with reality. Unfortunately for him, the party tended to see things Blatchford's way and both the conferences of 1895 and 1896 demanded negotiations with the SDF with a view to formal alliance, in spite of Hardie's opposition. In fact, in 1896 Hardie seemed to touch the very nadir of his fortunes when, at a by-election at Aberdeen, the local ILP refused to accept him as a candidate. His despair was such that he almost tendered his resignation from the party, only being dissuaded with some difficulty by a group of his colleagues led by Tom Mann.

But things began to improve, and in the years leading up to the end of the century Hardie regained some of his influence. This was partly due to changes in the upper echelons of the ILP where a number of prominent personalities, for one reason or another, took a less active part. Fred Brocklehurst, financial secretary from 1895-6, gave up his post because of illness; and Tom Mann and Pete Curran both decided to concentrate on union work. Hardie himself deplored these resignations as weakening the links with the trade union movement, but there is no doubt that his own position was stronger as a result. The men who now moved in, Ramsay MacDonald, Philip Snowden and J. Bruce Glasier, were less likely to challenge his authority.

Nonetheless the ILP had two serious problems to face between 1897 and the end of the century—the continued debate over the proposed alliance with the SDF and a disturbing drop in membership. As far as the former was concerned, Hardie was still out of step with the majority of the party. He had remained sceptical about the idea even when a joint conference of representatives from the two organisations had recommended fusion, followed by an ILP referendum in which there was a 5 to 1 majority in favour. He and the council delayed action on the grounds that only one-third of the paid-up members had voted and anyway the matter ought to be decided by the annual conference which, according to the constitution, was the party's ultimate authority. When the 1897 conference finally assembled, Hardie and the executive were criticised for their indecision. Both Hardie and Bruce Glasier spoke strongly against the idea of fusion, their main argument being that if the party wished to win over the trade union movement then association with the SDF would be fatal. In spite of this, conference wanted a two stage tie-up: first federation, then fusion after a decent interval. In the last resort two things killed the idea. First, the 1897 conference was persuaded that the question should be referred to another ballot of members with the proviso that a three-quarters majority was necessary for the proposals. This clearly stacked the cards heavily in Hardie's favour. Secondly, even had this been achieved, the fact was that the SDF itself was not interested in the idea and so negotiations for the time being ended.

More serious perhaps for the future was the decline in overall membership in the last three years of the century. The affiliation fees in the party's balance sheet show that the ILP lost nearly a third of its members between 1898 and 1900. In the balance sheet for the former year, from the sum of money paid by the branches, it seems there were slightly under 9,000 members but by 1900 there were only just over 6,000. Why was this? Hardie for his part thought it was due to the departure of Tom Mann's 'strong personality' (*Labour Leader* 7 January 1899). This does not seem convincing, because, as Pelling has pointed out, the departure of Mann and others from active positions in the party 'made for greater efficiency'. What seems a more likely explanation is that the overwhelming upsurge of imperialism and jingoism in the late 1890s, culminating in the South African War, diverted attention from the more mundane issue of independent working-class representation. But whatever the reason, it is very clear that, on the eve of its success in winning over some of the trade unions to the idea of a new labour party, the ILP itself was not in very good shape.

## [8] The SDF and the Fabians

While the ILP was in difficulties, the SDF was enjoying something of a revival. As we have already seen, the party had lost ground as a result of internal divisions and uncertain finances and little could be mounted in the way of an effective challenge at the 1892 general election. Nonetheless, in the last few years of the century the SDF could point to a definite increase in membership. Admittedly it is difficult to assess the true figures as there is a serious discrepancy between the numbers claimed by the officials and the numbers calculated from the amount paid in affiliation fees on the balance sheets. For example, according to the SDF's claims, their numbers more than doubled between 1894–5, from 4,500 to 10,536. Pelling however reckons that these are sizeable over-estimates, probably by as much as 50 per cent. Yet, if one takes the calculated figures from balance sheets, there is still a rising trend and, right at the end of the period, the number increases from 1,220 in 1897 to 2,680 in 1899. This was in marked contrast to the ILP which was losing members hand over fist. It is difficult to explain this convincingly. It has, for example, been argued by Pelling that the SDF was older, more firmly established and more obviously committed to socialism than the ILP. Also, the SDF had a strong power base in London and, apart from the influence of its branches, it had enough members on the London Trades Council virtually to control that body. In comparison, the ILP was, as yet anyway, a mushroom growth. More convincing perhaps is another argument, again advanced by Pelling, namely that the SDF had some very able men like Will Thorne in key positions in the trade union movement whereas the links between the unions and the ILP had been to some degree severed by the departure of Tom Mann and Pete Curran in 1896. Finally the SDF appears to have made a very good catch at this time by recruiting George Lansbury. Born in 1859, Lansbury was the son of a railway engineer. He had for a time run a small business in the East End of London and had then gone to Australia in the '80s only to return after a short period. He became involved in politics and, like so many in all sections of the working-class movement, at first had hoped to work with the Liberal Party. He had many personal contacts in it but his disillusion with Liberalism grew and was completed when he was pushed off an NLF Conference platform for advocating the eight-hour day. He thereupon joined the SDF, and with Hyndman, increasingly immersed himself in 'nursing' the parliamentary constituency at Burnley, becoming the leading figure of the party. In 1895, for example, he was not only organising secretary but also chairman of the party conference.

So, for these reasons, the SDF seemed to be making progress, while the ILP was slipping back. However, two contrary points should be made. In the first place, the SDF, though strong in London, did not cut much ice outside the capital and its total membership—whether one takes the claims of the officials or the number of affiliations on the balance sheet—was considerably lower than the ILP's. Secondly, the SDF generally speaking did rather worse in elections than its rival. At the 1895 election, four candidates stood: Hyndman at Burnley and George Lansbury at Walworth (London), the other two being at Salford South and Northampton. All came bottom of the poll, trailing very badly, with the exception of F. G. Jones at Northampton who just beat an Independent Liberal. Indeed, Jones' intervention was the only one that was effective in any sense for he undoubtedly split what might loosely be called the 'progressive' vote in the constituency and allowed the Conservative to take one of the two seats. Between the general elections of 1895 and 1900, the ILP fought four by-elections, doing very well in one (North Aberdeen in 1896) and performing fairly respectably in the others. The SDF fought only two, at Southampton in February 1896 and Reading, July 1898. At the latter, Harry Quelch got just over 3 per cent, and at Southampton the candidate could not even match this modest performance.

As for the Fabians, they seemed to be very much a declining force in the 1890s, for this was the period when the much-vaunted tactics of 'permeation' were exposed as being totally unworkable. They themselves and the early historians of the movement such as Edward Pease, made the most extravagant claims as to the extent of their influence. Sidney Webb regarded history as a river moving inevitably in the direction of socialism and the role of the society was to float with the tide, pointing the direction to others and removing obstacles from the stream. Shaw was if anything even more grandiose in his conceptions, claiming that the Fabians were the real manipulators of advanced thinking in the labour movement, the Liberal Party and the Progressive group on the LCC. Even at the time, there were some like H. G. Wells who poured scorn on these pretensions. But it is only comparatively recently that historians have really subjected these claims to critical examination—in particular A. M. McBriar (*Fabian Socialism and English Politics, 1884–1918*), Paul Thompson (*Socialists, Liberals and Labour, the struggle for London, 1885–1914*) and Eric Hobsbawm (essay on the Fabians in *Labouring Men*). Their work supports to a very considerable degree Wells' contemporary verdict.

Apart from the fact that the Fabians probably felt more at home in the middle-class milieu of the Liberal Party, their justification for 'permeation' was that it opened the door to immediate social reform, whereas any new independent party had little real prospect of success. This point was probably best expressed by Shaw speaking in 1895: 'It is far better to be an official Liberal . . . and do something, than to be an uncompromising Social Democrat and do nothing.' Basically, Shaw, Webb and their later apologists made three claims. First, in London, they were responsible for the radical reforming programme of the *Star* newspaper in the late 1880s and the policy pursued by the predominant Progressive group on the LCC. Secondly, by infiltrating the local Liberal associations, they had contributed significantly to the adoption of the Newcastle Programme by the Liberal Party in 1891. Finally, in Pease's opinion, the society's greatest achievement was to 'break the spell of Marxism in England'. As far as the first is concerned, it is certainly true that the *Star* from its foundation in 1888 conducted a vigorous campaign for 'war on privilege' and legislation 'to improve the lot of the masses of the people'. It is also true that the assistant editor, H. W. Massingham, was a member of the society but while he had some influence, it seems clear that the main driving force was the editor, T. P. O'Connor, whose crusading zeal appears to have owed nothing to Fabianism. Furthermore, even if one accepts the Fabians' view, the inescapable fact remains that neither they nor O'Connor could keep the paper on its radical path in the face of the protests of the majority of the shareholders in 1890 and again in 1891. As for the programme of the Progressive Party, both McBriar and Thompson are agreed that there is no evidence of direct Fabian influence. With regard to the second claim, a closer examination of the Newcastle document does not reveal much that could be credited to Fabianism. Amongst the rag-bag of causes to which the Liberals committed themselves, pride of place went to the good old middle-class stand-bys: Home Rule, Welsh and Scottish disestablishment, an end to plural voting and another campaign against the Tory landlords in the form of proposals to create district and parish councils, change the land laws and secure land for allotments. Predictably too the temperance lobby's commitment to Liberalism was confirmed by the proposal to introduce a local veto on the sale of alcohol. But the problem of social reform as it affected the urban working class hardly figured at all, apart from the acceptance of the principle of employers' liability for industrial accidents and a very vague commitment to secure some limitation of the hours of work. If this was all that 'permeation' could achieve then it would hardly seem worth the effort. Finally, Pease's claim has been crisply dismissed by McBriar on the grounds that Marxism had cast no spell in England and certainly the most superficial examination of the SDF's electoral achievement would bear this out. On the other hand, McBriar suggests that what the Fabians did achieve was the production of a brand of socialism which was peculiarly suitable for English conditions, where the country's comparative prosperity and general ingrained respect for constitutional proprieties made nonsense of Marxist talk of revolution.

But the real exposé of Fabian 'permeation' came when the Liberal government took office in 1892 and for the whole of its three years in power took no steps whatsoever in the field of social reform. The Fabians indeed soon realised the fraud and the measure of their disillusion is to be found in their pamphlet of 1893, *To Your Tents, O Israel!*, in which they attacked the Liberal record and declared themselves now ready to consider independent working-class action. In practical terms this meant cooperation with the ILP in the sphere of municipal politics. Here they did important and useful work in providing information and advice for the increasing number of ILP representatives on local authorities. Nonetheless it was a sad come-down after all the brave talk of 'permeation' and the benefits to be gained by the manipulation of the Liberal Party. But, as it happened, even this promising development did not last long, being destroyed by the Boer War. The ILP, and SDF as well, resolutely opposed the government, taking a somewhat rose-coloured view of the Boer States whose 're-publican form of government bespeaks freedom'. (Keir Hardie writing in the *Labour Leader*, 6 January 1900.) On the other hand, the Fabians gave cautious support to the imperialist mood, as expressed in the manifesto *Fabianism and the Empire* drawn up by Shaw in 1900: 'Until the Federation of the World becomes an accomplished fact, we must accept the most responsible Imperial Federations available as a substitute for it.'

To sum up, by the end of the century, the Fabian society seemed a spent force. 'All . . . [it] was fit for was to become a bureau of information for those engaged in following up the political programme that they had worked out in the eighties.' (Pelling, *Origins of the Labour Party*.) Its effective contribution to the foundation of the Labour Representation Committee in 1900 was minimal. Did the Fabians then achieve anything? McBriar, although exploding the myths surrounding the society, argues in his conclusion that they performed an important service by making the first sustained challenge to the philosophy of 'laisser-faire' and advancing the ideal of a society more consciously organised in which there should be a greater degree of equality than hitherto. 'Fabianism,' says McBriar, 'permitted Englishmen to swallow these pills without too much shock to their constitution.'


## [9] Local Developments

In considering the development of those groups working for independent labour representation, most emphasis has been laid on their activities as national political bodies. This has meant a temporary neglect of two important features of the movement; first, the part played by the socialist societies in local government politics, and secondly, the marked regional variations in their scale and progress. The ILP in particular recognised the importance of the field of local government and the valuable experience which might be gained there. As Fred Brocklehurst put it in 1900: 'Men and women who are daily occupied in administering the Poor Law, educational or civic affairs of the town, cannot escape the sobering influence of responsibility.' (*Clarion*, 21 April.) Some idea of the extent of the ILP's success in this sphere can be gauged from the numbers of local government representatives according to the party report of 1900. In this, they claimed to have in office throughout the country 63 town, 4 county, 36 urban district, 3 rural district and 16 parish councillors; 8 citizens' auditors; 51 members of boards of guardians; and 66 members of school boards. But the ILP was not the only organisation active in local government. One of the less noted results of the 'new unionism' was a keen interest on the part of the trade unions, working through the local trades councils, to secure representation on municipal and other councils. In the period 1889–91, no less than sixty new trades councils are known to have been established and they secured a threefold increase in the number of candidates returned in the period 1892–5. But the strength and influence of the local labour movement varied considerably and while it is difficult to get a full picture due to the paucity of research on the subject, an attempt must be made to sketch in these variations.

From what has been said about the foundation of the ILP, the main strength of the independent labour movement would appear to have rested in the industrial north. Here, as the Fabian Katherine Conway put it, writing in 1894, Liberalism had much less appeal to the politically conscious working-man: 'In London, he listens to the persuasive reasoning of the Progressives: in the provinces, face to face with Liberals of the Illingworth, Kitson and Pease type, he is doggedly independent.' Alfred Illingworth (MP for Bradford 1880–95), James Kitson (MP for Colne Valley, 1892–1907) and Sir Joseph Pease (MP for Barnard Castle, 1885–1903) were all employers or capitalists, exceedingly reluctant to make any concessions to the claims of labour, be they political or economic. The ILP's strength in the north was concentrated to a very high degree in Yorkshire. Of its 300 or so branches in existence in 1895, about one-third were in the county and a large proportion in the West Riding. The firm foundations here are revealed by the fact that even in the years of decline for the party from 1897 to 1900, the organisation continued to flourish, thanks partly to the energy and influence of Philip Snowden, working in the Keighley district from 1895 onwards. But even in Yorkshire, the independent movement had its failures. In particular, there was no progress in this period in winning over the miners in the South Yorkshire coal-field. Here, the main stumbling-block was the opposition of the Lib–Lab secretary of the Yorkshire Miners Association and also President of the national Miners' Federation, 'iron man' Ben Pickard. He was frankly suspicious of the suggestion which the ILP seemed to be making that the miners should subsidise other, less fortunate trade unionists. Well might Hardie characterise him as 'a man of few ideas, of a narrow, intolerant cast of mind, and altogether lacking in judgment or discretion'. This, however, could not alter the fact that Pickard's word was law and under him the miners regularly and solidly lined up with the Liberals. The failure of the ILP was duly blazoned to the world in the Barnsley by-election of 1897. The Liberal candidate, although a mine-owner, supported the eight-hour day and was duly backed by Pickard and his union. Curran, standing for the ILP, had difficulty in putting his case—for example at one village in the constituency he was driven off by the miners with stones and brick-bats. In the event he came bottom of the poll with 1,091 votes to the Conservative's 3,454 and the Liberal victor's 6,744.

In other parts of the north, progress was similarly patchy. In Lancashire, the cotton unions tended to be rather less militant than their brothers in the West Yorkshire woollen industry, for they had long since gained reasonable conditions. Furthermore, there was a strong working-class Conservative tradition in the county, which received notable expression when James Mawdsley, the Spinners' union secretary, stood as Conservative candidate at a by-election at Oldham towards the close of the century. The SDF had a number of branches in Lancashire and thought it worthwhile to contest two seats at the 1895 general election, but it will be remembered that neither Hyndman at Burnley, nor his colleague at Salford South was successful. Otherwise, the most promising developments towards independent labour representation appeared to be through the trades councils in Manchester and Liverpool. The history of both these bodies in the 1890s shows clearly both their interest in securing independent working-class representatives in local government and how they provided the organisation in which all the various socialist groups might cooperate in spite of their national rivalries. In Manchester in 1894 the council, prompted no doubt by Leonard Hall, a prominent local ILP member, had sponsored an alliance of local building and engineering unions with the district branch of the ILP to run candidates in the school board elections in the city and its near neighbour Salford. In 1897 it went a stage further. Having refused a suggestion of cooperation from the local Liberals, it sponsored a United Trades and Labour Party in which trades council members, individual unions and members of both the ILP and the SDF agreed to work together in support of candidates in local elections. In Liverpool there were similar moves. In 1892, as a result of pressure from its socialist members, the trades council formed a joint committee of its members with the local Fabians and the ILP, and in December of the following year a permanent Labour Representation Committee was set up to contest the municipal elections. Later, however, there appears to have been something of a set-back for in 1896 the trades council withdrew its members from the Representation Committee.

Outside industrial Yorkshire and Lancashire, the only other part of the north where it might be expected the political labour movement would have taken hold, was the coal-field of the north-east, Northumberland and Durham. Here the mining vote was the decisive factor in at least seven constituencies: Wansbeck and Morpeth in Northumberland; Mid-Durham, North-West Durham, Houghton-le-Spring, Chester-le-Street and Bishop Auckland in the Durham coal-field. In point of fact at this stage, the north-eastern miners were strongly Lib–Lab in their political sympathies. Burt and Fenwick of the Northumberland miners' union sat as Lib–Labs for the two Northumberland seats, and John Wilson, the Durham miners' financial and general secretary, represented Mid-Durham with Liberal backing, while the remaining seats were all left to the disposal of the local Liberal associations. The north-eastern miners had already secured a seven-hour day, which they did not wish to jeopardise by association with the socialist movement. The idea of independent political action had, for the time being at any rate, even less appeal than for their colleagues in Yorkshire.

There were two other areas where some progress, albeit halting, was made: Scotland and South Wales. In Scotland in the Glasgow area, the combination of markedly bad social conditions coupled with a fairly strong tradition of protest, were largely cancelled out by other factors. For a start, the miners, like their fellows south of the border were very pro-Liberal and reluctant to break their association with the party. Then there was the large Irish element in the population which had come in after the famine of the 1840s and was committed almost solidly to Liberalism by the overriding issue of Home Rule. Religion also tended to work against the socialist movement for the Catholic Church especially and the Church of Scotland to a lesser extent were hostile to its philosophy. The going was particularly hard, as Keir Hardie found in the 1880s. As with his later efforts in England, Hardie was anxious to secure the involvement of the trade unions in his political projects. In September 1891 the Scottish United Trades Council Labour Party was formed, to be run jointly by representatives from the trades councils and the Scottish Labour Party. Unfortunately the venture soon collapsed: the SLP men were excluded from the organisation's deliberations; an attempt to run candidates at the 1892 general election was not successful; and by the end of 1893 those still interested seem to have agreed quietly that further activity was pointless.

But, by the end of the century, there were signs of progress. In 1893, Hardie's Scottish Labour Party in effect became part of the ILP and from then on steadily recruited members and formed new branches, particularly in the Glasgow area. Its success was most marked in the field of local government in conjunction with the Glasgow Trades Council. This latter body dated from 1858, although its origins go back earlier, and it had for some time interested itself spasmodically in political matters. Together the two bodies were able to take advantage of the feuds within the Liberal Party between the Rosebery faction and the anti-Imperialists, and the ILP won no less than 10 seats on the 75 strong corporation in the municipal elections of 1898. The other event which showed that politically the working class in the west of Scotland was waking up was the Lanarkshire miners' strike of 1894. This was a movement against the coal-owners' attempt to reduce wages and it quickly spread to the whole of the Scottish Lowland coal-fields, involving 70,000 miners and lasting four months before the men were finally forced back on the employers' terms. But, although the strike was defeated, it had two important results for the future. First, it marked the emergence of Robert Smillie who formed the Scottish Miners' Federation and set himself the task of welding the hitherto weakly organised and divided miners into a coherent unit. Secondly, the clash with the predominantly Liberal mine-owners began the process of questioning the hitherto accepted links with the Liberal Party.

In South Wales there was a similarly delayed awakening of working-class political consciousness. K. O. Morgan, in his study *Wales in British Politics*, remarks that the working-class movement in the principality in the period after 1880 was characterised by both industrial and political feebleness. The main reason seems to have been that Welsh politics was dominated by two issues, nationalism and nonconformity. For the time being social issues were of little moment and the working-class leadership, such as it was, saw no reason to challenge traditional Liberalism. This attitude was perhaps most obviously represented by the miners' leader William Abraham, 'Mabon', who firmly believed there need be no real conflict between capital and labour. The political concomitant of this was, of course, Lib–Labism and in 1885 Mabon secured election as Lib–Lab MP for the Rhondda, a seat he held until 1920.

But, again as in Scotland, there were forces at work beginning to change this pattern. For a start, there was a marked impetus from the 'new unionism' which saw strong recruiting campaigns by dockworkers' and labourers' unions in the industrial centres of the south; and the formation of new trades councils at Newport, Barry, Neath, Merthyr Tydfil and Pontypridd and the revival of existing ones at Cardiff and Swansea. But of more significance was the conversion of the miners as a result of the strike of 1898. Even before this, there had already been some dissatisfaction with the quiescent policy so far followed by Mabon, and he was now overborne by something like a revolt amongst the men, demanding an end to the 'sliding scale'. This precipitated a bitter strike in which, unfortunately for themselves, the miners had no prospect of success for financial reasons. After five months bitter struggle, they were forced to give in. However, the stimulus the strike provided, both to a better organised trade unionism and a new political initiative, was of tremendous importance. Now the ILP was able to make some impact on a hitherto untapped area. Keir Hardie had always believed in the possibility of winning the Welsh for his cause, as he himself put it: 'Like all true Celts, they are socialists by instinct.' (*Labour Leader* 9 July 1898.) It seemed at last that he might be right. He personally led a band of ILP missionaries into the area and they made good progress in recruitment and the formation of branches, particularly in east Glamorgan. By the end of 1898, they had 31 branches with a total membership of 1,704 and, although this slipped back badly in the following year, there was still enough independent labour feeling in South Wales for Hardie to exploit in the Merthyr election of 1900.

But, of the areas where the idea of independent labour representation was making progress before 1900, perhaps the most surprising was London. It was surprising for two reasons. First, the London working class was far less homogeneous, less closely-knit and less well organised in a trade union sense than say the working class of the industrial north. Secondly, there was in London an advanced form of Liberalism in the shape of the Progressive Party which could mount a strong challenge for working-class support. That progress was made in London towards the ideal of independent representation was mainly due, according to Paul Thompson, to the tenacity of purpose of the SDF.

There were two areas in particular where socialism was firmly establishing itself, Bow and Bromley and West Ham. In the former, the driving force was George Lansbury and under his leadership the local SDF branch pursued an active and successful course in local government politics in the 1890s. Then, in the 1900 general election Lansbury, standing as an SDF candidate under LRC auspices, was able to make a not insignificant dent in the Conservative majority. In West Ham progress was even better. Even before Keir Hardie won the parliamentary seat of West Ham South in 1892, Will Thorne had secured election to the town council. The year of Hardie's success also saw seven 'labour' councillors elected to join Thorne. Other representatives secured seats on the school board and the board of guardians. These early successes though were followed by set-backs, in particular the morale-shattering

E.L.P.—3*

blow of Hardie's defeat in 1895, and there was a tendency, depressingly familiar in labour politics, for the various elements in the movement to react to defeat by fighting amongst themselves. Fortunately, this phase did not last long for representatives of the trades council, SDF, ILP (such as it was) and Christian Socialists formed a United Socialist and Labour Council, which not only had the inspiration of Thorne's leadership but also the services of a very effective electoral manager, J. J. Terrett. Substantial 'labour' gains were made in the last years of the 1890s, so much so that in 1898 the 'labour' men had a clear majority on the thirty-six-man council. Admittedly, this control did not last long and rather surprisingly, Will Thorne did badly in the 1900 general election. It is clear, however, that the cause of independen labour in West Ham, as in Bow and Bromley, had made tremendous strides forward.

Such then was the state of the independent political labour movement at the end of the nineteenth century. It does not present a very promis-ing picture: the groups were disunited, often quarrelling amongst themselves and making very uneven progress in establishing their organisations throughout the country. Yet, paradoxically, they were on the threshold of the first real break-through with the foundation of the Labour Representation Committee, the body which in the space of six years turned itself into the Labour Party

# Part IV

## The Foundation of the Labour Representation Committee 1900

### [10] The Idea of the Labour Alliance

Throughout his political life, Keir Hardie always insisted on the overriding importance of the idea of the 'labour alliance'. Any really effective independent working-class party must be based on an understanding with the trade union movement. The failure of his initiative in 1888 indicated the magnitude of the task and, to make matters worse, his natural allies, the 'new unionists', suffered serious setbacks. The defection of Burns, hitherto their most prominent leader, was followed by the economic recession of the 1890s which markedly reduced their strength and prestige. Admittedly the reverse was temporary but at the time the odds against Hardie seemed to have reached a level which would have daunted a lesser man. On the other hand there were some grounds for hope. All trade unionists, be they 'new' or 'old', were fully agreed on one burning issue—the eight-hour day. Yet, as the 1890s progressed, there seemed little immediate prospect of achieving this end. Perhaps this might prove to be the argument to convince the big battalions of coal and cotton in the TUC of the need for a new political party.

But, for the time being, progress was minimal. At the 1892 TUC Hardie had apparently secured a success when he carried a motion instructing the Parliamentary Committee to prepare a financial scheme for independent labour representation, but the opposition of the old guard Lib–Labs who still dominated the Parliamentary Committee ensured that nothing was done. The following year also saw developments which seemed promising. Delegates reiterated their commitment to the idea of a special political fund and even went so far as to decide to support only those candidates who accepted the principle of 'collective ownership and control of the means of production, distribution and exchange'. If this was not socialism, it was something very close to it. Yet, when it came to putting these principles into action, the TUC balked. When Hardie brought forward a definite motion calling for the establishment of a new working-class party, it was defeated by twenty-three votes. In spite of this set-back, the strength and prestige of the socialists in the trade union movement seemed to be reviving, and Hardie and his friends were hoping to capitalise on this by securing the election of Tom Mann as secretary at the 1894 congress. Their chances of bringing off this coup looked reasonably promising for, out of a total delegate body of 370, they reckoned no less than 80 were ILP members.

But now the old guard TUC leaders were alarmed and, led by James Mawdsley of the cotton union, ably assisted by Burns, they struck back to such purpose that the entry of the trade union movement into independent politics was delayed for another five years. They began the 1894 conference by securing a resolution instructing the Parliamentary Committee to revise standing orders ready for the 1895 meeting. Then, they brought forward three changes. First, the trades councils, which were predominantly 'new unionist' and socialist in composition, were to be barred in future from the TUC on the grounds that their members were already adequately represented through their national union bodies. Secondly, from now on delegates to the TUC could only be union officials or men actually still engaged on working at their trade. This was designed to remove Hardie and other ILP members from the trade union arena. This was a serious blow to his long-term plans, but it was ironic that the resolution also resulted in the removal of men such as Burns himself and Broadhurst. Finally, it was decided to introduce the principle of the 'card' vote whereby delegates did not vote as individuals but instead disposed of a number of votes according to the strength of their respective unions. This had the effect of further strengthening the power and influence of the large coal and cotton unions. These changes were duly approved by the 1895 TUC, the delegates apparently being convinced by Mawdsley's argument that unless these alterations were made, the movement might well become the dupe of unscrupulous political adventurers. Yet, in spite of this set-back, only four years later at the 1899 TUC the Railway Servants' Union succeeded in carrying its famous resolution instructing the Parliamentary Committee to summon the conference which established the Labour Representation Committee. The reason for this rapid change of tune was twofold. First, the leaders of the TUC became convinced that the position of the trade union movement was once more being seriously threatened and secondly, there was the growing realisation that Liberalism and the Liberal Party had little to offer the working class.

The growing anxiety and unease amongst certain sections of the trade union movement was the result of a number of factors. One of these was the structural changes taking place in some industries and the increasing mechanisation, both of which have already been dealt with in a previous chapter. (Part II, Chapter 3.) Secondly, it was becoming increasingly plain that some employers, encouraged perhaps by the example of their confrères on the other side of the Atlantic, were adopting a much tougher line towards the unions. This feeling was probably best expressed by the leader of the engineering employers, Colonel Dyer, writing to *The Times* in September 1897: 'The federated engineering employers are determined to obtain the freedom to manage their own affairs which has proved so beneficial to the American manufacturers.' At about the same time, the American, Henry Demarest Lloyd, who had given much time and energy to exposing the evil influence of the trusts in the States, gave it as his opinion that 'English employers are getting the opinion of American lawyers as to the American methods of dealing with labour troubles.' And as two famous strikes in the USA at the time showed, these methods were scarcely kid-gloved. In the Homestead strike of 1892 and the Pullman dispute of 1894, the employers not only took action in the courts, but had the assistance of State militia and even federal troops to put down the accompanying disorder.

The first overt signs that the employers were mounting a general and concerted counter-attack appeared with the establishment of associations and federations in a number of industries with the specific objective of checking the growth and powers of the unions. That of the engineering employers has already been mentioned, but also fairly typical was the Shipowners' Federation formed in 1890 which deliberately set out to prevent men from securing jobs if they were members of a union. Furthermore, it seems fairly certain that the shipping employers were largely responsible for the formation of a body calling itself the National Free Labour Association. The 'front man' was William Collison, who had hitherto pursued a somewhat varied, if not to say chequered, career as a soldier, dock-labourer, bus driver and union organiser. He claimed that he was protecting genuine trade unionists from what he considered were the evils of the 'new unionism' which had encouraged intimidation and other unlawful practices. He also argued that he was protecting 'the general body of Labour from the tyranny and dictation of Socialistic Trade Union leaders'. No doubt Collison himself believed this highflown justification but to his backers, not only the shipowners but also the railway companies, the Association was merely a convenient source of black-leg labour. Admittedly such an organisation could only be successful up to a point—it could, for example, only supply unskilled, or at best semi-skilled, men on any large scale. But its very existence—and the existence of bodies like it—lent colour and substance to the anxieties of many trade unionists. Nor was this all, for in 1898 there was formed the Employers' Parliamentary Council, whose objects were, according to *The Times*, 'free contracts and free labour'. This body had developed out of another, the Free Labour Protection Association formed in July of the previous year. The initiators included Lord Wemyss, who had sat on the Royal Commission of 1867 and then taken a pro-trade union view; Sir George Livesey of the South Metropolitan Gas Company; and Colonel Dyer. The engineering employers seem to have led the way but they were soon joined by representatives from a wide variety of industries—engineering, coal, cotton, building, printing, boot and shoe manufacturing and a number of others. In Wemyss's view, expressed in a letter to *The Times*, the new body would 'make members of Parliament . . . and the Board of Trade see that in labour and trade questions there are possibly two sides.'

But if there was a general tendency on the employers' part to harden their attitude, it was most marked in two industries—the boot and shoe industry as well as the engineering trade. Both had been, or were being, profoundly influenced by the mechanisation process which led to head-on clashes between management and labour. A third group of workers who found themselves under similar pressure were the railwaymen whose employers had always, almost without exception, taken an unyielding, hostile attitude to the development of trade unionism.

The boot and shoe manufacturers, like the engineering employers, had a well organised association, which had been spoiling for a fight for some time. In 1895 they got their opportunity when a strike began in one of the main centres of the industry, Northampton. The employers replied by declaring a lock-out which lasted over five weeks, involved 46,000 operatives and seriously weakened the strength of the union. The dispute was finally settled through the good offices of the permanent secretary of the board of trade, Sir Courtenay Boyle, but the fact remained that the employers gained almost all they wanted and the union membership declined substantially between then and the end of the century. Equally indicative of the general pattern, and if anything more serious for the whole working-class movement, was the defeat suffered by the Amalgamated Society of Engineers in the lock-out of 1897–8. The ASE had been pursuing a particularly militant line for some time and this trend was underlined by the election of George

Barnes as secretary in 1896. Barnes was a member of the ILP and was closely associated in the trade union movement with Tom Mann. On the other side, the employers under Dyer's leadership had recently (1896) organised their association and were ready to give battle. The issue that triggered off the conflict was a strike in the London area in favour of an eight-hour day, whereupon the employers declared a national lock-out which lasted from July 1897 to January 1898. Despite offers of financial support from other unions, the strain was too much and in the end the engineers were forced to capitulate. The significance of the whole episode has been succinctly expressed by Pelling in *A History of British Trade Unionism*: 'It was a humiliating set-back for a union which was still regarded as the foremost in the country, indeed in the world.' As for the railwaymen, they too suffered set-backs in the 1890s, though not perhaps so dramatically as their colleagues in the other two industries. The main railway trade union, the Amalgamated Society of Railway Servants, was unique amongst the country's leading unions for not being recognised by the employers. Now, under the capable leadership of Richard Bell who became secretary in October 1897, the ASRS mounted a strong campaign for recognition. In the following month a delegate conference considered the possibility of a national strike to force the companies' hand. The attempt to organise this was a complete fiasco; even the union's own newspaper argued that it was not yet strong enough to take on the employers with any hope of success. Admittedly, the editor, the Lib–Lab politician Fred Maddison, was forced to resign as a result of this indiscretion, but it did not alter the fact that he had judged correctly and the ASRS suffered a set-back which led to a significant decline in membership in the ensuing years.

Finally, there was a third element in the situation which caused trade union alarm. This was the question of the unions' legal status and in particular the liability of their funds and the right to make strike action effective by picketing. With regard to the issue of the unions' legal liability, a number of cases came before the courts in the 1890s from which no clear conclusion could be drawn. In the case of *Temperton* v *Russell* in 1893, a Hull building contractor was boycotted by the local builders' union for supplying materials to another builder with whom it was in dispute. Temperton, the victim of the boycott, accordingly brought an action for damages and his case was upheld. The principle of liability was reinforced by the decision in *Trollope* v *London Building Trades' Federation* in 1895–6, when Trollope's, a firm of builders, successfully sued the trade union for its action in putting them on a black list of allegedly unfair employers. But this trend was reversed in 1898 by the conclusion of a long drawn-out case, *Allen* v *Flood*. Flood was a carpenter employed in a shipyard on work supposedly reserved for boilermakers, and the boilermakers' secretary T. F. Allen threatened strike action if Flood were not dismissed. The firm dismissed him, where-upon he brought an action against the union secretary. The case went eventually to the House of Lords, where it was decided that, whatever Allen's motives, he had in fact committed no unlawful action and therefore the union had no case to answer.

This verdict not unnaturally caused great jubilation in the trade union world but unfortunately there was a much more serious challenge developing in the shape of an attack on the right to picket. The unions had hitherto assumed that they were on firm legal ground in establish-ing picket lines to ensure a strike's effectiveness, for Disraeli's Act of 1875 had expressly permitted such action provided it were 'peaceful'. The matter arose through the case of *Lyons* v *Wilkins* which was con-cluded in 1899. Lyons was a leather goods manufacturer involved in a strike with a small leather workers' union of which Wilkins was the secretary. When the union started picketing, Lyons obtained an injunc-tion against it, which was duly upheld in the Court of Appeal. Lyons then prosecuted Wilkins successfully, the judge arguing that it was illegal to 'persuade' someone to take part in a strike. On appeal, the judgment was upheld, one of the Appeal Court Judges commenting 'You cannot make a strike effective without doing more than what is lawful.' This was very serious. If nothing else, it meant that the unions no longer knew what their rights were. As the Liberal lawyer, R. B. Haldane, put it in 1903, after further anti-picketing decisions had been handed down in *Quinn* v *Leathem* and the Taff Vale Case: 'Speaking for myself, I should be very sorry to be called on to tell a Trade Union Secretary how he could conduct a strike lawfully. The only answer I could give would be that, having regard to the diverging opinion of the Judges, I did not know.' The unsettling effect of this on trade unionists and their leaders may well be imagined. Their reaction to this situation was twofold: first, they attempted to strengthen the trade union move-ment by forming in 1899 the General Federation of Trade Unions as a body to promote mutual support; secondly, some of them at any rate began to argue the merits of independent political action as the best long term means of securing redress.

## [11] The 1900 Conference

The second circumstance which helped Keir Hardie realise his idea of a new working-class party was the weakening of Lib–Labism in the last decade of the nineteenth century. In 1886, the Liberal Party had suffered a disaster of the first magnitude following the split over Home Rule and the loss of Chamberlain whose innate political dynamism in addition to his radical programmes might possibly have secured at least some portion of the working-class vote for Liberalism. But although this was a devastating blow, the fact remains that during the period 1886–1900 the party still had a chance to rebuild on the basis of mass working-class support. At first it seemed that this would happen. Thus T. R. Threlfall's establishment of the Labour Electoral Association was welcomed and encouraged by the Liberal leadership, particularly by the party organiser Schnadhorst and by Gladstone himself. Then there was the radical programme put forward by T. P. O'Connor in *The Star*, which has already been mentioned, and at least some, though not many, concessions were made to working-class aspirations in the Newcastle Manifesto. It would seem reasonable to assume that these moves contributed significantly to the Liberal recovery of 1892, which, though not by any means a sweeping victory, was a marked improvement on the 1886 position. But, unfortunately, the Liberals were not prepared to go far in meeting the working class. As we have already seen, the Liberal government of 1892–5 attempted nothing in the field of social reform and moreover failed to take up the key question of the payment of MPs. As for the policy of securing the adoption of working-class candidates by the local Liberal associations, by the mid 90s this was as dead as the dodo. Threlfall himself wrote in *The Nineteenth Century* in 1894: 'It is only a waste of time to advise the working classes to attend and make the caucus what they want it to be. . . . As it exists today, it is too narrow and too much hampered with class prejudice to be a reflex of the expanding democratic and labour sentiment.' Threlfall had good reason for disillusion. His organisation, which claimed to represent three-quarters of a million trade unionists in 1891, was totally ignored by the Liberals and, failing to secure any worthwhile concessions either at the election of 1892 or the one of 1895, simply disintegrated. Nor was Threlfall the only one to voice his disillusion. We have already noted Ramsay MacDonald's defection as a result of the Attercliffe election of 1894. On that occasion he wrote to Keir Hardie: 'Liberalism, and more particularly local Liberal Associations, have definitely declared against Labour.' The following year, we find him returning to the same theme in a letter to Herbert Samuel: 'We didn't leave the Liberals. They kicked us out and slammed the door in our faces!' At long last, events seemed to be breaking in Keir Hardie's favour.

Even at the nadir of his fortunes in 1895, when he had lost his seat in the general election and the TUC had just carried through its changes in standing orders to exclude the socialists, Hardie never entirely lost hope that his ideal could be achieved. Thus, writing of the TUC in the *Labour Leader* (22 February 1896): 'I still think this committee would be the recognised head of the socialist movement in Great Britain, leaving the ILP, the SDF, the Fabian Society and other organisations to carry on their propaganda in their respective ways.' But it was not until 1898 that reality came near to matching his hope. According to his calculations, the TUC that year was composed of a majority of socialists and of these something like 60 per cent were active ILP members. This may have been an over-estimate but, nonetheless, conference approved by a large majority a resolution urging support for 'the working-class socialist parties'. In addition, he was encouraged by the fact that the composition of the Parliamentary Committee had changed significantly in that the Lib–Lab element was weaker and that four of the thirteen members were either socialists or socialist sympathisers. Therefore, Hardie decided the time had come to strike. On 1 October 1898, the ILP Council, on his prompting, decided to approach the Parliamentary Committees of the TUC and the Scottish TUC to organise joint political action. On the same day, he spelt out clearly what he had in mind in the *Labour Leader*: 'What we should aim at is the same kind of working agreement nationally as already exists for municipal purposes in Glasgow. Trade unionists, socialists and co-operators, each select their own candidates, a joint programme having been first agreed upon, and then the expense of the campaign is also borne jointly.' As it turned out, the organisation which emerged conformed almost exactly to this blueprint for a federation.

In Scotland, the response was immediate and there was very little difficulty, following preliminary discussions, in convening a conference of interested parties which met in Edinburgh on 6 January 1900. Here, delegates from the Scottish TUC, the ILP and the SDF agreed on the desirability of independent representation, set out a list of reforms to be pursued and set up a rudimentary organisation—the Scottish Workers' Parliamentary Committee—to put the decisions into effect.

South of the border, the task was more difficult. In spite of what has been said about the position of the trades unions and the pressures pushing them towards the idea of a new independent party, the fact remains that there were still powerful groups opposed to the new policy. The miners and cotton unions of course were hostile to the proposals for reasons that have already become clear. Somewhat surprisingly, the engineers' attitude was rather equivocal. True, they, more than most, had been under pressure; they had in George Barnes, their secretary, an enthusiast for political action; and, in the course of 1899, they had already voted to establish a fund to run candidates for Parliament. On the other hand, the union's executive council was dominated by older, more conservative men than the secretary and it should not be forgotten that John Burns was an ex-member who still wielded considerable influence on the side of Lib–Labism. In fact, it was the Railway Servants who initiated action on the formation of a new party when the 1899 TUC assembled. Their resolution instructed the Parliamentary Committee to call a conference of representatives from the 'Cooperative, socialist, trade union and other working-class organisations,' to 'devise ways and means for the securing of an increased number of labour members in the next Parliament.' This was basically the work of the Doncaster branch of the ASRS working in cooperation with the editor of the *Railway Review*, Thomas Steels. Steels had said boldly in his journal some months before the conference met: 'The sending to Parliament of even one direct and independent representative by a powerful trade union . . . will make more for progress than the sending of fifty Liberals or Tories of the best type, because it will be unmistakeable evidence of labour's revolt.' (*Railway Review*, 3 March 1899.)

In the debate on the resolution, the ASRS was supported by James Sexton of the Liverpool dockers who drew attention to what he called the 'present disgraceful confusion' in labour politics and suggested this was the only sensible way to resolve it. The opposition of the coal and cotton group was voiced by W. E. Harvey of the Derbyshire miners and Thomas Ashton of the cotton spinners. Harvey in effect reiterated Pickard's view that there was no justification for the miners subsidising or underwriting other unions in political action: 'The matter was in their own hands and each society ought to get about teaching their members that it was their duty to pay for securing the end in view.' Ashton, aware of the strong tradition of working-class Toryism in Lancashire, was convinced that 'if their society were to interfere in politics, it would go down immediately.' At the end, on a card vote, those in favour of political action got home by a majority of just over 110,000 (546,000 votes for the motion, 434,000 against). The announcement was followed by scenes of great enthusiasm, and indeed its significance was tremendous. 'Labour's revolt' had truly begun.

It now remained to put the decision into effect. To do this a provisional committee of representatives of the TUC Parliamentary Committee, the Fabians, the ILP and the SDF was established to organise a conference to meet at the Farringdon Street Memorial Hall on 27 February 1900. Apart from the organisational arrangements, this committee, which seems to have been greatly influenced by Hardie and MacDonald working for the ILP and Shaw for the Fabians, produced a scheme suggesting the federation for political purposes of the trade unions, trade councils, co-ops and socialist societies. When the conference itself assembled, however, it very quickly became apparent that Hardie and his friends had by no means complete control. There were three other fairly distinctive groupings amongst the 129 delegates who, to a greater or lesser degree, opposed the ILP line. Naturally, Hardie had to count on the opposition of the SDF which produced for debate a rigidly Marxist motion calling for 'a distinctive party—separate from the capitalist parties based upon the recognition of the class war and having for its ultimate object the socialisation of the means of production, distribution and exchange.' This cut comparatively little ice but there was some support for it, mainly from the London representatives, which is not surprising in view of the strength of the party in the capital. At the other end of the political spectrum there was a group of trade unionists who, in Ramsay MacDonald's words, had come 'to bury the attempt in good humoured tolerance'. Finally, there was another group from the unions, whose main spokesman was Alexander Wilkie of the shipwrights union, who wanted political action but viewed with alarm the possibility that a new party be dominated by the members of the socialist societies. Their idea was to place the new organisation firmly under the aegis of the TUC Parliamentary Committee, whereas Hardie regarded this body as far too cautious if not conservative. Furthermore, they were not averse to the idea of establishing, or rather maintaining, links with the Liberals, whereas Hardie wanted complete independence.

But in the end, Hardie managed to get most of what he wanted and gained for the ILP the most influential position in the new group. First, he secured the principle of independence by getting the meeting to agree to the establishment of a distinct Labour group in Parliament with its own whips. Secondly, when the size and composition of the executive committee was finally established, he gained five of the twelve places for his nominees and, of the seven trade unionists who made up the remainder of that body, no less than four were known ILP sympathisers. Thirdly he successfully promoted the election of his chief henchman, Ramsay MacDonald, as secretary of the new organisation. Finally, he blocked a resolution which would have allowed the Parliamentary Committee to act on behalf of the trade union movement before individual unions decided to affiliate. How was Hardie able to achieve these striking successes? In the first place, it is not unlikely that his personal qualities of determination and sincerity influenced the delegates. Secondly, there was the fact that he handled the unions extremely tactfully and skilfully. He had always stressed the importance of good contacts between the ILP and the unions and when he went into the conference he had the open sympathies of most of the 'new unions' in addition to the ASRS, the boot and shoe workers and at least some sections of the ASE. Furthermore, he was very careful not to trample on the pro-Liberal sentiments of some of the other trade unionists. Thus, while his motion emphasised the new party's basic independence, it also laid down that a labour group might 'cooperate with any party which, for the time being, may be engaged in promoting legislation in the direct interests of labour.' Finally, there was the fact that Hardie and the ILP so clearly held the middle ground not only in this particular conference but in the working-class movement in general. Half way between the rigid Marxism of the SDF and the indeterminate Lib–Labs, they were almost bound to be the beneficiaries of a compromise on the issue of labour representation.

Thus, as a result of that meeting in London in February 1900, the new Labour Party was launched. After some further debate, it was agreed that its name should be the Labour Representation Committee and it was now ready to accept affiliations from socialist societies and trade unions. It was a beginning from which a great party was to develop but, in 1900, few would have dared to predict this. The LRC lacked funds, a proper administrative organisation and aroused very little attention in a nation more interested in the course of the South African War. Even those who helped to found it were none too sure. The Fabians predicted failure all along; the SDF soon decamped in dudgeon because its ideas had been largely rejected; and Blatchford's *Clarion*, though recognising a step forward, was very guarded in its optimism: 'At last, there is a United Labour Party, or perhaps it would be safer to say, a little cloud, no bigger than a man's hand, which may grow into a United Labour Party.' (10 March 1900.) The early years of the party's history were to show that this judgment was by no means unprophetic.

### PRINCIPAL EVENTS, 1880–1900

1881. The establishment of the Democratic Federation with H. M. Hyndman as its president

1883. The passage of the Corrupt Practices Act to restrict electoral expenditure

1884. The foundation of the Fabian Society. The Democratic Federation changed its name to the Social Democratic Federation. The passage of the Third Reform Act which enfranchised male householders in county constituencies. The secession of William Morris from the SDF to form the Socialist League

1885. The 'Tory gold' scandal. Failure of the SDF candidates in the general election

1886. The split in the Liberal Party over Home Rule. The TUC approved T. R. Threlfall's proposal for a Labour Electoral Committee (later renamed the Labour Electoral Association)

1887. Keir Hardie's attack on the Lib–Lab leader Henry Broadhurst at the TUC. Combined SDF and Irish demonstration ended in 'Bloody Sunday' in Trafalgar Square.

1888. The Mid-Lanark by-election: Keir Hardie's defeat followed by the formation of the Scottish Labour Party

1889. The formation of the National Union of Gasworkers and General Labourers by Will Thorne. The London dock strike followed by the formation of the dockers' union

1891. The Manningham Mills' strike in Bradford followed by the formation of the Bradford Labour Union

1892. Keir Hardie returned as 'independent labour' member for West Ham (South) in the general election

1893. The establishment of the Independent Labour Party following a conference at Bradford

1895. General election: failure of all ILP candidates and Hardie defeated at West Ham. Lock-out in the boot and shoe industry following a strike in Northampton

1897. Strike of London engineers for an eight-hour day precipitated a lock-out. Failure of attempts by the Amalgamated Society of Railway Servants to secure recognition by the employers

1899.  Final judgment in the case *Lyons* v *Wilkins* declared picketing illegal. ASRS motion for a conference on independent political representation carried at the TUC

1900.  Conference of trade unionists and delegates from the socialist societies established the Labour Representation Committee

# Part V

## The Progress of the Labour Representation Committee 1900–6

### [12] The New Party

The general tendency for both friends and foes alike to underrate the significance of the new party is not so surprising when one considers its first uncertain electoral venture in the general election of 1900. True, conditions were very much against a reasonable LRC showing. In the first place, the election was an attempt on the part of the Unionist government, prompted by its strongest personality Chamberlain, to capitalise on the Jingoism stirred by the South African War. In the atmosphere of extreme patriotism generated by Lord Roberts' victories in the preceding months, the 'left' — Liberals as well as the new Labour group — was hard pressed. Secondly, there was the time factor. The election came a bare eight months after the party's foundation and in that short space it had neither time to organise itself nor build up a body of worth-while candidates. Finally, and most important of all, was the shortage of funds: the LRC accounts show that a mere £33 was spent for the whole campaign, although individual candidates could and did spend quite large sums from their own resources. Thus Bell at Derby spent something like £900 and Hardie at Merthyr Tydfil found a grant of £150 from the chocolate manufacturer George Cadbury most useful, though his expenses were only one-third of Bell's.

Inevitably, given the circumstances, there was a marked tendency for LRC candidates to line up with the anti-war section of the Liberal Party and nowhere was this more marked than in Keir Hardie's constituency. Hardie himself felt very dubious about his chances in South Wales and had in fact allowed his name to go forward for the Preston constituency where he spent almost all of his time and energy in an unsuccessful attempt to shake the Conservative grip. In comparison, according to the *Labour Leader* (13 October 1900) he spent only 'eleven waking hours' in Merthyr Tydfil, yet secured election in the double-member seat along with the Liberal coal-owner David Thomas. The fact was that the third candidate, Pritchard Morgan, was a Liberal

Imperialist who dubbed both Hardie and Thomas as 'Pro-Boers'. Thus, Hardie, fighting on the platform 'Labour and Peace instead of Capital and War', undoubtedly received a good deal of support from anti-war Liberals who were strong in the area and could not stomach Morgan at any price. There were other examples of such cooperation. In the north, Fred Jowett received support from the local Liberals in Bradford and at Sunderland Alex Wilkie spoke on the same platform as the Liberal candidate G. B. Hunter, the shipbuilder. In the midlands, Richard Bell at Derby both looked for and received Liberal support. But there were also examples of friction between the two groups. At Gower in Glamorgan, John Hodge of the steel smelters' union tried to secure Liberal backing but was rebuffed by the local association and at Leeds East an LRC candidate with pronounced middle-class leanings, W. P. Byles, was opposed by a Liberal. So the equivocal nature of the relationship between the Liberal Party and organised labour, which had been a feature of politics in the preceding thirty years, was further underlined. This apart, the plain fact was that the new party had, electorally speaking, made a very modest start. Of fifteen candidates who went to the polls under LRC auspices only two—Hardie and Bell—were returned and a number of candidates who had looked to be well placed, fell by the wayside. Thus, besides Fred Jowett at Bradford, Ramsay MacDonald failed at Leicester, despite the alleged radical tradition of that city; Philip Snowden fought what the *Blackburn Weekly Telegraph* called 'a memorable campaign' but could come nowhere near unseating the Conservative. Perhaps most surprising of all was Will Thorne's defeat in Hardie's old seat at West Ham (South) where the forces of Labour had seemed to be securing a firm grip on the constituency.

The election of 1900 made even clearer the magnitude of the LRC's most urgent task, that of sheer survival. Given the strength of Lib–Labism, the danger was that the new body would go the way of the Labour Representation League of 1869 and the Labour Electoral Association of 1886, both of which had withered away and whose remnants had been absorbed by the Liberal Party. Admittedly the Lib–Labs were under pressure but they were not prepared to give up yet. They had the advantage of able and determined leaders like Burns and Pickard, whose prestige in the labour movement as a whole was very high. So anxious was the latter to avoid any tie-up between the miners and the LRC that in 1901 he introduced a new scheme to raise funds for the election of more miners' MPs, and this was accepted by the Miners' Federation in 1903. This was no surprise to the LRC and its supporters, but what did come as a nasty shock was the attitude of Richard Bell, who, almost immediately following his election, evinced clear Lib–Lab tendencies to the extent of launching a public campaign through the ASRS journal *Railway Review*.

Basically the Lib–Labs pursued two lines of action in an attempt to weaken and suborn the independence of the LRC. First, they sought to revive the proposal that the new group be brought under the control of the TUC Parliamentary Committee. This, it will be remembered, had been thrown out by the inaugural conference, but it was now brought before the 1902 TUC in the slightly modified form of a motion calling for the Parliamentary Committee to be accepted as the coordinating body for all labour representation. This was defeated but, undismayed, the Lib–Labs now tried a variation on the 'Trojan Horse' tactic by attempting to secure the affiliation to the LRC of a rival radical body, the National Democratic League. This had been established in October 1900 chiefly as a means of coordinating Liberal and Labour opposition to the Boer War. It is true that, for a time, the League attracted the sympathies of a number of men, such as Tom Mann and Bob Smillie, who were committed to the idea of independent labour representation but it soon came to be dominated by men such as Burns, Fenwick and Sam Woods. Their idea apparently was to secure the League's affiliation in the hope that it would act as a counter to the ILP's pressure for independence.

The issue came to a head at the 1903 annual LRC conference which was held at Newcastle. Here, the Lib–Lab sympathisers advanced a motion calling for the admission of 'any other organisation which is prepared to adhere to the objects of the Committee,' and one of the proposers made it clear that 'this vote was being taken specially on the question of the affiliation of the National Democratic League.' But when the motion came to the vote, it was decisively, if not overwhelmingly, rejected by 118 votes to 48. The Lib–Labs had in fact overreached themselves and their action had stirred up a large body of hitherto uncommitted delegates who were now prepared to back the ILP line of independence. For their part, the ILP members were only too ready to take the opportunity thus offered. They were well aware of the fact that the crux of the problem was finance: only give the LRC a proper fund to sustain its activities and it would be well on the way to real independence. Admittedly they had at first viewed the idea of a central fund with some suspicion and had even joined with the majority of the trade unionists to vote the idea down at the 1901 conference. But the following year saw a distinct shift of opinion and the Birmingham conference accepted a proposal by Pete Curran and James Sexton that a scheme for a levy on affiliated organisations be drafted for the approval of the trade unions. Now, taking advantage of the mood of indignation provoked by the Lib–Labs, Curran successfully carried his plan. At first the levy was voluntary and each affiliated organisation paid 1d per member, although Arthur Henderson had suggested 4d while Paul Weighill of the stonemasons' union had gone so far as to suggest one shilling. The following year, the annual conference made the levy compulsory. The fund was to be used to cover up to 25 per cent of candidates' election expenses and those who were elected would receive an annual grant of £200, while in return they were expected to accept the majority decisions of the group in Parliament. From now on the LRC executive had the means of promoting its own candidates and of retaining control over them if they were elected to Parliament. There was accordingly much less chance of the party degenerating into a mere appendage of the Liberals.

Even so there were elements in the situation which still made this a real possibility. The overriding issues of the day, particularly tariff reform, 'Chinese slavery' and education, made it difficult for Labour to distinguish itself clearly from the orthodox Liberal position. Perhaps more important was the size and nature of the Labour group in the Parliament of 1900–5. There were only five MPs all told: in addition to Hardie and Bell, David Shackleton, Will Crooks and Arthur Henderson were returned at by-elections between August 1902 and July 1903. Bell, as we have seen, soon proved a broken reed. He continued to commit indiscretions which the party was able to overlook until February 1903, when he revealed in an interview that he no longer believed in the idea of an independent labour group. This was followed in October by his refusal to sign the party constitution as laid down by the Newcastle conference and to all intents and purposes he had ceased to be a Labour member. The others remained but their attitude on this crucial issue of independence was doubtful. Shackleton's political views were very close to Liberalism. Will Crooks was conscious that a significant proportion of his majority at Woolwich was due to Liberal support. Henderson, as an ex-Liberal Party worker, undoubtedly felt the pull of Liberalism. Even Hardie himself seemed to be flirting with Lib–Labism. In the aftermath of the 1900 election, apparently believing that both major parties were on the point of collapse, he was thinking in terms of a new alliance of the Labour members with the pro-Boer

Liberals perhaps taking in the Irish. Even had this been a practical possibility, which is exceedingly doubtful, it is hard to see how Hardie could possibly have secured the return of sufficient independently minded Labour men to direct the new group along the road he wished it to go. Furthermore, at about the same time, he revived the old idea of offering John Burns the leadership of the existing Labour MPs. In March 1903 he wrote to the latter in terms so fulsome that the effect is slightly nauseating: 'With your magnificent voice, your rich imagination and attractive personality, you would rouse your fellows as no other man in public life could.' Needless to say the offer was not taken up but the very fact that it was made at all is indicative of the uncertain future of the Labour Party.

Apart from the hostility of the Lib–Labs, the other obvious difficulty under which the LRC laboured was inadequate organisation. At the outset, the LRC had no organisation at all. There was no proper office provision and the post of secretary was, initially at any rate, unpaid. It was fortunate that the party secured as its secretary an able and devoted man in the shape of Ramsay MacDonald. It is most unfortunate that the later, more controversial aspects of his career have tended to obscure, in some quarters at least, MacDonald's very real and vital services to the infant Labour Party. While Keir Hardie had done much to get it started, it seems doubtful if his particular brand of dogged leadership would have taken it very far in these first very difficult years, whereas MacDonald provided a very necessary element of subtlety and finesse. However, it should not be imagined that their markedly different approaches to politics meant differences of opinion. Indeed, the reverse was true, for Hardie had all along sought to secure the position of secretary for MacDonald and invariably backed him to the hilt in his determination to establish the LRC on a firm basis. Apart from the maintenance of independence, this was to be achieved in two ways: first by winning over the large sections of the trade union world that were still sceptical about the new party; secondly, by opening up some line of communication with the Liberals. Although Hardie insisted on independence, he had been particularly careful not to close the door on the idea of cooperation, while MacDonald saw it was essential to secure some working arrangement if the LRC were to make headway.

## [13] Towards the Labour Alliance

MacDonald and the executive committee's chairman, Frederick Rogers, were under no illusions about difficulties in their first task. Together they managed to draft an appeal to the trade unions which, couched as it was in fairly moderate terms, they hoped would win them more support. Basically, their main argument was that since industry seemed to be organising itself for political action, then the trade unions must do the same in self-defence: 'Today capital is federated for political as well as industrial purposes. The small business is being merged into the large . . . the result being that the control of capital over labour is enormously increased. This new power of capital is already represented in Parliament. . . . It has the ear of Ministers and can control the policy of parties. . . . It is fully alive to the fact that the great battles between capital and labour are to be fought on the floor and in the division lobbies of the House of Commons.' (23 March 1900.) And if any complained that they were exaggerating, MacDonald and Rogers could point to the activities of the Engineering Employers' Federation and the Employers' Parliamentary Council as evidence for their assertions.

The rate of union affiliation was slow as the various bodies had to go through the often cumbersome process of consulting their members. However, MacDonald was able to report to the executive committee meeting in May 1900, that, as a result of his appeal, unions representing over 187,000 members were prepared to join. Unfortunately this promising beginning was marred by a serious set-back. The Amalgamated Society of Engineers had originally backed the idea but now decided to postpone its decision. The conservatively minded executive committee of the union argued that although in a ballot of members there was a clear majority in favour of affiliation, since only 3,600 out of a total membership of 85,000 had bothered to vote, this could hardly be regarded as truly representative. Admittedly the set-back was a temporary one as the ASE eventually did affiliate in 1902 after much constitutional manoeuvring but the effect of the delay on the morale of LRC workers must have been considerable. However, MacDonald and Rogers redoubled their efforts. A second circular was despatched to all unions which had not bothered to reply to the first and in addition they started on a round of the various union annual conferences, pleading their case. The result was a slow but steady rise in the number of affiliations during the remainder of 1900 and the early part of the following year. Altogether in this period some 41 bodies representing over

350,000 workers came into the party. This was modest progress, as the figures represented well under one-third of the total TUC strength, but the next two years saw a dramatic improvement with the number of affiliated organisations rising to 127, representing nearly 850,000 workers, or 56 per cent of the TUC. This was due in part to the hard work of MacDonald but it was also to a greater extent the result of the Taff Vale case and its damaging effects on the legal position of the trade unions. Once these were understood, many of the waverers were prepared to commit themselves to the idea of independent political action and support for the LRC.

The Taff Vale Railway Company in South Wales found itself with a strike on its hands in August 1900. The immediate cause was the alleged victimisation of a signalman called John Ewington, but the two real issues were the men's demands for increased wages to meet the rise in the cost of living due to the South African War, and an attempt to secure the company's recognition of the Amalgamated Society of Railway Servants. Although the strikers' demands, which were soon officially backed by the ASRS, were reasonable, the company determined to fight them. Its general manager, Ammon Beasley, may not unfairly be described as a 'hard case'. James Holmes, the local organiser for the union, called him 'the TVR dictator', while a less biased observer, George Askwith, went so far as to say that he 'loved litigation for its own sake'. In effect he sought to check the union on two lines. In the first place, he tried to break the strike by importing black-leg labour and Collison's National Free Labour Association sent him about 200 men for this purpose. Then, when the ASRS tried to stop this by picketing, he turned to the law. He was probably well aware of the significance of the judgment in *Lyons* v *Wilkins* but in any case this was thoughtfully brought to his notice by the Employers' Parliamentary Council. Accordingly he applied for and gained an injunction against the ASRS and its officials for its picketing activities. This decision was reversed in the Appeal Court in November 1900, whereupon Beasley and the company took the case to the Lords, where, on 22 July 1901, judgment was given in their favour and, moreover, the principle was established that in such circumstances a union's funds were liable. With this behind it, the company could then go on to sue the ASRS for damages which were duly fixed at £23,000 and this, added to its own legal expenses, meant that the union had to meet a total bill of something like £30,000. This was all bad enough for the trade union movement but worse was to come. A fortnight after the Taff Vale decision, the

Lords handed down another unfavourable verdict in the case of *Quinn* v *Leathem*. Leathem was a Belfast butcher who had employed non-union labour and the local butchers' assistants' union tried to put pressure on him by organising a boycott of his business. As with Taff Vale, the case went in his favour at first, was reversed in the Appeal Court and finally upheld in the Lords.

From the LRC's point of view, these decisions were a godsend in its campaign to win over the unions, particularly when Balfour's government refused a request from Keir Hardie to pass legislation protecting union funds. On 1 August MacDonald issued a circular to the unions in which he argued: 'The recent decisions of the House of Lords . . . should convince the unions that a labour party in Parliament is an immediate necessity.' A month later, a special LRC sub-committee was set up to draft yet another message to trade unionists spelling out clearly the meaning of the Taff Vale judgment. Some members of the ILP even went so far as to claim that they could detect a carefully planned employers' conspiracy to destroy or at least cripple the movement. This was scarcely likely and the idea was dismissed by the more responsible leaders but some colour was lent to the socialists' exaggerations by the appearance in *The Times* of a series of articles called 'The Crisis in British Industry'. These were published between November 1901 and January 1902 and were the work of the paper's industrial correspondent E. A. Pratt. In them he drew attention to the failings of the British economy which he ascribed almost entirely to the baleful influence of trade unions and in particular their maintenance of restrictive practices and opposition to the introduction of new techniques. Undoubtedly the union leadership was seriously alarmed and was more prepared to listen to the sirens of independent political action but there is some evidence to suggest that the rank and file were hardly affected by the issue. It was at this point that the ASE held a series of votes in its branches to decide on the question of affiliation, only to find that in spite of the circumstances and the importance of the decision, less than 7,000 of the members bothered to turn out to record their preference. There was also the fact that, in the months following Taff Vale and *Quinn* v *Leathem*, there were two by-elections in which Labour candidates were standing—Bob Smillie at North East Lanark in September 1901 and Philip Snowden at Wakefield the following year. In neither contest does Taff Vale and its consequences seem to have been a significant issue; in fact it was hardly mentioned at all.

The worries of the union leadership were further increased by the ineffectiveness of action taken through what might be called the 'normal channels'. The Parliamentary Committee of the TUC in particular proved itself singularly incapable of organising an effective response. Its immediate reaction to Taff Vale was to suggest a rather complicated scheme of subsidiary companies for the express purpose of holding at least part of a union's funds so that this would restrict its liability. This however came to nothing as also did a suggestion that the TUC take the Blackburn Weavers' case to the Lords and challenge an injunction secured by the employers against picketing similar to that granted to the Taff Vale Company. The growing alarm was voiced at the 1901 Congress at Swansea and was dramatically expressed by John Hodge when he told the assembled delegates that 'he had made over his little possessions to his wife by deed of gift' lest they be deemed liable in some future trade dispute. Even this, however, did not stir the Committee to propose any really effective action and it was not until the following May that something was done when it attempted to put pressure on Parliament. The occasion was the debate on a motion put forward by the Radical-Liberal MP for Hexham, Wentworth Beaumont, and seconded by Bell 'That legislation is necessary to prevent workers being placed by judge-made law in a position inferior to that intended by Parliament in 1875.' In spite of massive lobbying of members on the day, the motion—inevitably perhaps in view of the opposition of the Balfour government—was lost by 203 to 174. The lack of urgency shown by the Parliamentary Committee was the final straw for some union leaders who, realising that fresh legislation was necessary, saw quite clearly that this could only be achieved by returning more independent working-class MPs. Therefore there was a veritable flood of affiliations in the course of 1902–3.

Of all the unions which affiliated in this period, the LRC's most impressive catch was the United Textile Factory Workers' Association, the major body in the cotton industry. Impressive not only because of its size of over 100,000 members but also because hitherto it had made a point of steering clear of party politics, and, along with the Miners' Federation, had been the most powerful influence working against the LRC in the trade union movement. The reasons for this change of heart were not merely concern over Taff Vale and fears of an employers' conspiracy. There were also local factors. It is important to notice the interaction of these, since it illustrates again the point that the rise of Labour as a political force was not uniform throughout the country and often depended on local conditions. In the cotton industry considerable irritation and alarm had been caused by two recent events. In 1899 a 'half timers' bill had come before the Commons to restrict children from working in the mills before they were twelve, and while this was an admirable piece of social legislation, it was much resented in parts of Lancashire where it resulted in a significant fall in the earnings of some operatives' families. The UTFWA had made a determined attempt to prevent this bill by mass lobbying but had failed. Two years later came the Blackburn Weavers' case, which has already been re-ferred to, and which cost the Northern Weavers, one of the associate members of the UTFWA, £11,000 in damages and legal expenses. This led immediately to demands from the Weavers that the main body should prepare plans for direct labour representation and these demands were echoed by the *Cotton Factory Times* two days after the debate on Beaumont's resolution in May 1902. Those who wanted this new initia-tive were no doubt encouraged by the fact that in February of the same year, Mawdsley, the cautious and Conservative-inclined secretary, had died. But what was probably the decisive influence was the pressure applied by a group of militant branches in Nelson and Colne in the north-east corner of Lancashire.

In June 1902 the sitting Liberal member for the Clitheroe division was raised to the peerage and the decision was taken to run David Shackleton, the vice-president of the Northern Weavers' Union, as an independent labour candidate at the ensuing by-election. The events which led to this show clearly the point that has already been em-phasised: the importance of the trades councils in organising political activity at the local level. Here the initiative was taken by the Colne council which already had run successfully candidates in the municipal elections in Colne in 1898 and Nelson in 1901. Early in 1902 a delegate conference of trade unionists, ILP and SDF representatives met at Nelson and it was decided first to adopt an independent candidate, then to adjourn for three months to consider possibilities and also raise necessary funds. The national ILP was quickly alerted to the oppor-tunity to make progress in an area where things had been difficult be-cause of the generally strong Conservative traditions amongst the Lancashire working class. The leadership soon realised the need to play the game very carefully, for a motion put to the delegate conference for 'a Labour and socialist candidate' had been soundly defeated. How-ever, it was hoped that the nomination might still be secured for Philip Snowden who had some local connections and seems to have had a fair measure of support amongst the delegates. In the event, as the day of the resumed conference drew nearer, it became clear that Shackleton had the confidence of the majority of the delegates. Accordingly, the ILP's Parliamentary Committee, meeting at Leeds the day before the Nelson conference was to re-assemble, decided, according to the ILP's official report, that 'Snowden should withdraw in Shackleton's favour provided the latter's position on the question of independence was satisfactory.' This was an extremely politic decision, for Shackleton's economic philosophy and his nonconformity gave him a marked leaning towards Liberalism, and at one point he had been secretary of a Liberal ward party in Accrington. A contemporary opinion described him as 'a very mild spoken gentleman, with ideas very little in advance of the average Liberal'. Obviously the ILP leadership was anxious not to ruin a chance of winning over one of the 'big battalions' of the trade union world by an over punctilious insistence on its principles. By stepping down gracefully, the ILP would be more likely to gain the confidence and respect of those union leaders who were still more than a little suspicious of it. There was another good reason for withdrawing on this occasion. The local Liberal association, though in a bad state, was anxious to fight the seat and had offered the candidature to a prominent radical, Philip Stanhope. Stanhope was a supporter of Lib–Labism but had indicated his willingness to stand should the Labour conference choose a 'socialist' and whilst this was not officially known it was generally suspected. Therefore, if the ILP were to persist with Snowden's candidature, it might succeed merely in splitting the Labour vote and ruining the chances of returning an additional MP. So, when the Labour delegate conference re-assembled at Nelson on July 5, Snowden declared his willingness to stand down in Shackleton's favour and the latter was duly adopted. The delegates then dispersed to set about organising some sort of machinery, having first decided that members of the bodies represented at the conference should be levied at the rate of 6d per annum to support Shackleton if he were elected. A number of election committees were set up, usually on the basis of the local branches of the weavers' union, and on 10 July, a meeting at Padiham formally established a Labour Representation Committee for the Clitheroe division. As it turned out, there was no contest. The local Liberal association still wanted to fight but Stanhope had already made it clear that he was not interested in challenging Shackleton and the Liberal chief whip, Herbert Gladstone, also gave no encouragement, so there was no Liberal candidate. As for the Conservatives, while strong in Lancashire generally, their organisation in Clitheroe was weak and when it became clear there was no possibility of a split 'progressive' vote, they too abandoned all thoughts of intervention. Accordingly Shackleton was formally returned as MP for the division on 1 August 1902. Now the patience and willingness to compromise exhibited by Hardie, MacDonald and the other ILP leaders, paid handsome dividends. The return of Shackleton marked an almost revolutionary change in the UTFWA's attitude to political representation. In the course of the summer of 1902, the union had held ballots on the issues of independent representation and a levy to support such activity, and overwhelming majorities in favour were secured in each case. From this it was only a short step to affiliation to the LRC. This was agreed in January 1903, and a delegation led by Shackleton attended the Newcastle LRC annual conference the following month. Here, to cap it all, Shackleton himself was elected to the party executive. The cotton union was the largest single body to join the LRC to date and was one of the most powerful, influential and best organised of the so-called 'old' unions. Its adhesion to the independent labour cause was a tremendous boost to morale and prestige.

But there was one large and well organised group of workers still aloof from the LRC—the miners. If they could be won for the party then the 'Labour Alliance' would be virtually complete and the LRC could really claim to speak for the whole labour movement. Up to 1906 there were encouraging signs that the miners were shifting from their previously hostile position but, despite redoubled efforts, Hardie and MacDonald found progress very difficult. The reasons for the miners' continued commitment to Liberalism were partly emotional and traditional and partly due to the influence of certain personalities in the unions. The strength of nonconformity, according to some observers, was particularly marked in the coal-mining areas, and this was necessarily a strong factor predisposing them towards the Liberals. Then again, in spite of the oft repeated adage that there is no gratitude in politics, it does seem in this case that the miners remained grateful to the Liberal government of 1880–5 for the extension of the franchise to the county areas. Most important of all was the strength of the leadership's opposition to the idea of any tie-up with the LRC. Pickard and Ned Cowey of the Federation, Burt and Fenwick of the Northumberland association and John Wilson, secretary of the Durham union, were all strong Lib–Lab men and it proved exceedingly difficult to shake their influence. Still, there were, by the early years of the century, signs of growing disillusion. Although the Liberals in theory were anxious to retain the miners' electoral support, in practice there were marked limits to how far they were prepared to go. The fact that between 1885 and 1900 the number of Lib–Lab miners' MPs fell from 6 to 5 is clearly indicative of this. Then, the miners' attitude to politics was severely practical and limited. They merely wanted specific reforms to improve their lot, such as an effective system of workmen's compensation and an eight-hour day. On this issue too, confidence began to weaken, for the Liberals were not winning elections and therefore lacked the power to meet the miners' claims. In any case, when they were in power they seemed too easily side-tracked from questions of practical reform by their obsession with Ireland. Taff Vale and its implications was also a factor in stimulating a new approach to politics, just as it had in other unions, and if the threat to union privileges was not yet clear to the miners as a whole, then doubts were removed by two further legal decisions directly affecting them. The first was the 'Stop-Day' case which began in 1901 and dragged on to 1905. It had become the practice in South Wales to bring out the miners for one day from time to time as a means of restricting output, thus maintaining prices and therefore wages. The South Wales Miners' Federation was now sued by the Glamorgan Coal Company and other owners for 'wrongfully and maliciously procuring and inducing workmen to break their contracts'. It seems that the employers' action had been encouraged by Beasley's success at Taff Vale and, as in that case, the matter went to the Lords who upheld the claim for damages. Almost simultaneously there was the Denaby Main Case in Yorkshire. Here the Denaby Coal Company obtained an injunction, ultimately upheld in the Lords, that the union had no right to pay strike benefit to members in dispute. Admittedly, the Company's parallel suit for damages, which also went to the Lords, failed but the overall effect of these decisions was undoubtedly damaging. Finally, economic factors added their weight. The prosperity during the South African War which had pushed wage rates up to a point where they were 20 per cent over 1888 levels now collapsed and, from 1902 onwards, a series of decisions by the industry's conciliation board cancelled out that gain. Further, a government decision to put a tax on exported coal in 1901, inevitably hit those areas involved in the export trade and some unemployment resulted, particularly in South Wales, Durham, Northumberland and the Fife field in Scotland.

As a result of these developments, pressure from the regions was building up and the first breach in Lib–Lab solidarity came as early as 1903 when the Lancashire and Cheshire miners decided to 'go it alone' and affiliate to the LRC. More serious for Lib–Lab prospects were the sudden and successive deaths of the two dominant personalities in the MFGB, Ned Cowey in 1903 and Ben Pickard the following year. Pickard's successor as president was another Lib–Lab sympathiser, Enoch Edwards of the Staffordshire Miners, but he had neither his predecessor's strength of character nor his outstanding prestige, and was thus less able to resist the growing movement for affiliation. The spearhead of this movement was mainly in South Wales and Scotland, although outside the Federation there were similar restless murmurings amongst the Durham men in the north-east. At the Miners' Federation conference in 1904, Edwards succeeded in disallowing a South Wales' motion for affiliation but the following year he had shifted his ground and actually recommended that a ballot of members be taken when this was again suggested by the representatives from South Wales, Scotland and Lancashire. Meanwhile, the Durham Miners' Association, irritated further by its failure to conclude a more favourable electoral deal with the local Liberal associations, had taken the decision in 1905 to make a modest donation of £80 to LRC funds. This was very encouraging to Hardie and MacDonald, but both men, in particular the latter, realised the need for caution and careful handling of the situation. In the event it was nearly another three years before the miners were fully convinced of the desirability of joining the organisation which by then was calling itself the Labour Party.

## [14] Relations with the Liberals: the MacDonald–Gladstone Pact

It could be argued that MacDonald and Hardie were not being entirely consistent in the pursuit of their second aim, that of gaining some sort of understanding with the Liberals. This was certainly true of Hardie for, while endorsing MacDonald's delicate and protracted negotiations with the Liberals, he remained deep down very uneasy. All along he had preached with fervour the cause of independence, in particular con-demning Bell's connection with Liberals, and yet he was nowhere near so rigid in practice as some of the purists in the ILP. Thus, immediately after the firm declaration made at the Newcastle conference in 1903, he seemed to shift his ground. With reference to the two-member con-stituencies, he said: 'If the Liberal Party would be content to select one candidate and would leave the Labour Party with one, that fact alone would be productive of good fellowship.' In March of the same year he went even further. This was the period when he renewed his approach to Burns (see Chapter 12) but earlier in the month he had tried to land an even bigger Liberal fish. On 3 March, in an open letter to Lloyd George in the *Labour Leader*, he had sought his support for what he called a new 'Party of the People'. Needless to say, there was no response.

MacDonald, on the other hand, approached the issue more coolly and clear-headedly. Partly this was due to personality and partly the result of past experience. MacDonald, like Hardie, had been snubbed by the Liberals, hence his conversion to the cause of independent Labour, but he never reacted with quite so much bitterness, nor had he broken off his close personal contacts with men like Herbert Samuel. His belief that, without an electoral understanding, the LRC would never make significant progress was generally borne out by the poor showing of Labour candidates in three-cornered contests in the period up to 1914. So, an understanding must be reached and he pursued this aim along two lines. First, he wished to repeat Bell's achievement in 1900 of persuading the Liberals to run in harness with Labour in two-member constituencies. Secondly, he hoped to build up sufficient strength in a limited number of constituencies to pressurise the Liberals into standing aside to allow the LRC man a straight fight with the Conservative. The possibilities on both counts were promising but MacDonald and Hardie had to be careful, as the purists in the ILP— amongst them Philip Snowden—were firmly against any sort of 'deal'. The negotiations had to be kept completely secret and so successfully was this achieved that, although there were suspicions of a Liberal/LRC pact there was no definite proof to substantiate any allegations. Indeed, until quite recently, Labour historians quite firmly and positively denied the existence of any such pact.

As for the Liberals, their national leadership was more than ready to respond. Herbert Gladstone had been impressed by the rise of the independent labour movement and realised only too well its full implications. A new departure was needed in the relations between the Liberal Party and the working class and Gladstone favoured two courses of action. He continually urged his party leader, Sir Henry Campbell-Bannerman, to pay more attention to the issue of social reform. In addition he was anxious to meet MacDonald half-way in the conclusion of an electoral pact. On this latter issue he had made his views clear as early as October 1901 when he declared: 'If I had the power and authority, I have no doubt that I could come to terms with the leaders of the Labour Party in the course of half a morning. . . . The difficulty lies in the constituencies . . . and in the unfortunate necessity of providing funds.' The following May he returned to this theme. Addressing a meeting of Liberal agents in Bristol he expressed the hope that 'the Liberal Party would be able to make an arrangement by which Labour would have greater and fairer opportunities of fighting seats at the next election than it had before.' But, as Gladstone himself had indicated, although he and Campbell-Bannerman might propose, in the last resort the local caucuses disposed and if events in three constituencies during 1901–2 were anything to go by, these bodies were still very reluctant to make any concession to Labour. In September 1901 MacDonald tried to claim the North Lanark seat for the Labour candidate Bob Smillie but, although the whips and national leadership made approving noises, the local association refused to cooperate, and the result was a split vote and a Tory gain. An attempt to get Snowden adopted by the local Liberals at Wakefield in March 1902 also failed for, although the association did not in the end put up its own candidate, it refused point-blank to issue any advice to its members to vote for Snowden. Finally MacDonald himself was snubbed when he tried to secure adoption as candidate for one of the Leicester seats. There were then difficulties on the Liberal side, but Gladstone was stirred to redouble his efforts to overcome them, particularly when the LRC's by-election success at Clitheroe was followed by another gain at Woolwich in March 1903.

The serious negotiations between MacDonald and Gladstone were not begun until the early days of 1903, and the pact was not finally concluded until September. At first there was no direct contact, MacDonald making his approach through George Cadbury and Jesse Herbert, Gladstone's secretary. MacDonald throughout stressed the growing influence of the LRC and pointed out the disastrous effects of its opposition throughout the country should the Liberals prove unfriendly. Herbert himself was particularly impressed by the LRC organisation and its ability 'to influence the votes of a million men'. Any hesitations Gladstone may have had were now overcome by two further developments. On 22 May, speaking in a debate on old age pensions in the House of Commons, Joseph Chamberlain made his first major public declaration outside Birmingham in favour of protection, thus beginning a controversy which led to his own resignation in September, divided his party and brought the next general election several years nearer. If the Liberals were to reap the full benefit of this, then they must put their own house in order as quickly as possible. The second development was the Barnard Castle by-election result in July. Here the local LRC had adopted Arthur Henderson, himself a former Liberal Party worker, to contest the seat on the retirement of Sir Joseph Pease. The local Liberal association, though seriously weakened by the secession of a substantial number of its members to Henderson, was pushed by Samuel Storey, president of the Northern Liberal Federation, to put up a candidate. The resulting campaign was marked by considerable bitterness and Henderson, doubting his chances in a three-cornered fight, at one point even suggested to MacDonald that he step down. In the end, he decided to carry on and was rewarded by a narrow victory of forty-seven votes over the Conservative with the Liberal coming bottom. Gladstone, the national Liberal Party leaders and the Liberal press had all favoured Henderson and for them indeed this was further proof, if proof were still needed, of the growing strength of the LRC. But before an understanding could be achieved, there was one final personal hurdle to overcome. Gladstone had to use his influence with the Leicester Liberals to persuade them to make a firm decision to promote MacDonald's own candidature. Once this was done, Gladstone moved speedily and some indication of his sense of urgency is shown by his seeking out MacDonald while the latter was sick in Leicester Hospital in September 1903. Here the two men agreed that the LRC should have a clear run in thirty constituencies and, in return, it should 'demonstrate friendliness' to the Liberals in those constituencies where it had influence. The pact was only to last for one election as any prolonged arrangement would clearly compromise the independence of the LRC which both Hardie and MacDonald were very anxious to avoid.

The successful conclusion of this 'entente', however, did not mean complete accord between the Liberals and Labour. On the contrary, 1904 saw the association put under some strain by developments in two by-elections. At Norwich, the local Labour committee, in spite of MacDonald's advice, insisted on running G. H. Roberts as a candidate against a Liberal and Conservative. The Liberal won handsomely, but both local and national leaderships regarded the Labour action askance. Even more productive of ill-feeling was the Scottish miners' decision to run John Robertson in the North East Lanarkshire contest in August, for not only was he supported by a number of prominent ILP men, including Hardie himself, but also by the Lib–Lab TUC Parliamentary Committee. Admittedly there was some justification for the Labour attitude as the Scottish Liberals had shown themselves particularly and consistently hostile to any claims for Labour representation. But, despite the strain caused by such local difficulties, the leaders on both sides decided to turn a blind eye and to look rather at the more encouraging prospects of cooperation in the general election.

As this election approached, the LRC was forced to reconsider its relationship not only with the Liberal Party but also with the Lib–Labs, and here too there was a willingness to forget old battles and line up, however uneasily, against the common Conservative enemy. The first real sign of this was in the West Monmouth by-election in 1904 where Thomas Richards backed by the South Wales Miners' Federation, stood as a Lib–Lab. After some hesitation the LRC executive committee decided that it too could support him, on the grounds of his declaration that 'he was the Labour candidate only and that if returned to the House of Commons, he would work with the Labour group.' (LRC Conference Report 1905.) In fact this declaration was highly misleading as Richards had already been adopted by the local Liberals and made full use of their machinery during the campaign. Nonetheless the incident proved to be a forerunner of a meeting between the LRC and the TUC Parliamentary Committee on 16 February 1905 which resulted in an electoral agreement sometimes called the Caxton Hall 'Concordat'. By this, LRC candidates were promised the 'loyal and hearty support' of the Lib–Labs; in return the LRC would follow the example of West Monmouth and support Parliamentary Committee candidates 'in so far as its constitution allows'. Later in the year, this *ad hoc* understanding was cemented by the formation of the Joint Board, comprising representatives of the LRC, the General Federation of Trade Unions and the Parliamentary Committee. In Parliament MPs of both groups came into much closer cooperation on such matters as the Unemployed Workmen's Act and the appointment of a Royal Commission on the Poor Law. The reason for this rapprochement was clearly political expediency, for neither side was prepared to budge from its position: the LRC continued to insist on independence, while the older generation of TUC leaders were still determined to maintain their long-standing connection with Liberalism. By these agreements, each tacitly recognised that the other was too strong to be ignored or suppressed and therefore cooperation was the only sensible alternative.

## [15]  The General Election of 1906

On 4 December 1905, Balfour, his party now a shambles as a result of the Tariff Reform controversy initiated by Chamberlain over two years previously, tendered his resignation to Edward VII. Campbell-Bannerman immediately took office as prime minister, but a general election was necessary as the Unionist party still had in theory a majority of seventy or more seats over Liberals, Irish and LRC members combined. The election was held in January and MacDonald's careful work over the past six years was put to the supreme test.

In addition to his other activities, MacDonald had also tried to encourage the development of local machinery. He received valuable assistance from Arthur Henderson who, throughout his career in the Labour Party, devoted much time in this field. There was a rather makeshift air about the party's local organisation in these years but this was, in part at any rate, the result of deliberate policy. The special committee set up to examine the matter reported in January 1901, advising against 'any uniform system of organisation for the whole country' on the grounds that '. . . some of our affiliated societies are already organised in certain constituencies. We think that these attempts should be encouraged by us, and be made the basis of a complete organisation later on.' Gradually local LRCs began to emerge, varying a good deal in character and composition, but very often based on the local trades councils. In the large towns and cities, the local LRC and the trades council were often in effect the same body. In county divisions, with more than one trades council, the organisation was necessarily a little more complex. However, although MacDonald felt it wiser to leave these local arrangements undisturbed and extend the party machinery on an *ad hoc* basis, clearly some direction and guidance were necessary. Thus, in 1903, he and Henderson issued an agents' handbook in which a model for local organisation was suggested. This in fact was the constitution of the Leicester LRC—significantly MacDonald's own constituency. It defined the object as uniting 'the forces of Labour in order to secure the election of Independent Representation on all Local and National Governing Bodies.' Representatives would be accepted 'from the Trades Council, Trade Unions, Cooperative Societies, ILP and other Labour and socialist organisations that are willing to work for the objects.' Nominations for candidatures were to be made by affiliated societies but 'The Committee shall have power, if it thinks advisable, to run candidates of its own where no candidate is nominated by an affiliated society.' The peculiar thing was that the local LRCs were not directly affiliated to the national LRC and a proposal that this should henceforward be allowed was defeated at the 1903 national conference. Henderson was particularly concerned by this as his position at Barnard Castle depended on such an organisation, known locally as the Labour and Progressive Association. Accordingly in 1904, he persuaded the party executive to place before the 1905 conference the following resolution: 'that in constituencies which are not covered by a Trades Council the Labour Association for the whole constituency will be eligible for affiliation.' With the executive's backing, it was duly accepted by the conference and by 1906 the number of such bodies has been variously estimated at between 70 and 100. Thus by the time of the general election, MacDonald, Henderson and their colleagues had succeeded in creating at least the skeleton of a national political machine.

This awareness of the importance of organisation was matched by an equal concern with matters of policy. As early as 1903-4, MacDonald and Henderson were giving active consideration to the formation of a platform. In April of the latter year, they called a meeting of prospective candidates at which a number of issues became agreed party policy: free trade; an end to 'Chinese slavery'; licensing legislation; nationalisation of railways; payment of MPs; representative government for South Africa; a reversal of the Unionist education policy; and an extension of the principle of workmen's compensation. However, the election manifesto eventually drawn up by MacDonald turned out to be a rather nebulous document, particularly when compared with that issued by the Parliamentary Committee on behalf of the Lib–Labs. Basically it was simply an appeal for more Labour members and although protection and Chinese labour were condemned and mention made of the social problems of poverty, bad housing, unemployment and the rights of trade unions, there was no specific programme of legislation outlined for the electorate's consideration. On the other hand the Lib–Lab platform presented a precise and comprehensive programme of social change: a Trades Disputes Bill to reverse recent court judgments; the amendment of the Workmen's Compensation, Truck and Unemployment Acts; legislation to improve working-class housing; the payment of state pensions at sixty and an eight-hour working day. Yet perhaps MacDonald was right not to stress the issue of social reform for it would seem that, amongst many sections of the electorate, this was of comparatively small moment. What mattered most was tariff reform and a general feeling that the Tories had out-stayed their welcome.

As for the working of the electoral pacts, the Caxton House agreement with the Lib–Labs generally held up well, but in some parts of the country local zealots on both sides did their best to upset or nullify the MacDonald/Gladstone arrangement. The LRC had 50 candidates in the field (plus the 5 put up in Scotland by the Scottish Workers' Representation Committee) and of these, 32 were allowed a straight fight with the Conservative. The pact worked most successfully in Lancashire where the Liberals had made no headway against a strong Conservative machine with a substantial working-class following, and at the 1900 election, the Unionists held 47 of the county's 58 seats. The Lancashire Liberals, not surprisingly, were anxious to secure LRC support and were prepared to accept the claims of their candidates. Cooperation was cordial and fairly complete, though difficulties did arise. For example, in Manchester the local ILP was keen to run Fred Bramley first in the city's eastern division against Balfour, even though it had been agreed to leave the Liberal there a clear run. In the end the local branches only desisted on the intervention of Keir Hardie himself who, in a letter, pointed out that whatever their personal feelings they were 'in honour bound to work in harmony with the local LRC'. On the eastern side of the Pennines it was a different story and the local leaderships conspicuously failed to reach a working arrangement. One explanation suggested for this was the comparative shortage of two-member constituencies in Yorkshire and it is significant that in such constituencies, like York and Halifax, terms acceptable to both sides were fairly easily arranged. On the other hand, in some of the West Riding centres like Bradford, Leeds and Huddersfield where the ILP was particularly strong, the local Liberals accused it of splitting the vote in traditionally radical areas. In Leeds a highly embarrassing situation developed at the end of 1905. After some confused negotiations and much unpleasantness the Liberals had agreed to give the LRC candidate, James O'Grady, a clear run in the eastern division on the understanding that there would be no LRC men against their candidates in the other city seats. But, following a good performance in the November municipal elections, the local LRC demanded to run candidates in the south and west seats and while MacDonald was prepared to countenance the former, the latter was held by none other than Herbert Gladstone. MacDonald now had to pull every string he could to stop this unexpected development jeopardising the whole agreement. He secured the support of O'Grady but that was insufficient and in the end only a minatory letter to the local LRC secretary, J. D. Macrae, early in December 1905, did the trick. In it MacDonald warned '. . . my executive will even go to the length of publishing a condemnatory resolution in the newspaper if you insist locally on a third candidate.' The limited working of the pact in Yorkshire is best shown by the fact that of the 6 LRC candidates, 4 had three-cornered fights. Elsewhere in the north, the story was a mixed one: in the two-member seats of Newcastle and Sunderland, LRC and Liberals ran in harness and were returned, while Arthur Henderson was given a clear run at Barnard Castle, as was Isaac Mitchell at Darlington. On the other hand, Stockton-on-Tees was a three-cornered battle and at Jarrow Pete Curran actually found himself contesting the seat against the Liberal with the Conservative standing down. In Scotland, even more than in Yorkshire, the local Liberals set their faces implacably against any cooperation and both the 4 LRC and the 5 SWRC candidates had to fight three-cornered contests. In the south of England, where the LRC was weaker and had comparatively few candidates, the working of the pact was obviously less of a problem and in general where the local party could put in a strong claim—as at Leicester, Norwich, Woolwich, West Ham and Chatham—this was accepted by the Liberals.

Although it was fairly clear at the time that there was a strong swing from right to left as the country approached the 1906 election, nevertheless the actual results seem to have taken most contemporary commentators by surprise. This was particularly true of the performance of the LRC. Of its 50 candidates, 29 were returned and this figure was raised to 30 when J. W. Taylor of the Durham miners, who had won Chester-le-Street, declared his adhesion to the Labour cause immediately after the election. The overwhelming majority of the successful candidates—two-thirds to be precise—came from the north of England; two from the midlands; two from London; and three from the rest of southern England. Scotland provided two while Wales, in latter days regarded almost as a Labour Party pocket borough, sent but one, Keir Hardie duly retaining his seat at Merthyr. The vote polled by all candidates was 329,748, or only 5·9 per cent of the total votes cast, but, by concentrating on a small number of constituencies, the LRC had secured the maximum effect: each of the candidates on average polled 39·9 per cent of the votes. This was a tremendous improvement on the results of five years before and reflected great credit on the

LRC's leadership, particularly MacDonald but also Hardie who gave full and loyal support to his colleague. But there was still a long way to go before the Labour Party became a truly national party and not just a sectional pressure group clinging to the Liberals' coat-tails. Just as contemporaries had tended to underrate the significance of the emergence of the LRC in 1900, now some of them swung the other way. Thus the somewhat hysterical letter written by the defeated Unionist prime minister to Lady Salisbury on the aftermath of the election, in which he claimed that 'C-B [i.e. Campbell-Bannerman] is a mere cork dancing on a current he cannot control.' The history of the Labour Party over the next eight years was to show that the current was not nearly as powerful as Balfour feared.

# Part VI

## The Labour Party's Early Years 1906–14

### [16] The Aftermath of Victory 1906–8

Immediately following the success in the general election of 1906, the LRC executive committee recommended the adoption of a new title, 'The Labour Party', and this was accepted by the annual conference meeting on 15 February. Already the group's MPs had met to elect a leader (or rather, a chairman), a secretary and a chief whip. Here there was some difficulty. From a practical point of view it was obvious that some form of leadership was necessary if the group was to retain any semblance of coherence and, more important, its independence. On the other hand, there was a strong feeling amongst the members that the concept of leadership was somehow undemocratic and care must be taken to prevent one man from making party policy or imposing his will on the rest. Indeed, far from being free agents, the MPs were expected to take their instructions from the annual conference. This concept, while laudable perhaps in theory, was less effective in practice and events were to reveal that it was a source of weakness to the party in these early, difficult years. As it happened the election of the first chairman was a cause of confusion both at the time and later. According to the now generally accepted account, the two candidates for the position, Hardie and David Shackleton, tied on a show of hands and again on a secret ballot until finally a second ballot took Hardie home by just one vote. In spite of this, some later Labour historians—notably Raymond Postgate in his *Life of George Lansbury*—have stated that Hardie's election was more or less unanimous and there was no serious challenge from anybody else. In any case, the vote was a triumph of sentiment over sense. As Snowden put it, Hardie only got in because some of the trade union MPs who would normally have gone for Shackleton voted the way they did 'because they felt his [i.e. Hardie's] great services in building up the political Labour Party deserved recognition.' Shackleton was much the more capable man for the situation facing Labour in 1906 whatever Hardie's services in the past. Hardie had already shown that he was no Parliamentarian and to lack of aptitude was added the natural slowing down effects of ill-health and advancing years. As it was, during Hardie's tenure of the chairmanship, much of the work of leadership and organisation devolved on Shackleton, who accepted the post of vice-chairman, and also on Henderson and MacDonald, respectively elected chief whip and secretary.

Apart from these initial difficulties over the leadership, this period in the party's history was also marked by a determined effort to establish the principle that it should, in Philip Snowden's words, 'take its directions from the Resolutions of the Party Conference'. The main protagonist of this view was Ben Tillett. At the 1905 conference his motion to secure this was defeated on an individual and a card vote but he and his supporters continued their attacks undismayed. At the 1906 conference one resolution called for the meeting to instruct MPs to take action on the issue of trade union rights and the following year Tillett himself introduced a resolution that 'The Executive shall organise a Committee within the House of Commons of Labour Party members to instruct and advise its fellow members'. Finally in 1908, he published his ill-timed blast *Is the Parliamentary Labour Party a Failure?* in which he sought to undermine the position of its leaders. 'Sheer hypocrites', 'softly feline in their purrings to ministers', and 'press flunkeys to Asquith' were some of the choicer barbs he flung at them. This was followed once more by resolutions at successive conferences calling for more effective control. But although Tillett had sufficient following to create trouble within the party on this issue, he never succeeded in securing the passage of any of these resolutions. The opposition to him was very strong, including not only MacDonald and Henderson but also Curran and Hardie. Hardie indeed was so adamant that MPs' freedom of action should be preserved that, in 1907 when the conference passed a resolution on women's suffrage with which he disagreed, he declared: 'if the motion . . . was intended to limit the action of the Party in the House of Commons, he should have seriously to consider whether he could remain a member of the Parliamentary Party'. In fact, this selfsame conference in the debate on Tillett's motion finally arrived at a compromise which proved to be generally acceptable; namely that the conference should give its opinion on certain issues and lines of action but that the PLP must be left with discretion in the timing and method of achievement.

Inevitably there was a marked feeling of euphoria in Labour circles following the unexpectedly good showing of the party's candidates in the election and in the period immediately following some further important successes were secured which served to heighten this mood. In the first instance, the party seemed to be wielding considerable influence in Parliament. The most immediate issue for Labour was a bill to reverse the Taff Vale decision and the Liberal Party had previously committed itself to tackling this question along lines laid down by the TUC Parliamentary Committee. The latter was in favour of a measure granting the unions complete freedom from liability for actions committed during a strike in addition to a clear definition of the right to picket. However, when it came to introducing a measure, influential members of the cabinet, in spite of past promises, now had doubts. In the end the government's measure proposed that a union's funds would be liable if it failed to repudiate, or alternatively, authorised a tort. Further, the duty of defining such an action, or deciding whether or not the union had authorised it, was to be left to the courts. This was quite unacceptable to the labour movement as it thoroughly distrusted the courts and could not accept their impartiality following the decisions culminating in Taff Vale. So, the Labour Party and the TUC Parliamentary Committee under Shackleton's leadership, immediately took up the issue by introducing their own proposals two days after the government bill. There then followed in the course of the debate a minor sensation when no less a person than Campbell-Bannerman, the prime minister himself, declared in favour of the Labour Party's bill. This development seems to have been largely because Shackleton had approached C-B behind the scenes and had secured an assurance of his support. The ground had now clearly been cut from under the legalists' feet and an amended bill was introduced incorporating the principle of immunity. Thereafter, Shackleton, in cooperation with a group of back-bench Liberal sympathisers, kept close watch throughout the committee stage to see that no hostile amendments crept in. The bill then passed its third reading in the Commons without a division. A rather perfunctory attempt to amend it in the Lords was checked and it received the royal assent on 20 December. Thus the Labour group had won a great initial success and much of the credit was due to Shackleton's astute manoeuvres.

The other legislation of the 1906 session for which Labour claimed credit concerned school meals, workmen's compensation and unemployment. In the first case, although Labour MPs had urged action, the Liberal government did not in fact need much persuasion. The result was the Education (Provision of Meals) Act which rather cautiously allowed local education authorities in England and Wales to provide school meals, and these were to be free for necessitous children. In spite of the permissive nature of the measure, within four years 96 local authorities were actually operating such a scheme and by 1914 some 158,000 children were being provided for. On the vexed question of workmen's compensation (for accidents incurred at work) the Labour Party and the trade unions were not so much concerned to establish a new principle as to extend one already accepted, albeit on a limited scale. The previous government, as a result of pressure applied not only by the unions but also by its colonial secretary, Chamberlain, had passed a measure in 1897 and an extension to this had been secured in 1900. What the labour movement now wanted were three things: a further extension of the scope of the law to cover all workers; the acceptance of the principle that employers be compelled to take out insurance to cover the possibility of accidents; finally that 'industrial diseases' be recognised as giving a worker the right to compensation. When the Liberal government came to tackle the problem in the Workmen's Compensation Act of 1906, most of what was wanted was duly carried, with the exception of compulsory insurance. As a result of the pressure applied, the number of workmen entitled to compensation was increased by 6 million whereas the government had originally only intended to increase it by 2 million. On the question of diseases, the measure included a schedule of six and provision for more to be added by departmental order. Finally, Labour pressure on the question of unemployment produced a vote of £200,000 to finance relief works under the Unemployed Workmen's Act of 1905.

These triumphs, however, were to be followed by a period of frustration. During the course of 1907 and 1908, the Labour members in Parliament took up the issues of unemployment and pensions without securing much success. On the former they found it quite impossible to prod the minister responsible, John Burns, into any sort of action. When they introduced their own 'right to work' bill in 1907 it did not even reach the second reading and an attempt the following year was only marginally more successful. With old age pensions it was a similar story. In spite of Labour pressure, the chancellor, Asquith, resisted until he had secured a surplus in his budget sufficient to cover a rather niggardly scheme. Only in one respect could Labour claim any credit and that was when the government at last decided to sponsor a bill providing for an eight-hour day in the coal mines. Even here it might be argued that it was not so much political as industrial pressure which secured the concession. As Herbert Samuel, one of the ministers, remarked: 'If the bill is not to be passed ... it means a coal strike.'

But outside Parliament the period 1906-8 saw the Labour Party at last succeed in securing the affiliation of the miners' union, the MFGB. The miners' disillusion with their traditional Liberal allies had continued to grow. In 1905 there were powerful demands from the Lancashire, Scottish and South Wales coal-fields for a ballot of the union on the issue of affiliation. Accordingly in 1906, a vote was held and although the opposition carried the day, the majority was a comparatively narrow one of under 10,000 on a 57 per cent poll, and encouraged those in favour to renew their efforts the following year. At the Federation's conference, the South Wales representatives talked of following the example of Lancashire and Cheshire and taking independent action, while the socialist group suggested the issue be settled on a card vote, knowing full well that this way the combined weight of South Wales, Scotland and Lancashire would be decisive. However, the Lib–Labs were still strong enough to prevent this suggestion and instead it was agreed to have a second secret ballot which was duly arranged for the following year. On this occasion, a rather higher poll, 69 per cent, produced a handsome majority in favour: 213,137 for, 168,446 against. The opposition, as in 1907, was centred in the more prosperous midland coal-fields but they were now overborne by the larger majorities in favour of affiliation in the north. The reason for the marked reversal was probably twofold: the election of so many Labour MPs in 1906 and the successes secured in Parliament must have had a powerful 'bandwagon' effect; in addition the growth of the ILP in the northern coal-fields undoubtedly contributed to the greater militancy there now expressing itself in political terms. However, in spite of this considerable, if not overwhelming, expression of opinion, the Lib–Labs were not beaten yet. When the Federation conference assembled in October 1908 and the president, Enoch Edwards, recommended action on the vote, they demanded yet another ballot and that affiliation should only be sought if this produced a two-thirds majority in favour. The delegates by this time were convinced of the correctness of the course of action and, after defeating the Lib–Lab resolution, they went on to approve Bob Smillie's motion that they apply for admission. As a concession to the Lib–Labs, it was agreed that no immediate changes were to be made as far as their MPs were concerned, except that in future their candidatures would be under Labour Party auspices. By December the negotiations between the MFGB and MacDonald were complete and the Labour Party was substantially reinforced by the addition of 550,000 new members. There was also a hefty financial contribution from the miners' union to the party's Parliamentary fund. Thus Keir Hardie's dream of the 'Labour Alliance' was at last realised in its entirety, for now there was no major grouping of organised workers outside the Labour Party.

## [17] A Period of Difficulty 1909–14

If the first three years of the Labour Party's existence saw it make significant if limited progress, the period from 1909 to the outbreak of the World War was one of manifold difficulty and virtual absence of achievement, at least in the Parliamentary or electoral sense. Certainly no legislation went on to the statute book which the party could fairly claim to have initiated or even influenced to any real degree and, in the country, attempts to increase its strength in by-elections ended almost invariably in depressing failure. Even in the honeymoon era immediately after the 1906 election things had been difficult. For example, between 1906 and 1908, 10 by-elections were contested, all but 2 being three-cornered fights, and the Labour candidate came bottom of the poll on no less than 5 occasions. The sole victory was the remarkable feat of Pete Curran in a four-cornered fight at Jarrow in June 1907, where the intervention of an Irish Nationalist undoubtedly took a large number of votes which would otherwise have gone to the Liberal. From 1909 the going, already hard, got progressively harder. The victory of Joseph Pointer at Attercliffe (Sheffield) in May of that year was a lucky one which, like Curran's at Jarrow, was the result of special local circumstances, in this case the appearance of two Conservative candidates and the consequent split in the right wing vote. The following year, with its two general elections, seemed, on the face of it, to have strengthened Labour's position for the number of MPs was increased to 40 in January and then to 42 in December. But appearances were deceptive, for these figures included the miners' MPs, following the decision to affiliate in 1908, and in fact the Labour Party failed to hold 4 of the mining seats, while 7 of its sitting MPs were defeated in the January election. At the second contest at the end of the year, the party could only put up 62 as opposed to 85 candidates, the result not only of the strain of two general elections in one year, but also the blow to the party's finances dealt by the Osborne Judgment (see below, page 111).

Yet, paradoxically some of the lost ground was regained—three seats lost in the north-west were more than balanced by two gains in London and one each in Scotland, Cumberland and the north-east. But this minor revival proved to be a temporary phenomenon for, from 1911 onwards, the by-election failures continued. Between then and the outbreak of war, official Labour candidates fought no less than 14 contests, all of them three-cornered, and on each occasion came bottom of the poll, sometimes very badly adrift from the Liberal and Conservative. Perhaps the worst result was the one at Hanley in July 1912, hitherto comfortably held by the MFGB President Enoch Edwards. This was now lost as a result of internal divisions, with the Labour candidate securing barely 12 per cent of the total poll.

One explanation for this melancholy decline is the more aggressive policy now initiated by the Liberal Party. In Parliament they took up the cause of social reform with renewed vigour and thus stole Labour's thunder. In the country they showed themselves less disposed to continue or extend the Gladstone policy of making seats available to Labour. On the issue of social reform, in particular the acute questions of pensions and unemployment, it had seemed in the course of 1907–8 that the Liberals were running out of steam as neither Asquith nor Burns seemed willing to take really effective action. Even when the Poor Law Commission finally produced its long awaited report in February 1909, thus re-kindling interest in the matter, Burns and his department were still opposed to action. Admittedly he had a faint excuse since the members could not agree on their conclusions and so issued two reports. The majority wanted to keep the Poor Law system but abandon the harsh, basically deterrent principles of 1834, in addition to renaming it 'Public Assistance' and transferring its administration from the boards of guardians to the county councils. On the other hand, the minority report, signed by Beatrice Webb, George Lansbury, Francis Chandler (secretary of the carpenters' union) and H. R. Wakefield (later Bishop of Birmingham) was, for the time, a revolutionary document. It was inspired and masterminded by the Webbs and, beginning from the now obvious and well documented fact that large sections of the population lived in poverty, it argued that the state or community should take steps to prevent destitution rather than merely relieve it. In practice, this would mean a comprehensive scheme of social reform including a proper system of child care and education; protection against sickness, disablement and unemployment; the establishment of a 'national minimum'; and a reasonable income for the aged. But, if all this was

too much for Burns, it was the opportunity for action which was joy-
fully seized by two other ministers in the Liberal cabinet. In the re-
shuffle which followed the resignation and death of Campbell-Bannerman, Lloyd George became chancellor of the exchequer and Winston
Churchill president of the board of trade. From their new positions
they launched a campaign to improve the lot of what Churchill called
'the left-out millions'. Lloyd George's contribution was the implementation of the old age pensions' scheme, the inception of a redistributive
taxation system in the Budget of 1909 and the National Insurance Act
of 1911. While his colleague assisted him with the last measure, he himself was responsible for establishing labour exchanges and, with the
Trade Boards Act, the first attempt to regulate conditions in certain
industries like tailoring and chain-making, where 'sweating' was
prevalent. Thus the Liberals, at any rate temporarily, regained the
initiative in a field which Labour claimed as its own. True, Henderson
might, half jestingly, criticise Churchill's labour exchanges as 'the Right
to Work bill in penny numbers' and some sections of the party led by
Snowden might castigate the contributory principle enshrined in the
National Insurance Act, but the Labour leaders were only too well
aware that this was the best that could be achieved at present and, to the
world at large, it was clear that Labour members followed where the
Liberals led. As for the situation in the country, Labour's electoral
record outlined above is significant evidence of its dependence on the
Liberals and the latter's reluctance to make further concession on the
lines of the 1906 pact. Admittedly, MacDonald and Henderson negotiated a fresh agreement with the then Liberal chief whip, J. A. Pease, for
the elections of 1910 but, following the affiliation of the miners, the
Liberals were not prepared to allow seats formerly held by Lib–Labs to
go by default and, on occasions, were able to win them back, as in the
Hanley by-election referred to above. Furthermore, whenever Labour
put up a candidate in a three-cornered fight, invariably he lost and
often came a very bad third. In the first general election of 1910 of the
forty Labour MPs returned only one had Liberal opposition and that
was from an unofficial candidate. Clearly, Labour held its seats only by
courtesy of the Liberal Party.

In another very real sense Labour was the prisoner of the Liberals.
Until 1910, the party not only insisted on its independence and
freedom of action, but was also able to practise this to the full—a fact
which was ostentatiously proclaimed to the world by the Labour MPs
sitting on the opposition benches with the Unionists when the 1906

Parliament assembled. From 1910 all this was changed as a result of the general elections which returned the two major parties with almost equal strength. Now they could scarcely indulge themselves in the luxury of opposition lest they inadvertently turn the government out. Further, although it was true that the government was dependent on Labour votes, it relied to an even greater degree on Irish support which was only given on the understanding that Asquith would tackle the Home Rule issue. Once this was joined the government found itself entangled in so much constitutional and political difficulty that the interests of Labour, in particular the question of social reform, were pushed into the background. This in turn was particularly serious for the party because at this point it received a serious blow which required rapid legislative action to prevent its very existence from being threatened. In 1909 the final judgment in the Osborne case was handed down by the House of Lords.

In the words of a recent account (Clegg, Fox and Thompson, *A History of British Trade Unions*) this decision threatened 'the very right of unions to undertake political action'. The whole point of the 'Labour Alliance' which Hardie and MacDonald had worked so long to attain was that the unions would provide the essential power base for working-class independent action, in particular money for electoral organisation and the maintenance of MPs in the Commons. Now, on the very morrow of the achievement of their aim, it seemed as if the whole thing was to be set at naught. In fact, the Osborne case was not the first attempt to check the involvement of the trade unions in politics. In 1906 a South Wales miner called Steele sued his union, the South Wales Miners' Federation, for using funds for political activities without his consent. He lost his case, both in the county court (March 1906) and then on appeal to the King's Bench Division (January 1907) but this apparently did not deter a group of ASRS members who objected to their union's affiliation to the Labour Party. They were led by the Walthamstow branch of the union and in particular its secretary W. V. Osborne who, in July 1908, appealed to the High Court for an injunction against the union's political activities on the grounds that these were 'ultra vires'. Following the precedent of Steele's case, the court found against him but on appeal in November of the same year, this was reversed and the Lords upheld the Appeal Court's ruling in December 1909. Osborne himself and the case became a centre of much controversy. Some said that this was another manifestation of the great anti-union anti-socialist 'conspiracy'. The Webbs claimed that he was 'liberally financed from capitalist sources' but others, particularly later commentators, have tended to dismiss this view. Whether Osborne was merely what he claimed to be, a loyal Liberal, or was the tool of sinister interests inimical to the working-class movement, made no difference to the political effects. The sudden restriction on its main source of revenue obviously reduced the Labour Party's ability to fight elections and to maintain its MPs once elected. It has been suggested that the effect on the funds was neither so immediate nor so drastic as had previously been thought. Nonetheless, the sharp reduction in the number of candidates for the December election of 1910 shows clearly that the injunctions secured against unions by those following in Osborne's footsteps were beginning to bite. What was even more serious was that, due to the Liberal Party's troubles over Home Rule, it took the Labour members some time to persuade it to take action to mitigate these effects. Eventually, in 1911, Lloyd George dealt with the problem of Labour members on reduced salaries by instituting the state payment of MPs, but this was only granted on the understanding that in return they would support his National Insurance measure, which was not to the taste of some of them, nor to that of their following in the country. But it was not until 1913 that the Liberals finally brought forward a measure to deal with the wider problem of the trade unions' involvement in politics. Here again, the movement did not get what it wanted, namely a complete reversal to the status quo such as the Trades Disputes Act of 1906 had provided. Instead the unions were now allowed to maintain a political fund, but a ballot of members had to be taken first and the fund must be kept completely separate from the general finances with members having the right to refuse payment if they so wished. This was the best Labour could secure in the circumstances. Recently, it has been argued convincingly by A. J. P. Taylor in *English History 1914–1945* that while this measure was designed precisely by the Liberals to restrict the Labour Party's development, in fact it had the reverse effect, substantially expanding rather than restricting its finances: 'The political fund could not be used for anything else. In the old days a union felt generous when it subscribed £100 to the Labour Party. Now it thought nothing of handing over £5,000 . . . [and] the income of the Labour Party multiplied by ten overnight.' This, however, does not alter the fact that for most of the period from 1909–14, the party was seriously weakened as a result of the Osborne Judgment.

Finally, in addition to these troubles there was the problem of considerable internal dissension. The Labour Party in its early days, like the Liberal Party of the 1860s, was not so much a homogeneous group as a coalition and, like all coalitions, was subject to considerable tensions which at times threatened to splinter the public façade of unity. Indeed, there were times when not even a façade could be maintained. Thus, W. J. Braithwaite, one of the civil servants engaged in the preparation of the 1911 National Insurance Act, commented on the party's leaders: 'They don't speak for their men, don't know what their men want, and can't bind their men to obey—rather difficult people to deal with.' Some of the leaders were well aware of the extent to which this impaired the party's image. MacDonald, exasperated by the experiences of his first year in office as PLP chairman, warned delegates at the 1912 party conference that serious problems were being created by openly expressed differences between the members. In part, these divisions might be explained in terms of left and right, and reflected the divergent views of the ILP on the one hand and the trade union lobby on the other. The issues at stake were twofold: the ILP militants wanted a definite commitment to socialism and a harder, more aggressive line against the Liberals, whereas the trade unionists evinced no great enthusiasm for either course. With almost monotonous regularity, the former brought forward their socialist resolutions at party conferences between 1901–8, but with equally monotonous regularity these were defeated. Generally delegates would agree that the socialist society was an ideal to strive for but they were not prepared to write this officially into the constitution. The cause of the left, however, received a great stimulus in July 1907, when, in a by-election at Colne Valley, Victor Grayson was returned as an 'independent socialist' after a three-cornered contest with a Liberal and Conservative. By any standards his impact was devastating. In effect he constituted himself into a one-man pressure group, a spokesman for a minority, but a growing minority, who were already uneasy and disappointed with Labour's performance even so soon after the electoral and legislative successes of 1906. He was a member of the ILP and was backed by the local branch, but the Labour Party refused to endorse his candidature and when he was returned he reciprocated by refusing to sign the party constitution. The violence of his approach to politics not only attracted the following of the ILP activists, it also made his name known throughout Europe. He made his mark during the debates on the 'right to work' Bill in 1908 when he first blasted the Labour leadership for its lukewarm attitude and then created a scene on the floor of the House which led to his suspension on 15–16 October for the rest of the session. Completely unabashed, he set out on a tour of the country to stir up discontent against the Labour leaders, calling for much more drastic action than they were prepared to contemplate. 'Parliament,' he said in a speech at Keighley on 24 October 'all along had passed measures for the good of the people only when dragged from their hands by riot and bloodshed.' His attacks on MacDonald were very much in the nature of a personal feud and the effect on the ILP was such that, in the course of 1909, MacDonald, Hardie and Snowden decided they could no longer continue to sit on its executive. All this was highly embarrassing and disruptive but fortunately for the party his career was short. Increasingly his judgment was affected by heavy drinking. In the election of January 1910 he lost his seat and the following year led the ILP extremists into a new party formed by coalescing with the Social Democrats and called the British Socialist Party. This body in turn continued the miserable, feuding tradition in which all British left wing groups seem fated to follow and it divided in the early stages of the First World War.

Grayson's departure, however, by no means signified the end of trouble on the Labour left and after 1911 the activists drew into their ranks some prominent and highly respected personalities in the movement. Thus the ILP campaign against Lloyd George's National Insurance Act was led by Philip Snowden who objected strongly to what he called a step towards the 'servile state'. Then, George Lansbury struck out on his own in ways that proved embarrassing to the official leadership. In 1912 in typically generous, but muddled, fashion he resigned his seat at Bow and Bromley to fight it again on the issue of women's suffrage. Not even his outstanding local reputation was sufficient to reverse the electoral swing against Labour and the Conservative overturned his majority of 863, replacing it with one of 751 in a straight fight. But not only did Lansbury gratuitously present a seat to the Conservatives, also in 1912 he began publishing the *Daily Herald* which became the organ of the left wing and was far superior to and far more influential than the stodgy official publication the *Daily Citizen*. Finally giving further comfort to the left wing rebels was the openly expressed sympathy of Keir Hardie who at this time felt his loyalties painfully torn between his fundamentalist socialist beliefs and the need to support the official leadership in the case of party unity.

Trouble on the left was matched by trouble on the right, from the more conservatively minded trade union leaders. In 1905 they had attempted to pass a resolution expelling the socialist societies and the trades councils and although this proved unsuccessful, there were some who feared their influence over men like Henderson and Shackleton. Keir Hardie, writing to Bruce Glasier in December 1908, gave voice to these fears: 'I suppose we are in for another year of Henderson's chairmanship, which means that reaction and timidity will be in the ascendancy. . . . Then, when the miners come in the Annual Conferences will be controlled by Coal and Cotton and . . . that means more reaction. There are times when I confess to feeling sore at seeing the fruits of our years of toil being garnered by men who were never of us, and who even now would trick us out.' Hardie's concern certainly seemed justified by the outcome. The adhesion of the miners, with their traditional Liberal sympathies only lately abandoned, was not entirely a gain for the party, particularly in areas like the north and east midlands where Lib–Labism continued to flourish in spite of assurances to the contrary. From the date of their adhesion to the Labour Party until as late as 1912, there was incessant bickering on this issue. Labour Party men in the constituencies claimed that in a number of cases at the 1910 elections, miners' candidates were not properly adopted and moreover did not make it clear they were standing as 'independents'. In some constituencies there were serious differences of opinion between the MFGB lodges and the party's local organisation. In others, sitting miners' MPs refused to countenance the establishment of a separate Labour organisation, sometimes with disastrous results. The collapse of the Labour vote in the Hanley by-election of 1912 was partially a consequence of such a situation. But, as it turned out, this proved to be a watershed in the relations of the MFGB and the party. The shock of the result brought the former hard up against the realities of the political situation and it was apparent that they must close ranks if the party were to survive. The situation was also improved by the election of Bob Smillie as president of the Federation—as always a strong exponent of independent political action—and of an executive with a clear majority of Labour sympathisers. Nonetheless, for much of the period immediately before the war, the miners' reluctance to make a complete break with Liberalism was a source of weakness.

However, the real issue on which the trade union leaders parted company with the rest of the party was the National Insurance Bill, which they enthusiastically supported since the unions were to be brought in to help administer the measure. This, they argued, would not only enhance their prestige and give opportunities for the recruit-

ment of new members, but would also take the strain off their own benefit funds. In the negotiations between the government and the labour
movement on this issue in the course of 1909–10, there were complaints
that Shackleton and the Parliamentary Committee of the TUC were
negotiating directly with the ministers and keeping the Labour Party in
the dark. These and other criticisms seemed to have profoundly irritated
Shackleton and, partly as a result, he decided to leave politics and accept a post as a civil servant on the new National Insurance Commission. Thus did internal conflicts not only have a weakening effect
but also brought about the resignation of a man, who, despite the
doubts expressed as to his loyalty, was one of Labour's ablest politicians
and would leave a gap which it would be difficult if not impossible to fill.

All this was serious enough but what was even worse was the rise of
an influential group in the trade union movement which went even
further than Tillett, not merely questioning the record of the Labour
Party, but suggesting that any political action was futile. The argument
ran that the working class could do far more for itself, and far more
quickly, by aggressive industrial action than by the slow process of
building up an effective Parliamentary party. Ultimately the Syndicalists, as they were known, aimed at a general strike which would have the
effect of paralysing the country and giving them control of the state. The
idea seems to have originated in France in the mind of Georges Sorel,
but there were also American influences at work. Daniel de Leon, a
leading American Marxist, had been preaching something similar and
his work was widely known in Britain, particularly in Ireland and on
Clydeside. In 1910 the movement secured the support of the veteran
Tom Mann who had recently returned from a lengthy stay in Australia
and was an enthusiastic convert to the cause. He almost immediately
began publishing a monthly journal, the *Industrial Syndicalist*, and
established an organisation called the Industrial Syndicalist Education
League for propaganda purposes. Furthermore, he was quickly joined
by his former colleague in the dock strike, Ben Tillett, and by the
sailors' and firemen's union chief, Havelock Wilson. Their activities
helped to trigger off industrial conflict for a period of two years, reaching a climax in 1912 and only really checked when the Port of London
Authority under its hard chairman, Lord Devonport, succeeded in
defeating a strike called to prevent its employment of non-union labour.
The causes of this movement, which was to revive after the war, were
various and details need not concern us. It has already been pointed
out that wages generally in the five years before 1914 were stagnant

while prices were rising, and this in itself is probably sufficient explanation for the support the Syndicalists were able to attract. There was also
the general violent tone of politics and the penchant for 'direct action'
which had been exhibited by the 'Ditchers' in the Lords, the suffra-
gettes and the two Irish factions and which seemed to some degree at
any rate to succeed. But from the Labour Party's point of view, the
fact that a section of its support was clearly throwing it over, regarding
it as a broken reed, was potentially disastrous. Indeed, Devonport
certainly did not realise it, but his success in checking the strike movement in 1912 probably did more to maintain the party's existence at a
critical stage in its fortunes than has been generally admitted.

But even in this very difficult period in Labour's history at least some
progress was made. At last, something was done to provide a stable and
effective leadership. The totally unsatisfactory idea of rotating the PLP
chairmanship now came to be questioned. Between 1906–10, there were
three chairmen, successively Keir Hardie (1906–8), Arthur Henderson
(1908–10) and George Barnes (1910–11). These constant changes in
themselves, together with the incapacity of Hardie and the suspicion
with which the socialist elements viewed the trade union leaders,
Henderson and Barnes, were a serious source of weakness. Henderson in
particular was convinced that some more satisfactory arrangement
must be devised and he was equally convinced that there was only one
man who could lead the party effectively: MacDonald. MacDonald
was acceptable to the 'left' as an ILP man and a close colleague of
Hardie's. On the other hand, his stand against the extremists in the
ILP had endeared him to the trade union leaders, as ever fearful of too
close a commitment to socialism. But MacDonald for his part was not
keen, or so he said, objecting particularly to the disunity of the party
and the irresponsible independent line often taken by Keir Hardie.
But, if Philip Snowden is to be believed, MacDonald's protests were not
to be taken seriously and in fact he and Henderson had between them
worked out a neat little backstairs deal by which he would be elected
chairman, at the same time resigning his post as secretary to Henderson. With MacDonald, the Labour Party acquired in R. T. McKenzie's
words 'its first real leader'. Not only was he effective in the House—'a
born Parliamentarian', according to A. J. Balfour—but he soon established a tremendously strong ascendancy over the other Labour MPs
and the party as a whole. Beatrice Webb, in her usual cutting manner,
explained his success as being due to the fact that he was 'more than a
match for all those underbred and under-trained workmen who sur-

rounded him on the platform and faced him in the audience'. She felt
that, as 'long as he chooses to remain leader of the Labour Party he
will do so'. McKenzie argues that with the election of MacDonald and
his retention of the chairmanship over the next few years, the party
'was well on the way to accepting a relationship to their "chairman"
almost indistinguishable from the traditional relationship between the
older parties and their respective leaders.' But all this was changed by
the outbreak of the war and MacDonald's break with the majority of
his followers on the issue. Nonetheless, he served the party well in this
period and almost all sections and shades of opinion recognised the
achievement of his leadership. Admittedly, he did nothing to provide
the party with an effective philosophy. His socialism was of a somewhat
bland, not to say nebulous, kind and was clearly coloured by his
Liberal background and the maintenance of his links with a number of
Liberal friends. Indeed, in a book *Socialism and Society* published in 1905,
he had expounded the rather comfortable theory that Labour was the
natural and inevitable successor to Liberalism: 'Each new stage in
evolution retains all that was vital in the old and sheds all that was
dead. . . . Socialism, the stage which follows Liberalism, retains everything of permanent value that was in Liberalism by virtue of its being
the hereditary heir of Liberalism.' Moreover, for MacDonald, the
Marxist class war which the ILP activists wanted to fight was irrelevant
and, pursuing his evolutionary analogy still further, he declared:
'Socialism marks the growth of society, not the uprising of a class.'
Certainly there seemed to be much truth in these arguments for Labour
often found itself following Liberal philosophy willy-nilly, particularly
on foreign and imperial matters, as well as in the field of social reform.
Not everyone found this as comforting as MacDonald and Victor
Grayson touched the responsive chords of a significant number in the
labour movement with his brief, hell-raising campaign. Nor indeed was
it just the firebrands on the ILP left who thought thus. The intellectuals
of the Fabian Society voiced similar criticisms. In 1905, Cecil Chester-
ton, in the publication *Gladstonian Ghosts*, complained: 'You cannot
have an independent party with any real backbone in it without independent thinking.' And again, writing in the privacy of her diary in
1912, Beatrice Webb criticised MacDonald for 'being sceptical of all
the reforms which he is supposed to believe in' and then added with
remarkable foresight: 'If we could see into MacDonald's mind I don't
believe it differs materially from John Burns' mentality.'

# [18] The Party in the Country

By 1914, Labour's strength in the country was developing significantly in four areas: the industrial north; parts of London; Clydeside; and South Wales. Here, in the period from its foundation in 1900 to the outbreak of the First World War, the party was able to build on the foundations laid by the pioneers of the previous generation whose activities we have already examined (see Part III, Chapter 9). Outside these areas Labour made scarcely any impact at all.

In the north, in Lancashire, it received its biggest boost following the adhesion of the big battalions of the cotton unions. The details of their conversion at the Clitheroe by-election have already been recounted (see Part V, Chapter 13). Suffice it to add that the textile workers' influence together with the local Liberals' almost total commitment to the MacDonald-Gladstone arrangement were the major factors ensuring that, during this period, the north-west returned the most Labour MPs: 13 in 1906 and January 1910 and 10 in December 1910. The position here was further strengthened by the early adhesion of the county's miners to the LRC in 1903. On paper, the miners' potential electoral strength looked promising: they formed more than 40 per cent of the constituency in 3 cases (Leigh, Newton and Wigan); more than 20 per cent in 2 (Ince and St. Helens); and about 11–12 per cent in 3 others (Ashton-under-Lyne, Eccles and Radcliffe). Industrial relations in the coal-field were bad and this was reflected in political action. Accordingly the LCMF candidates were returned in 2 constituencies in 1906 and 4 in January 1910, although the second election of that year saw 2 of the seats lost.

On the other side of the Pennines the situation was rather different. The West Riding woollen towns were, of course, the original power base of the ILP and the successful consolidation of its position brought its reward in the 1906 election when three seats were won at Bradford West, Leeds East and one of the two Halifax seats. All three were retained throughout the period but the local activists were not satisfied and frequently demanded a more aggressive line against the Liberals. This led to the particularly embarrassing challenge to Herbert Gladstone in the 1906 Election (see Part V, Chapter 15). Further south in the coal-field the spread of Labour influence continued to be slow and hesitant. At the beginning of this period the ILP had only one sizeable branch in the whole of the coal-field, at Hemsworth near Barnsley and, moreover, it found great difficulty in discovering an issue which could be exploited to stir the miners to abandon Lib–Labism. However, the ILP activists could and did seize on the Denaby Main Case (see Part V, Chapter 13) and they could also point to the fact that by the beginning of the century the electoral pact originally worked out between the Yorkshire Miners' Association and the Liberals back in 1885 was blatantly unfair. The miners clearly deserved more representation than the one seat—Ben Pickard's constituency at Normanton—granted them in return for their support for Liberal candidates in the rest of the coalfield.

The death in 1904 of Pickard, the Lib–Lab anchorman, provided the ILP with an opportunity it did not neglect. Its increasing influence was soon shown by the growth in the number of branches. By mid-1904, seven new ones had been formed and the process continued over the next eighteen months, by which time it has been calculated that there was at least one branch in every important mining centre. Another indication of the way things were going was the annual gala in June when the ILP organised an unofficial platform, on which Keir Hardie appeared, and this, according to some observers, was the greatest success of the day. Sooner or later there was bound to be a major clash between the ILP and the old guard. In April 1904 the union's council agreed that it should sponsor five more candidates and the ILP immediately began a campaign to secure the nominations either for the LRC or for their own men under the sponsorship of the union. Then in October of the same year a group of ILP colliers, calling itself the South-West Yorkshire Independent Labour Party Federation, meeting at Wakefield, demanded that independent labour candidates should be adopted at Osgoldcross, Hallamshire, Barnsley, Rotherham and Sheffield (Attercliffe). The proposal was endorsed by the council of the YMA but it was not entirely to the taste of the Lib–Lab leadership. The local Liberals in turn were reluctant to make any concessions but in the end, after much manoeuvring, they agreed that the miner's nominee, John Wadsworth, would be accepted as a Lib–Lab candidate at Hallamshire but would make no concession in any of the other seats. The ILP came out of the whole affair very badly. In the first place, one of their leaders, Herbert Smith, had seemed to have a very good chance of succeeding Pickard at Normanton but in view of the need to appease the Liberals the miners' leaders instead put up William Parrott for the vacancy. Then, the local miners' lodges had wanted Smith as candidate against the sitting mine-owner Joseph Walton at Barnsley, but once again the leadership intervened and the proposal was defeated on the union

The Labour Leader.

cartoonist's view of Keir Hardie. But Hardie himself neither liked nor was capable of ercising the concept of leadership.

Unsuccessful pioneers of Socialism Great Britain: William Morris and (opposite) H. M. Hyndman.

This early propaganda effort expressed the Labour movement's alarm at the effect of the judicial decisions culminating in Taff Vale. But the poster (opposite) points out that even after the Trades Disputes Act (1906) there is much to be done.

The early ILP membership card is typically elaborate.

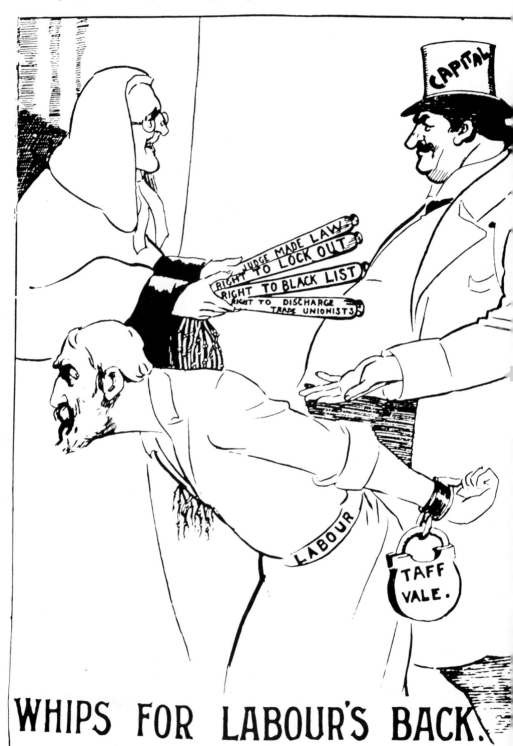

WHIPS FOR LABOUR'S BACK.

SWEATING

LAND MONOPOLY

TRADES DISPUTES ACT
FAIR WAGES
FEEDING CHILDREN
WORKING
COMP

PRIVILEGE

THE LABOUR PARTY STILL AT I

This is to Certify that

Samuel Hague

is a member of the

National Independent Labour Party

for the year 1895.

National Administrative Council:
Pete Curran.    Leonard Hall.
Enid Stacy.    J. Tattersall.
G. S. Christie.

J. Keir Hardie, President.
J. Lister, Treasurer.
Fred Brocklehurst, Fin. Secy.
Tom Mann, Secretary.

# MERTHYR TYDFIL BOROUGHS

### ❧ GENERAL ELECTION, 1910. ❧

# "TO THE MERTHYR LABOUR REPRESENTATION ASSOCIATION

**COMRADES,**

In response to your invitation I am willing to again become your **Candidate.** This is the fourth time you have so honoured me, and, if again elected, I shall continue to do what I can to **REPRESENT and SAFE-GUARD YOUR INTERESTS.**

The events of the past few weeks in the Aberdare and Rhondda Valleys must have shown you anew that a Liberal Government is first and foremost a **CAPITALIST GOVERN-MENT.** If the Bloodshed and Riotous Conduct of which the police have been guilty had taken place under a Conservative Government **every Liberal Platform would have rung with denunciation of the wicked Tories;** but, because it is the LIBERALS who are RESPONSIBLE there is a

# CONSPIRACY OF SILENCE IN THE PRESS, AND EVERY LIBERAL SPEAKER IS DUMB.

The **HOME SECRETARY** not only **DEFENDS THE ACTIONS OF THE POLICE** and **REFUSES an ENQUIRY** into the charges against them but also **EULOGISES** the **HOOLIGANS** in **UNIFORM**, whilst **LIBERAL M.P.'s**, with few exceptions, back him up by their Votes in the Division Lobby.

As a consequence of this the **MEN ON STRIKE** are **BELIEVED** by **Millions of People** who **KNOW NOTHING OF THE FACTS** to be **WILD, RIOTOUS, DRUNKEN, WORTHLESS SCAMPS**, whereas the very **OPPOSITE IS THE TRUTH.** THE MILITARY and POLICE have been sent to **HELP** the **MASTERS** to **CRUSH THE MEN.**

## THE TRICK WON'T SUCCEED.

During the Contest I shall be a good deal in other Constituencies where Labour Men are being opposed. Both Parties fear the presence in Parliament of Labour Men whom they can neither **SILENCE** nor **CONTROL.** I want to see the **NUMBER** of **SUCH MEN INCREASED**, so that **POLITICAL HYPOCRITES** of the **CHURCHILL TYPE** may be **UNMASKED**, and the Health, Comfort, Safety, and General Well-being of the Working Class promoted. I know you will **HOLD THE FORT** for **LABOUR** in my absence.

Fraternally Yours,

# J. KEIR HARDIE."

MERTHYR TYDFIL, Nov. 28th, 1910.

Printed and Published by The LABOUR PIONEER PRESS, Ltd., Williams' Square, Glebeland, Merthyr Tydfil.

Reprinted October 1975 to mark the 75th Anniversary of the Labour Party    Printed by Oxley Printing Group Limited  Bournemouth and London

**Left: Victor Grayson, the first of many left-wing 'hell-raisers'. Above: Keir Hardie's December 1910 election address indicates the strain on Labour Party/Liberal relationships at this time.**

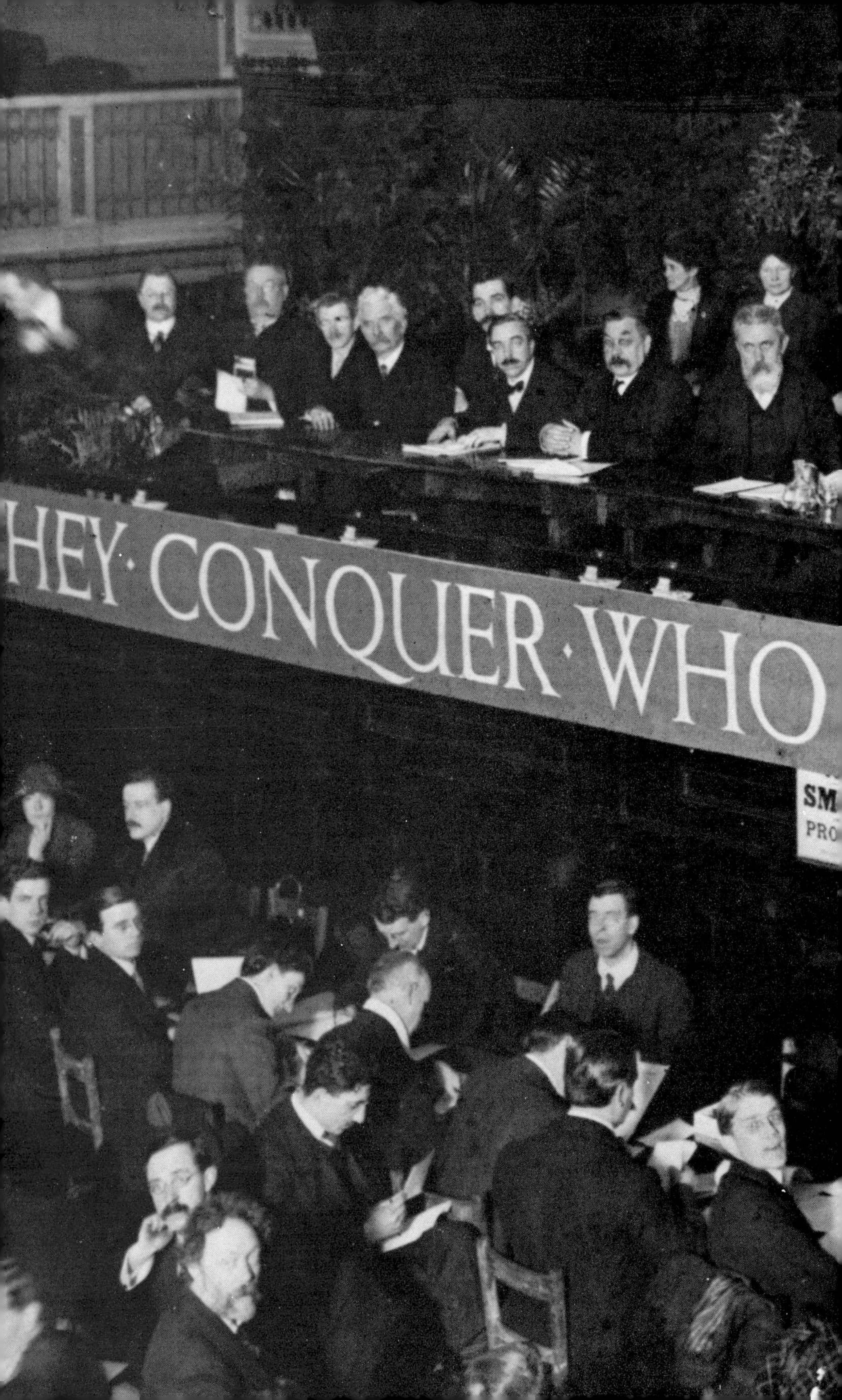
HEY · CONQUER · WHO

Labour Party Conference, Birmingham, 1912. Turner presides on the platform with Henderson and MacDonald to his immediate right and Hardie one place along on his left.

Arthur Henderson's campaign at Widnes in 1922 and (below) Henderson with the Webbs at t 1923 party conference. Opposite: how the Labour Party encompassed strangely dissimilar personalities. Keir Hardie enjoys Fabian support at Merthyr in the persons of Mr and Mrs B Shaw, while J. H. Thomas (below, right) and John Wheatley step out in fraternal harmony.

A Group of Labour MPs, probably taken shortly after the 1922 election, with the Clydesiders well represented. On the back row are Maxton (third from left), Kirkwood (middle) and Johnston (second from right); Shinwell is in the middle of the second row. Ex-Liberal and future minister, C. P. Trevelyan is at the extreme right of the back row.

On his way to the top: MacDonald (centre, raising hat) leaves the 192[ ] party conference with the first Labour government soon to take offi[ ]

# TO-DAY-UNEMPLOYED

PUBLISHED BY THE LABOUR PARTY 33, Eccleston Square, London, S.W. & PRINTED BY VINCENT BROOKS DAY & SON LTD 48 Parker St. Kingsway. London WC2

**Unemployment: a recurrent theme in Labour's propaganda throughout the early period of its history.**

council. Not surprisingly the ILP reacted strongly in the face of these disappointments and there was a determined attempt in 1906 to disrupt the Miners' Association/Liberal alliance by fierce attacks on the two Lib–Lab candidates, Fred Hall (who had succeeded Parrott) and Wadsworth. The Lib–Labs countered this by using their votes on the union council to block a resolution for affiliation to the LRC. But increasingly opinion at the grass roots was turning against them and when in 1906 the MFGB held its ballot on the question of affiliation, the Yorkshire miners voted in favour by a majority of just under 5,000. Furthermore in 1907, when the Labour leaders, Snowden, Hardie, Crooks and Stephen Walsh were invited to speak at the annual demonstration, it was noticeable that their speeches went down with the audience far better than those of the Lib–Labs. Finally in the 1908 ballot, the majority in favour of affiliation went up to over 12,000.

In view of these developments, the ILP was now confident that it had virtually complete control of the Yorkshire miners' vote and that the way was clear for a substantial expansion in political representation in the area of the coal-field. But the Lib–Labs in the union continued to resist the ILP faction with some success for a further two years and the latter suffered a pronounced set-back in 1910. When the preparations were being made for the first general election of that year, the ILP wanted to contest no less than seven seats on an independent basis. This proposal was strongly opposed by the Lib–Labs on the grounds that the Osborne case had so weakened their position that this was no time to undertake further political commitments, nor was it wise in the circumstances to challenge the Liberals. There was too the position of the sitting MPs, Wadsworth and Hall, to consider. They were still Lib–Lab in their sympathies and wished to retain the support of the Liberals in their constituencies. These arguments carried the day and the YMA decided to contest only one additional seat in the Yorkshire coal-field at Morley where Herbert Smith was duly adopted as the candidate. However, at Holmfirth, where there was a sizeable number of miners amongst the electorate, the local LRC, independently of the union, decided to run William Pickles of the painters' union. Neither candidate did well, coming third in both cases but, from the point of view of the Labour activists, Smith did particularly badly. It has been calculated that there were some 5,000 miners on the register and Smith polled only just over 2,000. The Liberal was a clear winner with over 8,000 and the Conservative managed 3,395. The immediate result of this débâcle was a general review of the union's electoral policy and, in a ballot of the members, it was narrowly agreed that no additional parliamentary candidatures should be promoted.

But the set-back was only temporary and the ILP soon bounced back undismayed. In 1911 it began to campaign for a reversal of the ballot and the following year saw what was to prove the final showdown in the YMA between its protagonists and the Lib–Labs. The occasion was a by-election at Holmfirth in June when the Liberals suggested that the miners' nominee should go before the Liberal association for its approval. After a fierce clash between the two factions, the union decided to run the candidate, William Lunn, independently and although he lost, he all but doubled Pickles' vote in January 1910. This was really the end of the alliance between Liberalism and the Yorkshire miners. It was followed rapidly by a number of actions which confirmed the YMA commitment to the Labour Party. At the turn of the year 1913–14, the union branches voted to fight seven extra seats at the next general election—i.e. nine altogether counting the two seats already held. And in the course of 1914, LRCs in the constituencies named responded to the union's initiative and candidates were duly adopted. In August it was agreed to establish a central committee in constituencies the union had decided, or might decide, to fight, and a full-time agent was also appointed for the Normanton, Hallamshire and Holmfirth divisions. Thus, by 1914, industrial Yorkshire—the West Riding textile towns and the coal-field—while not yet returning anything like the number of MPs from Lancashire, was beginning to emerge as a very important power base for the Labour Party.

In the north-east, as in Yorkshire, a lot depended on the attitude of the powerful, well-organised miners' unions and, once again, the outcome of the struggle was to depend to a very great extent on the activities of the ILP enthusiasts. For a variety of reasons the miners in this area had not hitherto shown any marked signs of radicalism in politics. But in the early years of the century their attitude began to change, largely for economic reasons. Wages fell markedly as a result of conciliation board decisions in the slump following the Boer War and the north-east coal-fields were particularly hit by a tax on exported coal in the budget of 1901. Not only were wages further depressed but some measure of unemployment also resulted.

In Durham the ILP had succeeded in establishing a number of branches in the 1890s and by the early years of the century, there seem to have been some sixteen in existence. This number was rapidly increased following the appointment of a very able organiser, Matt Simm, to cover the whole of the north-east. By 1906–7, there were no less than sixty branches and the party report for 1906 confidently asserted that 'the county of Durham especially is in the very van of the movement for labour and socialism'. Working with Simm was the energetic Thomas Richardson, who, from his base in the powerful Usworth and Washington branch, conducted a highly effective progaganda campaign amongst the Durham miners and succeeded in infiltrating ILP members into key posts in the union. In 1901, ILP members of the Durham Miners' Association formed an organisation called the Durham Labour Council which was expressly designed to fight local government elections. This it did with some success. The following year it held a conference at which doubts were expressed about its continued existence due to the strong criticisms of the Lib–Lab element in the union but it was decided to carry on with its activities and, within a very short time, it had become a sort of unofficial LRC for the whole county. Then, in 1903, came the triumph of Arthur Henderson in the Barnard Castle by-election (see Part V, Chapter 14) which was a tremendous boost to the ILP campaign for independent representation, although not all of them saw it that way. According to them, Henderson had to a great degree compromised his independence by his promise to support the DMA's Lib–Lab candidates in the next general election—a concession designed to secure the support of the miners who formed just over one-third of the electorate in the Barnard Castle division.

At the same time as the ILP was making progress, the Liberals were in a state of disarray. Early in 1903, the president of the Northern Liberal Federation, Sam Storey, decided the time had come to check the growing ambitions and pretensions of the Labour interest in the north-east. He was supported by the majority of the Liberal associations in his organisation, no less than 18 of the 23 affiliated endorsing the policy. The Barnard Castle election was the first attempt to put this into practice and proved a serious set-back to his initiative. Moreover, the policy was deplored by the Liberal Party's national leadership, its central machine and most of the press. The upshot was that Storey and the treasurer of the Northern Federation resigned immediately after the electoral fiasco and the Liberal Party in Durham was left in a confused and seriously weakened state. From the Liberal point of view this was bad enough, but what was worse was that simultaneously the DMA—or some elements in it—began to question the value of their twenty-year alliance with Liberalism. The understanding dated back to 1885, when, in return for its support for other Liberal candidates, the DMA had been granted the right to nominate candidates for two constituencies, Mid-Durham and Houghton-le-Spring. In fact, as things turned out, only the former was held by a mining candidate, the secretary of the DMA, John Wilson, a staunch Liberal and very much opposed to socialism and the idea of independent labour representation. As in the case of Yorkshire, the arrangement was manifestly disadvantageous to the DMA, for there were several other constituencies where the miners formed a significant percentage of the electorate. The decision to challenge this set-up was partly due to the changing economic circumstances and partly the propagandising of the ILP, but the final straw seems to have been the Taff Vale decision. Demands for independent representation were now increasingly heard. For a time, Wilson and the Lib–Lab element in the union managed to hold them off. In March 1903, the Durham Miners' Council decided to run two more candidates, but on the Lib–Lab ticket, and three months later the same body threw out a resolution for affiliation to the LRC. The following year saw the success of the union's treasurer, John Johnson, in a by-election at Gateshead, but although a member of the ILP he was adopted by the Liberals and MacDonald dissuaded the local LRC from putting up a candidate as such action would clearly compromise both his recently concluded entente with Herbert Gladstone and his long-term aim to win the miners to the Labour cause. Later in 1904 an attempt by the ILP to get an LRC candidate adopted in North-West Durham failed due to the obdurate opposition of Wilson and the weakness of William House, the president of the Durham Miners who was himself an ILP member. But despite Wilson's stubborn rearguard action, time was running out for the Lib–Labs. Successive wage reductions in February, May and November, against which the union was unable to take effective action, gave the ILP an opportunity which it seized with both hands. Its meetings were better attended and its membership in the union rose significantly. The first open signs that the DMA was changing its political allegiance came in 1905 when it made its dispositions for the now inevitable general election. It first agreed to make £80 available from its funds to the Durham Labour Council, which was in effect a donation to the LRC, and then it decided to run an ILP member, J. W. Taylor, as an independent at Chester-le-Street. At the general election Taylor won the seat easily and almost immediately declared his adhesion to the LRC group in Parliament. From 1906 onwards, the ILP men gradually fastened their hold on the union, and in 1910 they were able to precipitate the final public and irreparable breach between the DMA and the

Liberals, when, at the January election, the latter not only refused to give House a free run at Bishop Auckland, but also decided this time to oppose Johnson at Gateshead. But unfortunately control of the union did not necessarily mean success at the polls. Between 1910 and the outbreak of war, Labour candidates in Durham did very badly indeed. Liberal sentiments among the rank and file miners in the constituencies remained quite strong and it became clear that much more was needed in the field of organisation and propaganda before Durham could be accounted a safe power base.

In Northumberland, the Lib–Labs, led by Burt and Fenwick, were if anything in an even stronger position. There seems to have been comparatively little ILP activity in the area in the 1890s and it was not until Matt Simm's arrival that any signs of progress were apparent. Under his guidance, the number of branches rose by more than threefold in the space of eighteen months (though even then only numbering thirteen); individual members began to make their presence felt at union lodge meetings; finally a newspaper, the *Northern Democrat*, with Simm himself as editor, was launched. This growth of ILP influence was illustrated when it secured two major successes in the union against the Lib–Labs: in 1907, the NMA voted overwhelmingly to join the MFGB; and the following year there was also a majority in the ballot in favour of affiliating to the Labour Party. But unfortunately when an attempt was made to translate this into political terms, the ILP found itself up against a brick wall. An attempt to ease out Burt and Fenwick, when both refused to stand as Labour candidates in 1910, was an abysmal failure. The most the ILP faction could achieve was the NMA's agreement in 1912 to choose independent labour candidates for whenever the two veterans retired, and also to cooperate with the ILP and other unions in the formation of local LRCs.

In England outside the industrial areas of the north, the most promising field for Labour endeavour continued to be in London. Altogether it has been calculated that by the early years of the century, 12 local 'independent' parties had been established, and if one then adds a number of others which were either Lib–Lab or divided between the two, then the total of 'labour' parties rises to 20. Furthermore, right at the end of the period, representatives of these groups, the trade unions and trades councils came together to form the London Labour Party. But the promise of success must not obscure the fact that progress at first was limited. In 1907 the Labour Party could only claim 10 per cent of its membership in London which itself contained 20 per cent of the country's population. Electorally speaking, there were never more than 70 metropolitan borough councillors before 1914, while on the LCC the number of independent representatives rose to 3 in 1910, but had slipped back to 1 by 1913. Such halting progress was due in part to the strength of the SDF and the Fabians and the relative weakness of the ILP in the capital. Neither of the former groups was entirely committed to the Labour cause, although some of the Fabians, like the Webbs, were gradually coming to accept the idea.

Of the local Labour parties the most successful in electoral terms were West Ham and Woolwich. In the former, Will Thorne held Keir Hardie's old seat with fairly comfortable majorities throughout the period 1906–14 while Will Crooks sat for Woolwich from 1903 apart from the eleven months between the elections of 1910. There was also progress in Poplar where George Lansbury did well in the Bow and Bromley constituency in 1900 and won the seat in 1910 only to throw it away two years later. All three parties also took a keen and effective interest in local government, regularly securing the return of candidates to the municipal councils and boards of guardians. Equally important, and perhaps the explanation of their success, was the concern displayed for organisation. At West Ham it was based on the local trades council while Woolwich had a relatively sophisticated system of committees at ward level. In addition, Woolwich and Poplar were two of the earliest local Labour parties to develop the idea of individual membership, thus anticipating an important feature of Arthur Henderson's reforms of 1918. But in organisational terms probably the most significant development in the capital was the establishment of the London Labour Party, a body over and above the local groups. This project had been mooted for some time but it was not until May 1914 that a conference met on the initiative of the London Trades Council to put it into effect. By the end of the year it had secured the adhesion of the great majority of Labour's affiliated membership in London. This was of great importance for the future. Under the leadership of Herbert Morrison it became the instrument of a growing Labour predominance in the capital's politics. On the LCC Labour first ousted the Progressives as the main alternative to the Conservatives and then won absolute control in 1933—a control which it never relinquished throughout the remainder of the LCC's existence.

In the rest of England there was little significant development. In the general election of 1906 the whole of southern England (excluding London) and the midlands returned 5 of the Party's 30 MPs and proportionately did only marginally better in the 1910 elections when 10 members were returned on both occasions. Particularly disappointing was the failure to make much headway in the coal-fields of the north and east midlands where the miners' attachment to Liberalism remained particularly strong. The prevalence of Lib–Labism here was strikingly revealed almost immediately following the MFGB decision to affiliate to the Labour Party in 1908. In July of the following year at the Mid-Derbyshire by-election, J. G. Hancock, the general secretary of the Nottingham Miners stood as a 'Labour' candidate, but his endorsement by the local Liberals and his almost entire reliance on their machine during the election made his standing rather uncertain to put it mildly. Further confirmation of this was provided by the losses in by-elections of mining seats at Hanley (July 1912), Chesterfield (August 1913) and North East Derbyshire (May 1914).

Apart from the coal-mining areas of the midlands, the other districts where the possibilities of Labour progress seemed most promising were where there was a concentration of the members of two unions which had been in at the foundation of the LRC—the ASRS and the National Union of Boot and Shoe Operatives. In the case of the former, the two constituencies concerned were Crewe and Derby. Of the two, Crewe had the greater concentration but, strangely enough, the cause does not appear to have made much impact and the seat was not contested until a by-election of July 1912 when J. H. Holmes came bottom in a three-cornered fight. Even in a radical union like the railwaymen, the adherents of Liberalism were not inconsiderable, and furthermore, they had the inspiration of Richard Bell who retained his general secretaryship until 1910. With his retirement from the union and from politics also, there came an opportunity to regain his seat at Derby. This J. H. Thomas, the assistant general secretary, succeeded in doing in 1910.

The heaviest concentrations of boot and shoe workers in the midlands were in Northampton and the surrounding districts and Leicester. In the former little progress was made due to a strong Liberal element in the electorate and the continued presence of the SDF. The latter in fact contested both seats in the two-member constituency in 1906 and in the first election of 1910, but without success, although the performance in 1906 when their candidates secured roughly 20 per cent of the total vote was quite respectable. An attempt in the neighbouring Wellingborough seat in the December 1910 election by T. F. Richards, hitherto a prominent figure in the Leicester branch of NUBSO, was heavily defeated in a three-cornered contest securing less than 10 per cent of the turn-out. In Leicester matters turned out more favourably. The NUBSO branch was the largest in the country and was fairly heavily penetrated by ILP enthusiasts. To make the situation even more favourable the ILP branch itself was one of the strongest and best organised in the country. No doubt it was factors such as these which prompted MacDonald to try his luck in the constituency. He was defeated in 1900 but succeeded in 1906, and again in 1910, holding second place to the Liberal. Here, however, as in the case of Derby, the electoral arrangement with the local Liberals in a two-member constituency contributed significantly to Labour's success.

In Scotland the most promising areas continued to be the lowland coal-field and Clydeside. In the coal-field, Bob Smillie continued the hard work already begun in the 1890s to win the miners from Liberalism. He had played a prominent part in the formation of the SWRC, in 1900 being elected its first chairman, and increasingly throughout its short and unhappy history that body came to be dominated by the Scottish Miners' Federation. Unfortunately the separate existence of the SWRC was a bone of contention between it and the LRC for the latter felt that unnecessary duplication ought to be avoided, while the Scottish body claimed that the LRC was not entitled to the affiliation fees of the Scottish membership of its affiliated trade unions. Attempts in 1905 by Hardie and Smillie to smooth over the differences failed and the two bodies continued to operate side by side with the SWRC gradually dwindling away until it finally disappeared when the miners' union joined the Labour Party in 1909. During those years, its electoral record in the coal-field was far from impressive in spite of strong concentrations of miners in a number of constituencies. North East Lanark was contested unsuccessfully on no less than three occasions and nothing was achieved in the four seats fought in 1906, although Smillie performed quite creditably at Paisley. These disasters, coupled with severe financial difficulties, went a long way towards undermining the SWRC's separate existence and within three years it was eliminated. In the following general elections (1910) the Scottish miners, now, like the rest of the MFGB fully affiliated to the Labour Party, did marginally better. True, the indefatigable Smillie could do no better than third place in Mid-Lanark both in January and December, and his colleagues in the neighbouring constituencies were even more heavily defeated. Furthermore, with two elections following so quickly and the implications of the Osborne case just coming to be realised, the strain was such that the Scottish miners only fought three seats altogether in December.

But in one of these, West Fife, they scored, at long last, a well deserved success. William Adamson had done very well here in January, coming second, and now in December with the Conservative standing down he won by some 700 votes.

On Clydeside at the turn of the century the ILP was experiencing serious problems. Its leadership lacked dynamism; its organisation was slack and inefficient; it wasted a good deal of its time and energy feuding with the SDF; it was making little or no impact on the large Irish community; finally, trade union opinion, as expressed in the powerful and influential Glasgow Trades Council, was wary of committing itself to Labour. Nonetheless, a start was made in laying the basis of future Labour successes on the Clyde and the credit for this must go to three men: John Wheatley, Thomas Johnston and Emanuel Shinwell.

Wheatley's achievement was the building of a bridge between the labour movement and the Irish. This, given the hostility of the Catholic Church towards socialism and the appeal of Liberalism on the Home Rule issue, was a difficult task, but Wheatley, as an Irishman and a Catholic, was peculiarly fitted for it. He had come to socialism as a result of his personal experiences in the poverty-stricken mining communities on the outskirts of Glasgow—he himself worked in a pit from the age of eleven for some years—and of his own wide reading. Physically he was unprepossessing. Arthur Marwick describes him as 'a chubby owl behind his pebble lens spectacles'. But he was endowed with considerable ability, shrewdness and drive. He was active in ILP circles from about the turn of the century, although he did not become a fully paid-up member until 1907. In the course of 1906–7 he formed the Catholic Socialist Society which soon began to attract large attendances at its meetings and involved Wheatley in keen and often bitter controversy with the Catholic clergy. On one occasion late on a Saturday, a drunken mob, urged on by his local priest, burned him in effigy. But his propaganda was beginning to have an effect, and, particularly after 1910, evidence of local elections seems to show that the Irish Catholic vote was steadily transferring its allegiance from the Liberals to Labour. His own political career advanced in these years. In 1909 he was elected to the Lanark County Council and the following year saw him on the Glasgow City Council. His power and influence in the ILP was also growing and his position here was particularly strengthened in 1910 when that much misunderstood but forceful personality, Jimmy Maxton, became one of his closest collaborators.

The second of our trio, Thomas Johnston, was the only native-born

E.L.P.—5*

Scotsman amongst them, hailing originally from Kirkintilloch, outside Glasgow. Like Maxton, he represented the middle-class 'intellectual' element in the Scottish ILP having graduated from Glasgow University. He was no forceful controversialist like Wheatley or Maxton, being of a rather shy and retiring disposition, but his special contribution was most vital, for he organised an effective system of propaganda. In 1906, he inherited a small printing works, and he seized the opportunity to embark on a highly successful venture into political journalism. He began publishing a weekly called *Forward*, which, in a matter of three years, due to his vigorous policy, had a circulation of approximately 10,000. His single most effective effort was an attack on the Scottish aristocracy in a series of articles, entitled *Our Noble Families*, published in his periodical in the course of 1908–9. He later reprinted these in the form of a book which had sold something like 100,000 copies by 1914. The object of this particular exercise was to stir up and win for Labour the other large important element in Glasgow's population, the refugees from the Highlands who had been driven there by the Scottish lairds' 'clearance' policies earlier in the nineteenth century.

Finally, in Emanuel Shinwell there was the means by which official trade union support could be mobilised for Labour through the Glasgow Trades Council. Born in the East End of London, he had moved at an early age to Glasgow via South Shields. He became a delegate on the council in 1906 and soon built a reputation for himself as an able and enthusiastic speaker in the cause of political action. In 1908 he became vice-president and was able to carry a radical-sounding declaration in favour of this, but, in practice, it was not implemented due to the caution of the council's secretary, George Carson, and the representatives of the engineering and ship-building unions who largely made up the membership. So, for all his combative and persuasive approach it is doubtful whether Shinwell would have made much progress with his fellow trade unionists had it not been for outside circumstances which spurred them to action. In 1908, Clydeside suffered a sharp and sudden shock when a recession in shipbuilding produced unemployment on a scale not experienced for something like half a century. Board of Trade figures put the rates at something like 28½ per cent in shipbuilding and 25 per cent in engineering. The destruction of the sense of economic security built up over the previous decades was a very real factor in the switch from Liberalism to independent Labour.

As the slump lifted in 1910, the ILP, under Wheatley's leadership, campaigned vigorously for members amongst trade unionists, although it had to face considerable competition from the Socialist Labour Party, one of the groups to emerge from the SDF schism of 1903. Here, however, Wheatley scored a notable success when he succeeded in 1909 in winning over to his side the influential David Kirkwood. Gradually Wheatley's design unfolded itself. He proposed first that the ILP and trades council should cooperate to secure more working-class representation on the city council, and in January 1911 a joint body was established with Shinwell and Carson representing the trades council. In May of the same year, further discussions between the two organisations led to the formation of the Glasgow Central Labour Party which held its first meeting on 18 May. By 1912 this body had been recognised as controlling all the labour movement's electoral activities in the city. At the same time not only did Wheatley create a party but he tried to provide it with a programme—a programme based on a scheme to improve Glasgow's deplorable housing which was not only expensive but, through overcrowding, contributed to the hideously high mortality rates in some of the central areas. Admittedly the plan, which envisaged council house-building out of the profits of the city tramways, provoked divisions within the party and when placed before the city council was inevitably and heavily rejected. But, despite this set-back, by 1914 the situation in the Glasgow area was beginning to look quite promising.

In Wales, progress continued to depend on the attitude of the miners. Their growing political awareness was stimulated not only by particular events like the Taff Vale and Stop Day cases, but by a general deterioration in industrial relations in the coal-field. The South Wales Miners' Federation, formed after the 1898 strike, was soon infiltrated to a considerable degree by the ILP which had hitherto only maintained a very precarious footing in east Glamorgan. Prominent amongst the campaigners for socialism within the union were three men: Vernon Hartshorn, C. B. Stanton and James Winstone. Their task was made rather easier by a number of factors, social, personal and political.

In the first instance the twin influences of nonconformity and Welsh nationalism which had done so much to bind the Welsh miners to Liberalism were now beginning to lose their hold. This was due mainly to the rapid anglicisation of the Glamorgan coal-field in the last quarter of the nineteenth and the early years of the twentieth century. In 1871 there were 34,000 employed in the field whereas by 1911 this number had risen to 150,000, mainly immigrants from England. To these newcomers, the old issues of disestablishment, education and temperance meant little or nothing. They were far more concerned with 'bread and butter' matters of employment, wages and general conditions of work, and hence more likely to gravitate to a party which placed a high premium on such matters. Then there was the personal division between the Lib–Lab leaders of the union: the president, the veteran Mabon, and his vice-president, William Brace. The two had clashed bitterly in the early 1890s on the issue of the sliding scale, when Mabon had used his influence to break a strike of hauliers called by Brace, and even when they came together to run the SWMF a certain measure of antipathy remained. Finally, as always, the Lib–Labs were let down by the reluctance of the local Liberal parties to play ball on the issue of additional representation. Under Pickard's scheme, the Welsh miners reckoned they were entitled to at least three extra seats and in particular had their eyes on Gower, South Glamorgan and West Monmouth. In the first case, the Liberals refused point blank to cooperate and in the second only accepted the miners' candidate after the intervention of Herbert Gladstone. Admittedly, West Monmouth was a happier story for Thomas Richards was adopted and returned at a by-election in November 1904.

But, in spite of these developments, the issue remained in balance for some time yet and the SWMF's relationship with the Labour Party was highly equivocal. In 1906 while it gave financial backing to Winstone standing at Monmouth in the general election and went on to vote in favour of affiliation in the MFGB ballot, at the same time four of its members secured election to Parliament as Lib–Labs. It was not until 1908, when the miners as a whole finally voted to affiliate to the Labour Party, that this uncertainty was resolved and the four SWMF MPs transferred their allegiance from the Liberals. But even this did not mean all was plain sailing, and from 1909 until the outbreak of the war little further progress was made. This may have been due to the comparative popularity of syndicalism in South Wales, but the strength of Liberalism remained an important factor. While it is true that there was a relative decline of nonconformity in Wales, the Chapel retained a good deal of influence, particularly in the mining valleys, and in politics this was invariably exercised on the Liberal behalf. Until this alliance of nonconformity and Liberalism was completely broken, Labour could expect only limited success.

Apart from the miners, there were two other groups of workers whose sizeable concentrations in Wales afforded a potential powerbase for independent action, the tinplatemen and the dockers. In neither case did Labour have much success. John Hodge, whose Steel Smelters' union had absorbed many of the tinplate workers, tried his luck at Gower in 1900. He failed, mainly due to the hostility of the local miners, and the cost, £1,200, meant the experiment was one not to be repeated. In the case of the dockers, Swansea, along with Bristol, was one of the main centres of Ben Tillett's Dock, Wharf, Riverside and General Labourers Union and it was here that Tillett attempted to advance his personal political ambitions having failed previously to secure election at East Bradford in 1892 and West Bradford in 1895. At first things looked promising. In 1898 an independent labour candidate was elected to the borough council and the following year Tillett received a useful addition to his strength when he succeeded in recruiting some of the tinplatemen who were reluctant to come under Hodge's domination. In 1900 the number of local councillors rose to five and shortly afterwards a local LRC was formed. Yet, surprisingly perhaps in view of this apparently solid progress, it was not deemed worth-while to attempt the parliamentary seat until the January 1910 election, and then Tillett performed wretchedly, polling only 1,451 to the Conservative's 4,375 and the Liberal victor's 6,020. The reason for this fiasco seems to have lain partly in the superior resources of the Liberal candidate, the wealthy Anglo-German industrialist, Alfred Mond, and partly in Tillett's own shortcomings as a leader and organiser.

The case of Swansea was paralleled in other major centres of population in South Wales. In Cardiff and Newport Labour made scarcely any headway in this period. On two occasions, 1904 and 1907, Cardiff Trades Council passed, with large majorities, resolutions in favour of contesting parliamentary elections on an independent basis, but in neither case did anything concrete materialise. In Newport, there was slightly more effective action. A local LRC was formed in 1901 and four years later the trades council sponsored Winstone's unsuccessful candidature at Monmouth to which reference has already been made. Only in one place, Merthyr Tydfil, could it be said that Labour made consistent progress. Here, Keir Hardie polled well in the four general elections, holding one of the two seats until his death. This success was matched in local elections in the borough, the best year being 1905 when all twelve Labour candidates were elected and a Labour councillor became the mayor.

This then was the state of the party at the grass roots in 1914. It was, in some respects, a situation full of promise for in several areas Labour was making a serious challenge to Liberalism and its adherents in the working-class movement. Looking back over the years it becomes apparent that it was in this period that the foundations were laid for later success in London, the north-east and the west of Scotland. But the progress was patchy and, as in Parliament, after the tremendous boost of the 1906 election there was something of a reaction. Some of the new supporters became disillusioned at the failure to secure quick results and the Liberals proved to be no easy touch, fighting back strongly to regain seats which Labour had presumed were its own. Finally, and most important of all, it was still a long way from being a truly national party, and if this end were to be achieved then clearly some attempt must be made to establish an organisation to cover not only the heavily urbanised, industrial districts, but also the country as a whole. As it turned out, the next four years were to provide the solution to this problem.

## PRINCIPAL EVENTS, 1900–14

1900.  General election: two LRC candidates (Keir Hardie and Richard Bell) returned out of fifteen

1901.  Final judgments by the House of Lords in the cases of Taff Vale and *Quinn* v *Leathem*

1902.  David Shackleton returned unopposed at the Clitheroe by-election

1903.  Annual LRC conference established a proper party fund to be provided by levies from the affiliated bodies. LRC candidates returned in by-elections at Woolwich (Will Crooks) and Barnard Castle (Arthur Henderson). A secret electoral understanding concluded between Ramsay MacDonald for the LRC and Herbert Gladstone for the Liberals

1906.  General election: 30 LRC candidates returned. The name now changed to the Labour Party and Keir Hardie elected as the first chairman. The passage of the Trades Disputes Act to reverse the Taff Vale decision

1907.  Victor Grayson returned as 'independent socialist' in the Colne Valley by-election

1908.  Miners' Federation voted in favour of affiliation to the Labour Party

1909.  The Osborne case

1910.  General election (January): 40 Labour MPs returned. The beginning of industrial unrest, the syndicalist movement. General election (December): 42 MPs returned although fewer candidates were put up

1911. The National Insurance Act caused divisions between the trade unions and the socialists. The introduction of payment of MPs mitigated some of the effects of the Osborne judgment

1912. The system of rotating the parliamentary leadership ended with MacDonald's election as chairman

1913. Trade Union Act allowed unions to establish a political fund under certain conditions

1914. The formation of the 'triple alliance' (miners, railwaymen, dockers and transport workers) to facilitate a general strike

# *Part VII*

## Labour and the First World War 1914–18

The labour movement's immediate reaction to the outbreak of European war in August 1914 was one of disapproval, yet paradoxically the war did much to advance the party's cause and ensure that in the five years following the peace it replaced the Liberals as the main alternative to Conservatism. As a result of the war Labour became accepted, almost, one is tempted to say, respectable, though that perhaps would be going too far. Nevertheless this acceptance was made very clear in three respects. In the first place Labour's collectivist ideas, hitherto exercising limited influence, now came to be embraced generally, if somewhat reluctantly. Secondly, the government, faced with the problem of organising the country to fight a war on a scale never before envisaged, was compelled to take the trade unions—the backbone of the Labour Party—fully into its confidence. This fillip to the unions' prestige was matched by an expansion in membership, financial strength and real power. Finally, in an attempt to secure a stable political framework at home, the ruling politicians decided that Labour's leaders must take their place in a national coalition and this, of all the developments, was probably the most striking.

Yet, at the same time Labour had to face serious problems. One result of the war was to open up divisions within the movement which placed a considerable strain on the party and cost it for some years the leadership of its most capable politician, Ramsay MacDonald. Fortunately in the last resort these feuds were resolved and, thanks to the constructive work of Arthur Henderson, the party emerged in 1919 a more coherent, united body with a properly organised national machine and an agreed statement of policy. It now remains to us to consider these developments in some detail.

## [19] The Acceptance of Labour 1914–16

The acceptance of Labour's collectivist ideas was probably due not only to the war but also to the activities of other groups influential in politics. There was, for example, a small section on the Liberal left, including Chiozza Money, Clement Edwards and Francis Channing, which had for some years previously canvassed the desirability of railway nationalisation and in 1907 had formed the Railway Nationalisation Society. On the other side of Parliament, a group of Conservatives, influenced by the memory of Disraeli and, more recently, by Joseph Chamberlain, had also toyed with collectivist ideas. Finally, there was a group of very capable civil servants such as Braithwaite, Beveridge and Sir Hubert Llewellyn Smith who approved the idea of some measure of state intervention in industry and society. Such men were in a distinct minority before 1914, but, with the outbreak of war, it became apparent to all, except the dyed-in-the-wool 'laisser-fairists', that the government would have to take some action in regulating industry and the life of the community in general. So in August 1914 the railways passed under government control, now being subjected to a body called the Railways Executive Committee under the president of the board of trade. This was soon followed by other actions: restrictions were placed on the chemical industry; under the Defence of the Realm Act (DORA), the government empowered itself to take over munition factories if necessary; and a Royal Commission was set up to consider the control of sugar supplies.

It must be emphasised that many remained uneasy at this interference and the government's measures were often tentative. Thus, for example, the arrangements regarding the railways left the day-to-day running still essentially in the hands of the private companies and while the president of the board of trade in theory supervised the committee's work, in practice control was exercised by the acting chairman who was the general manager of the London and North Western Railway. In the event, the labour movement while deriving satisfaction and justification from the implementation of its ideas felt increasingly that such action did not go far enough. The TUC unanimously adopted a resolution which described the railway arrangements as 'partial, vague, and unsatisfactory in character' and called for 'legislation having for its object the effecting of complete national ownership of the railways'. The official Labour organ the *Daily Citizen*, commenting on the work of the Sugar Commission, pointed out that the country was adopting

'collectivist experiments urged for so many years by the labour movement' and then went on to hope that the principle would be extended
and maintained for the future. 'If it be necessary for the state to guard
the poor from exploitation now, will it not be sound policy to continue
the experiment during what we hope will be the long years of unbroken
peace?' But Labour was to gain little satisfaction either on the issue of
further nationalisation or on control of prices, and there was still a long
way to go to the ideal of the collectivist state. Yet, however tentative the
moves, it did mean that the party's thinking was not so far out on a limb
as it had hitherto seemed.

More important from a practical point of view was the government's
acceptance of the trade unions as partners in the war effort and ultimately of Labour politicians as colleagues in the administration. This
anxiety for cooperation was most marked in Lloyd George who was
fully aware of the needs of the situation long before he took over from
Asquith as prime minister. It is true that in August 1914, the trade
union movement had proclaimed an industrial truce in the face of the
outside threat, but it was not long before two issues arose which created
tensions and made some sort of understanding between the government and the unions absolutely essential. These issues were 'dilution'
and conscription. By 'dilution of labour' is meant the waiving of rules
and conditions of entry into skilled employment and thus the use of
semi-skilled or unskilled labour, often juvenile or female, in jobs previously reserved to craftsmen. The industry most obviously affected was
engineering and the Amalgamated Society of Engineers was coming
under increasing pressure to relax its craft rules. In spite of the justification of the exigencies of war, it was only natural that the trade unions
should look on such developments with suspicion and seek assurances
that 'dilution' would only last the duration of the conflict. Fortunately
the heat was taken out of the situation by Lloyd George who was then
chancellor of the exchequer in Asquith's government. Together with
Runciman, the president of the board of trade, he called a meeting
with Henderson and several leading trade unionists at the treasury
from 17–19 March 1915. The result was the so-called Treasury Agreement which, together with an understanding reached separately with
the ASE a week later, was to cover almost the whole of British industry,
with the sole, though significant, exception of the mines. On their part,
the unions agreed to eschew all industrial practices which might hinder
war production. Disputes would be settled by arbitration and 'dilution'
was accepted. In return Lloyd George promised the agreement would

only be for the duration of the war; action would be taken to check the profits of munitions manufacturers; and a body was to be set up under Henderson's chairmanship to advise the government on labour questions. The whole package was given legal status by the Munitions of War Act, which Lloyd George piloted through Parliament when he became minister of munitions in the reconstructed Asquith ministry. The significance of this for the prestige of the trade union movement was immense but as a practical solution to the problem of labour relations in wartime, the measure was not entirely successful. As we shall see, it did not prevent unrest in the country particularly in South Wales and on Clydeside.

On the issue of conscription the reaction of the labour movement was not entirely consistent. The manpower demands of the western front had begun to cause Kitchener at the war office considerable concern during the course of 1915 but the government hoped to avoid the issue of compulsion by persuading men to volunteer under the Derby Scheme of October. The previous month the TUC had passed a resolution which seemed to imply—though the language was not entirely clear—that the labour movement would have no great objection should conscription ultimately be necessary. However when, at the turn of the year, the government decided to introduce a conscription bill, opposition erupted immediately and a special party conference meeting on 6 January 1916 passed a resolution against the bill calling on Labour MPs to oppose it in all its stages. Apparently it had become widely feared that a measure of military conscription would be followed by similar legislation in the industrial field and that workers would be placed directly under army control and receive only army pay. The government in fact carried two conscription measures in 1916. The first in January covered single men, the second in May extended the principle to married men, and on neither occasion did heated protests from the labour movement serve to deflect the ministers from their course. But, even so, the government found it expedient to make an important modification in its plans. Both the Derby Scheme and the two acts of 1916 had made provision for the exemption of key industrial workers and in the course of 1916 the power to grant exemptions was vested in a committee known as the Manpower Board. Friction between the Board and the unions over this culminated in a serious unofficial strike in the engineering industry in Sheffield in the middle of November. Following discussions, the ASE and the government decided that the whole business of granting exemptions should, for the time being at any rate, be left in the hands of the unions, who would issue 'trade cards' to denote those exempt from military service. This, as a number of historians have pointed out, was a remarkable concession by the government to organised labour.

It was also of prime importance that, during these years, Labour became accepted politically as well as industrially. It has already been pointed out how, by the Treasury Agreements of March 1915, Henderson was to chair a special committee to advise ministers on the labour question. This temporarily placed him in a rather equivocal position but matters were soon clarified when in May Asquith offered him the cabinet position of president of the board of education. At the same time two other Labour MPs were given junior positions: William Brace as under-secretary at the home office and G. H. Roberts as a government whip. Henderson himself was not too sure whether to accept. He realised fully that in effect the government was seeking to purchase in advance through him the support of Labour for its necessarily unpopular measures. This, he felt, could easily lead to his own loss of influence within the movement. In fact, there was immediate opposition to the whole idea, led chiefly by the ILP element but also taking in some of the trade unionists who stressed the virtue of maintaining independence at all costs. However, when it came to a vote, following a joint meeting of the National Executive and the Parliamentary Labour Party, the majority was for accepting Asquith's offer. According to Snowden the MPs were on balance against, believing that 'such a step as joining in a Coalition Government was so opposed to the constitution of the Labour Party that it was felt a decision ought not to be taken without the sanction of the Party Conference.' In spite of this suggestion, Henderson decided to act on the vote and join the government. This decision was duly endorsed by the TUC meeting in September and by the party conference in the following January. But Henderson's forebodings were at least partly realised. He brought upon himself much odium, particularly in Wales and on Clydeside, for his forays into the industrial relations field on the government's behalf, and the issue of conscription twice brought about threats of withdrawal from the coalition.

Yet, despite the apparently uncertain value of Labour, Lloyd George, when he succeeded Asquith, was even more determined than his predecessor not only to maintain its presence in the government but to extend it. Lloyd George reckoned that he needed Labour not only to fight the war but also to underwrite his political future. He calculated, quite rightly, that without its support he could not form a government. On the morning of 7 December 1916 he met the NEC and PLP in joint session and presented a package which was highly attractive to many of them. He proposed a new inner cabinet solely for the direction of the war in which Labour would be represented and intimated his intention to offer a further half a dozen or so positions in the government to Labour MPs. As to policy, he proposed new government departments for labour and food distribution. He hinted at a further extension of the principle of state control particularly in the fields of mines and shipping. Finally he even suggested Labour's direct and separate representation at the peace conference. Not everybody amongst the Labour leadership was impressed by this performance. According to Beatrice Webb, her husband felt that 'Lloyd George was at his worst—evasive in his statement of policy and cynical in his offer of places in the government.' When Lloyd George had finished, the meeting adjourned but later the same day reassembled to debate what action to take. In this discussion, according to Snowden, the most telling arguments were on the side against participation and yet, strangely, the meeting finally broke decisively in favour, by 17 votes to 12, though the Webbs give the figures as 18 to 12. Both Snowden and Mrs Webb were quick to suggest that Lloyd George's offer of 'jobs for the boys' had done much to influence the verdict. As the latter put it: 'To enjoy an income of £4,000 a year, or even of £1,600, for a year or two means to any Trade Union official personal independence for the rest of his life.' To be fair there were more disinterested motives influencing the party. Thus Mrs Webb refers to a feeling—or 'illusion' she calls it—that Labour ought to continue in the coalition in the hopes of influencing government policy and in particular the peace terms. Henderson for his part made much of the national interest argument. According to Snowden, he claimed that 'If Labour were to take no part in the new Government it would give to the Allies the impression that the country was divided and not behind the new Government.' The decision was followed by Henderson's elevation to the small inner war cabinet while John Hodge became Minister of Labour and George Barnes Minister of Pensions. Minor posts were filled by Brace, Roberts and James Parker. Later, J. R. Clynes became under-secretary at the food ministry and (in 1918) took on the position of food controller. The decision to accept Lloyd George's terms was rubber stamped by the next party conference in January 1918 by a large majority: 1,849,000 to 307,000. In spite of Mrs Webb's talk of 'illusions', Labour's participation in the wartime ministries was important, not least because it gave politicians the chance to show their paces as administrators, a chance which they exploited generally to good effect. Arthur Marwick in *The Deluge* makes the point clearly: 'Henderson, Clynes, Barnes and Roberts made nonsense of the tale that, good as Labour chaps might be on wages and hours of work, they were not fit to govern.'

## [20] Feuds and Unrest 1914–17

The progress outlined above was real but it is also true that at the same time the party and movement were experiencing quite serious internal difficulties. Until these were resolved its emergence as a truly effective national political organisation was delayed. These difficulties came from two sources: the socialist wing of the party, represented chiefly by the ILP, was opposed to the war, or, at very least, opposed to the way it was being waged; further, while the movement's leaders became more closely associated with the government, there sprang up an unofficial leadership at the local level which, to put it mildly, was not always so keen on the official policy of cooperation. Both these developments proved an embarrassment, though they looked more serious than they were, being resolved ultimately with comparatively little difficulty.

For a brief time the whole labour movement agreed with Bob Smillie's reputed gibe that its part in the war was merely to try 'to stop the bloody thing!' On 30 July, as the crisis gathered momentum, Labour MPs at a meeting endorsed a resolution in favour of staying out of the approaching conflict. Two days later, the British sections of the Second International, which included the Labour Party, drew up a manifesto denouncing the war. It was quite clear at this stage that British socialists in general, and the ILP in particular, based their hopes for peace on the famous resolution passed by the conference of the Second International back in 1907: 'If war threatens to break out, it is the duty of the working class in the countries concerned and of their Parliamentary representatives . . . to use every effort to prevent war. . . . Should war nonetheless break out, their duty is to intervene to bring it promptly to an end, and with all their energies to use the political and economic crisis created by the war to rouse the populace from its slumbers, and to hasten the fall of capitalist domination.' The thinly veiled call to revolution certainly struck a discordant note as far as MacDonald and the other Labour leaders were concerned, but they fully accepted the main pacifist message. On 2 August a great rally was organised in Trafalgar Square and both Keir Hardie and Arthur Henderson spoke powerfully for peace. Moreover, as he made clear in the debate on the war in the Commons on the afternoon of 3 August, MacDonald was hopeful that the Liberal government would see the error of its ways before it was too late: 'Whatever may happen, whatever may be said about us, we will take the action . . . of saying that this country ought to have remained neutral, because in the deepest parts of our hearts we believe that that was right and that that alone was consistent with the honour of our country and the traditions of the party that are now in office.' But all was in vain. The International, for all its brave words, ratted on its principles. The French socialists supported their government and in Germany the Social Democrats' enthusiasm for voting war credits was such that the Kaiser was moved to make his famous remark that now he could 'see only Germans'. As for British opinion, it was changed overnight by the German invasion of Belgium. On 4 August the Labour Party, after some hesitations, gave its support to the government's declaration of war, whereupon MacDonald resigned his position as party chairman and Henderson was elected in his place. This decision inaugurated a division in the party which rapidly hardened along the old, thinly concealed lines of ILP socialists versus middle-of-the-road trade unionists.

Throughout the late summer and early autumn of 1914, the split gradually became more clear cut with the pacifists very much in the minority. At first those supporting the government made it quite clear that this support was qualified. Thus, the party circular issued on 7 August was highly critical of Grey's pre-war policy for being 'bound to increase the power of Russia . . . and to endanger good relations with Germany'. The foreign secretary was further criticised for committing Great Britain to support France without securing the endorsement either of public opinion or of Parliament. In addition the circular stressed the overriding need for 'peace at the earliest possible moment'. But the end of August and the beginning of September saw the official pro-war line established with no concessions to the pacifists. On 24 August the trade unions unilaterally declared an industrial truce for the duration of hostilities and five days later the Labour Party declared its approval of a similar arrangement in the electoral field. By early September, Will Crooks probably summed up the majority feeling most accurately when, at an inter-party recruiting rally in London, he declared 'he would rather see every living soul blotted off the face of the earth than see the Kaiser supreme anywhere.' The growing commitment to support the war finally crystallised in the manifesto of 15 October signed by the majority of the party's MPs and the TUC Parliamentary Committee. Clearly intended as a counterblast to the pacifist activities of the ILP it stressed the need for the fullest participation in the national effort.

Equally as the official policy hardened, so too did that of the ILP dissidents. The latter were now openly preaching the view that the war was the result of the activities of militarists on both sides and that the British government was as much to blame as anybody. On 13 August, they even went so far as to issue a declaration for international socialism in which, in spite of all evidence to the contrary, they referred to the German Social Democrats as 'faithful friends'. By the end of the month the rift in the labour movement was clear and the ILP and the recently affiliated BSP formed the pacifist wing led by five of the ILP's seven MPs: Hardie, MacDonald, Snowden, Jowett and Thomas Richardson. Unfortunately for themselves, the pacifists laboured under a number of difficulties. In particular not only were they a minority, and a highly unpopular minority at that, but they themselves were also divided. MacDonald, once the highly respected leader both inside and outside the party, now became so thoroughly hated that he was openly accused of defeatism, pacifism and even actual treachery. As a result there were very few places where he might appear in public and be given a fair hearing. Herbert Morrison in his autobiography has recorded particularly vividly how dangerous it was to express anti-war sentiments: 'My audience was very hostile. I spoke amid a great deal of violent and angry heckling. Ultimately I was dragged off the platform and taken by force to a nearby pond. . . . However, when the police intervened . . . although my pince-nez glasses were flung into the water, I was not.' The extent of feeling against the pacifists was also illustrated electorally late in 1915. In September, Keir Hardie had died which left his seat at Merthyr Tydfil vacant. In view of the electoral truce, the ILP assumed that their candidate James Winstone would be unopposed, particularly as he had the strong support of the South Wales miners. However, at this stage, a pro-war faction decided to intervene and put up C. B. Stanton against Winstone. In the ensuing contest, he won easily polling 10,286 votes to Winstone's 6,080.

Amongst the pacifists themselves part of the trouble was the division of opinion between the ILP and the BSP. The former agitated for a negotiated peace but the latter were prepared to go much further and increasingly talked of revolution on the lines laid down by Lenin as the only means of ending the war. But the division was not quite so simple as that, for within the ILP itself there were varying shades of opinion and some confusion of thought. Thus, while MacDonald and Hardie felt the government had mishandled Britain's entry and continually urged the need for a negotiated peace, equally they felt there could be no going back. MacDonald, speaking at Leicester on 7 August 1914, declared: 'Whatever our views may be of the origin of the war, we must go through with it.' A week later, Hardie at Merthyr Tydfil emphasised the need for national unity as 'the lads who have gone forth to fight their country's battles must not be disheartened by any discordant notes at home.' On the other hand, there were those who took a more un-compromising view, arguing that the Allies were just as bad as the Central Powers, that whoever won, the working class would be the losers, and therefore, come what may, they would make no contribu-tion whatsoever to the war effort. This was almost certainly the ILP majority line and it received widespread publicity, since Glasier, Brock-way and Johnston, the editors of the party's three journals, all sub-scribed to it. In addition, this viewpoint was supported by George Lansbury in the *Daily Herald*.

Hampered then by these difficulties, it is not surprising that those opposed to the war found it uphill work to educate the rest of the labour movement. However, almost at the outset of their campaign they achieved what in retrospect was clearly an important success. There was on the left wing of the Liberal Party a small group of MPs who were profoundly shocked by the government's revelations of its pre-war policy and thereby found themselves substantially in agreement with Mac-Donald and the ILP. Accordingly the leaders of this group, in particular E. D. Morel, C. P. Trevelyan and Arthur Ponsonby, joined with MacDonald in September 1914 in setting up an organisation known as the Union of Democratic Control. It demanded that certain important steps be taken in the future to secure the maintenance of peace, notably the democratic control of foreign policy, the reduction and control of armaments, the establishment of an international peace-keeping organisation and an end to the exchange of territories without the con-sent of the native population. The long-term significance of this mani-festo was that it was to provide the basis of Labour's foreign policy after the war and thus lead to the defection of many Liberals disgusted by what they considered to be their party's betrayal of true Liberal principles. In the short run, it meant close cooperation between the UDC and the ILP although with little immediate success.

From a practical point of view, the ILP sought to implement its pacifist policies by keeping the Labour Party out of the Asquith and Lloyd George coalition governments. The basic argument against participation was that Labour would be committed to the support of other parties' policies and would lose the confidence of its supporters in the country. In addition to these fears for the party itself, Snowden also claimed Labour would be doing the country a service by staying out and providing 'independent criticism, which at a time like this may often be the most valuable service a small party can render to the nation.' (*Manchester Guardian*, May 1915.) But these views, as we have seen, were discounted and the party duly entered office under Asquith. At the end of 1916 on the accession of Lloyd George, virtually the same pattern of events was repeated. The ILP, backed by the BSP, expressed its contempt for Lloyd George's package deal but the matter was settled at the January 1917 conference by the trade union block vote. As if to emphasise the set-back, this conference saw two further blows against the ILP: first, a motion calling for an immediate negotiated peace was almost as heavily defeated as the one disapproving participation in the coalition; secondly, there was a suggestion that election to the National Executive should be altered in such a way as virtually to exclude the representatives of the socialist societies. This, for many ILP members, must have been almost the last straw. Already there had been talk of them disaffiliating from the Labour Party and a motion had actually gone before the ILP conference in 1916 only to be rejected. MacDonald himself now seems to have considered this as a serious possibility. Writing in *Forward*, a month or so after the conference, he declared: 'I am not going to sneak about and bargain for trade union votes for ILP candidates for the Executive. . . . If a split were to come owing to the oppressive use of the block vote of some of the larger unions, I would do what I could to form a new Labour combination for political purposes.' Thus, by the beginning of 1917, the Labour Party, based as it was on a federal alliance of the trade unions and the socialist societies, seemed to be on the verge of disintegration.

Serious as this was, it was not the whole story. Not only was there ill-feeling between the pro- and anti-war factions, but in the country at large there was considerable rank and file unrest which found vivid expression particularly on the Clyde and in South Wales, although other areas were also affected. This rank and file movement reached a climax on two occasions, in 1915 and 1917. In the second instance, which came at a crucial point in the war, the government was sufficiently disturbed to set up a special commission to discover the causes. Its report, which was made on a regional basis, laid most emphasis on the cost of living. Admittedly wage rates during the war went up quite sharply, so much so that some sections of the press were full of stories of working-class affluence expressing itself in the purchase of consumer goods. Even later economic historians writing more cautiously have concluded that at the end of the war wages were as much as 10 or even 20 per cent ahead of the parallel price rises. But on the other hand, there does appear to have been something of a time-lag before wages reached this happy state and, moreover, the rise in prices, though general, seemed most marked in food. By the early part of 1917 bread had reached a level four times greater than its pre-war price. Meat had doubled in price by the summer of the same year and, according to E. M. H. Lloyd (*Experiments in State Control*) when the government got round to rationing it, 'a certain part of the population, especially in Scotland, and in some country districts, did not choose or could not afford to purchase the full amount to which their ration entitled them.' The overall position was summarised plainly by the government commission's report for the north-eastern region. 'It is no doubt true that in some industries wages have risen to such an extent as largely to compensate for the increased cost of living, but there are workers whose wages have been raised very slightly, if at all, and some whose earnings have actually diminished, and on these the high food prices have borne heavily.' Further, as the war went on, not only did food cost more, but some commodities were increasingly in short supply and this too was a potent cause of ill-feeling, as much as anything due to the inconvenience of queuing. In April 1917, *The Observer* reported that in Edmonton 'there were bread and potato queues of such length that the police had to regulate them, and newcomers had to inquire which was the particular queue that they wanted.' In December of the same year *The Times* claimed that women, often accompanied by their children, queued for margarine from 5 o'clock in the morning and that, in southeast London, one of these margarine queues was estimated at 3,000 and 'one thousand of these were sent away unsupplied'. The frustration of those left unsupplied may well be imagined and this was certainly not an isolated instance.

Food prices and shortages were not the only major grievances. There was also considerable ill-feeling over the workings of the Munitions of

War and Conscription Acts. 'Dilution', inevitably perhaps, continued to be a problem. It may well have been whole-heartedly accepted by the national trade union leadership who were satisfied by government assurances that it would apply only to war work and would cease at the end of hostilities, but local opinion was not always so trusting and it does appear that in some cases, where employers tried to exploit the situation and extend dilution to their private work, these suspicions were justified. Also, of course, there was the special resentment of the skilled workers, particularly in the engineering industry, who found that as a result of dilution the differentials between themselves and the semi-skilled were narrowing quite markedly. Another major issue arose over 'leaving certificates'. The Munitions of War Acts restricted the mobility of labour by a clause which declared 'A person shall not give employment to a workman who has within the previous six weeks . . . been employed on or in connection with munitions work . . . unless he holds a certificate from the employer by whom he was last so employed that he left with the consent of the employer.' The government's apparently reasonable intention was to prevent employers poaching from one another the rather limited number of skilled workers, but it was rightly resented, for while the employee could not leave his job without permission, at the same time the employer still retained the right to dismiss him if he wished. The trouble over the Conscription Acts was at root due to a widespread fear that military conscription would be followed by industrial conscription, even the institution of military discipline within the factories. The issue had been shelved by the 'trade cards' agreement of 1916 which, in effect, gave the unions power to grant exemptions from military service to their members. But then in April 1917, the Lloyd George government, worried by the increasing man-power demands, rescinded the 'trade card' scheme and set up a new ministry of national service which began combing out the skilled men from the factories for service in the army. While the unfriendly or cynical may well declare that the resulting complaints were merely those of shirkers and quite unjustified, the fact remains that many in the rank and file of the labour movement seem to have regarded the government's action as a breach of faith. Finally, among the immediate factors causing resentment, there seems to have been a fairly wide-spread feeling amongst the working class that they were carrying the greater part of the burden of the war and that other people were doing rather well out of it. In concrete terms this expressed itself in complaints about profiteering, particularly by the shopkeepers putting up their prices, and the factory owners who were generally reckoned to be making small fortunes out of munitions' contracts. Certainly there was some evidence to justify the suspicion that not all were making equal sacrifices. Upper and middle-class life in general went on much as before with at times quite ostentatious displays of wealth and undue concern for trivialities. Admittedly some people did feel uneasy or even guilty and would have agreed with the *Times* military correspondent Colonel Repington, that in the eyes of posterity 'we should be considered rather callous to go on with our usual life when we were reading of 3,000 to 4,000 casualties a day.'

So, the discontent of the rank and file grew and as it did so, there was borne in on the men a growing feeling that their official leaders had let them down. In short, they had sold out to the employers and the government. With this feeling strengthening it was only a matter of time before the ordinary trade unionist turned to local leaders to redress his grievances. There began then the rise of what Arthur Marwick has called 'an informal labour movement' with its first most obvious manifestation on Clydeside in 1915. The trouble began in February when the Cathcart engineering firm of Weir's was paralysed by strike action for bringing in American workmen at higher rates of pay. It is important to notice that the strike, which soon spread to involve some 5,000 engineers, was not organised by the national officials of the ASE but by a committee of shop stewards. The dispute was soon settled, but the committee which had been formed on an *ad hoc* basis now decided to make itself a permanent body, the Clyde Workers' Committee, with the aim of opposing the new Munitions of War Act. Their view of the act and of their national leadership who had accepted it was stated bluntly in a manifesto: 'The support given to the Munitions Act by the officials was an act of treachery to the working classes. Those of us who have refused to be sold have organised the above committee. . . .' In addition to their expressed determination to oppose dilution and other attacks on the traditional rights of labour, the shop stewards also argued strongly in favour of 'workers' control' of industry, not to mention the maintenance of 'the class struggle until the overthrow of the wages system, the freedom of the workers and the establishment of industrial democracy have been obtained.' The chief personalities on the committee were Willie Gallacher, the chairman, half Scots, half Irish and a leading light in the Glasgow branch of the BSP, and David Kirkwood, treasurer, chief shop steward at Parkhead Forge and a close confidant of John Wheatley. The growing tension on the Clyde and the near certainty of a serious

strike breaking out at any moment so worried the government that at
Christmas it sent Lloyd George north in the hope that he could save the
situation. Unfortunately, for once Lloyd George's brand of spell-
binding oratory did no good. Nor was a private approach to the shop
stewards much more productive, and when, in March 1916, there was
further trouble at the Parkhead Forge culminating in an eighteen-day
strike, the government decided on repressive action. The Glasgow ILP
paper *Forward* had already been suppressed for daring to publish an
account of the fiasco of Lloyd George's Christmas meeting and now
Kirkwood and a number of his colleagues were prosecuted under the
terms of the Munitions of War Act. The upshot was the deportation of
ten of the shop stewards to Edinburgh and other towns where they were
to live under police supervision, while a number of others, including
Gallacher, received prison sentences of between twelve months and
three years. This, for the time being at any rate, ended the trouble on
Clydeside and there was comparative peace for the remainder of the
war.

But Scotland was not the only place where there was serious industrial
trouble in 1915. Almost simultaneously unrest developed in the South
Wales coal-field. Here the men were about to negotiate a new wage
settlement with the employers and were annoyed by the latter's attempt
to fob them off with a temporary war bonus which had just been
agreed upon for the whole British coal industry. As on the Clyde it was
a case of a local militant leadership at odds with its own union as well
as the employers. The MFGB had approved the war bonus scheme and
was against the strike, but the Welsh miners were much more influenced
by a body calling itself the Unofficial Reform Movement. The leaders,
mainly young men and disillusioned alike with the national union
leaders and the politicians of the Labour Party, had come together in
1910 as a result of the bitter Cambrian strike of that year. They now
preached a more radical class war against the owners and publicly
advocated the exploitation of the war situation to secure their pay
claim. The government at first tried mediation, but then, when the
miners persisted and named the strike day (July 14), the big stick was
waved and the strike declared illegal under the Munitions Act. Far
from frightening off the miners, this merely exacerbated feelings and
made them more determined to go through with it. The stoppage
lasted for five days, and at the end of that period, the government was
forced to capitulate lest the war effort be seriously disrupted. Lloyd
George, accompanied by Henderson, went down to Wales, virtually

cap in hand, and the miners got what they wanted. Thus Clydeside and South Wales established in 1915 a pattern of local, unofficial labour action, a pattern moreover in which the shop steward, previously a minor cog in the trade union administrative machine, now played the leading part. This was perhaps inevitable. As the official leadership grew more distant and apparently more in the pocket of the government, grievances would be brought increasingly to the shop steward whose prime strength lay in the fact that he was in close continual contact with the men he represented.

The second major outbreak of unrest came in the spring of 1917 and affected mainly the engineering industry throughout England, though on this occasion Scotland remained quiet. There had in fact been a foretaste of the trouble to come in the previous October when a Sheffield engineer named Hargreaves was conscripted into the army in spite of official union protests. Whereupon the local shop stewards seized the initiative and called a strike involving 10,000 skilled engineers, causing the military authorities to back down hastily and release Hargreaves after the stoppage had lasted a mere three days. This success strengthened the militants' hand and paved the way for a great wave of unofficial strikes led by local shop stewards which began on 3 May at Rochdale. The immediate cause was the attempt of a local employer to extend dilution and this together with the other grievances ensured widespread support. A week later the trouble spread to the rest of the country and some 250,000 engineers were involved for a period of up to a fortnight. The government reaction on this occasion was better judged than previously, possibly because it was acutely conscious that the war was at a very critical stage. At first, it seems to have toyed with the idea of repression, for a number of leaders were arrested. Then, however, a more conciliatory line was adopted. No charges were preferred against the arrested men and steps were taken to elucidate the causes of unrest. Once these were made known in the reports published in July, the newly appointed minister of munitions, Winston Churchill, took prompt and vigorous steps to meet the working-class grievances. Significant concessions were made on the issues of dilution and leaving certificates, and fairly substantial bonuses were made payable to both skilled and piece workers in the munitions industry. This effectively damped the trouble down, but it did not mean the end of the shop stewards' movement and steps were taken to establish a National Administrative Council which came into existence following a conference in Manchester in August 1917. But although there was to be further working-class ill-feeling, particularly over conscription, the government's prompt concessions had drawn the sting and there was no further overt trouble during the war.

By the middle of 1917 then, in spite of considerable progress in some important respects, Labour seemed in quite serious difficulties. Until these were resolved, there was a very real danger of a serious reversal. In fact, the last fifteen months of the war saw not only a reunification of the party but also the execution of a badly needed reorganisation which did much to place it in a stronger position in the post-war period.

## [21] Reunification and Reorganisation 1917–18

In the first place, it should be pointed out that the divisions in the movement were not in reality quite so deep as they seemed to the casual observer. For example, both pro- and anti-war factions in the party maintained throughout the conflict a useful link with each other through the medium of the War Emergency Workers' National Committee. This body was established early in August 1914 'to mitigate the destitution which will inevitably overtake our working people while the state of war lasts.' (Labour Party Circular, 7 August 1914.) Admittedly the party was wrong in believing unemployment to be a likely side-effect but, as we have already seen, there were other economic and social issues affecting the working class and both pacifist ILP men and patriotic trade union leaders could concentrate on these and forget for a time their differences over the war. Then, there was a considerable measure of agreement between the two factions on the nature of the peace settlement to follow. Many even of the pro-war faction fully accepted the UDC/ILP demands for a 'just' peace in general terms and, more specifically, could agree on the liberation of Belgium and the fulfilment of nationalist aspirations in Alsace, Poland and the Balkans. Also, it was true that, for the most part, there was nothing in the way of a witch-hunt of the minority and relations on a personal level remained cordial. Even when Labour conferences rejected the policies and motions of MacDonald and Snowden, they did so with gracious tributes to their integrity, although the 1917 conference with its proposed new executive council election procedure did go some way towards spoiling this happy atmosphere. Finally, even the division between shop stewards and official union leaders was more apparent than real, and this is shown clearly by the way in which the ranks closed at the end of the war.

However, the event which acted as a catalyst and brought the divergent elements of the party and the movement together was the Russian revolution. This was very much in the nature of a paradox, for at first the revolution seemed more to drive the factions wider apart.

It was understandable that the anti-war group should receive the news of the Russian revolution with considerable enthusiasm. For a start, it marked the overthrow of a government which they and indeed most of the labour movement, not to mention Liberals, regarded as a foul tyranny. More to the point, it opened up the possibility of a negotiated peace, for this was one of the demands voiced early on by the powerful Petrograd Soviet. But not only did the revolutionaries demand this of their own government, they were ready to suggest ways and means of putting pressure on other countries, hence their call on the morrow of the February revolution for an international socialist conference which would agree on peace terms and then force the respective countries to accept them. In the early months of 1917 this projected meeting, which was to be held in Stockholm, was a matter for discussion amongst socialists everywhere not least in Great Britain. Left-wing approval of the events in Russia and the suggested new initiatives in foreign policy found memorable expression in a meeting at Leeds on 3 June organised jointly by the ILP and the BSP with the backing of George Lansbury and the *Daily Herald*. Here MacDonald and Snowden, apparently temporarily infected by much wild talk of a parallel revolutionary movement in Britain, made uncharacteristically flamboyant speeches which they afterwards regretted. The meeting concluded by approving the Russian revolution, calling on Great Britain to accept Russian foreign policy and deciding to set up district workers' and soldiers' councils on the Russian model. For all practical purposes this was so much hot air, but the impact at the time was quite considerable, coming as it did immediately after the unofficial strikes in May.

The official Labour Party reaction to all this was more cautious. Certainly the leadership disapproved wholeheartedly of the Leeds affair and took care to stay well clear of it. But the Stockholm conference project soon caused considerable disagreement and eventually in May it was decided that a special delegation—G. H. Roberts, MacDonald and William Carter of the MFGB—should go to Russia on a fact-finding mission to assist the party in making up its mind. But, in the event, it was denied this first hand report, for although the government issued the necessary passports, when the delegates turned up to take ship at Aberdeen, they were prevented from sailing by representatives of Havelock Wilson's seamen's union who had suffered terribly at the hands of the German U-Boats and as a result were violently opposed to the idea of a compromise peace.

Meanwhile those who supported the Stockholm conference received a powerful boost when no less a person than Henderson declared himself in favour. This change of heart had come about as the result of a visit to Russia in May on the government's behalf with the object of keeping Russia in the war. But Henderson returned convinced that Russia was just about finished and that the Stockholm project was worth pursuing as a possible means of pressurising Germany into genuine peace negotiations. In the circumstances it was now decided to hold a special party conference on the matter which assembled on 10 August. Henderson spoke powerfully and persuasively in favour of participating in the Stockholm meeting and his motion was duly carried by 1,846,000 to 550,000. But when it came to a discussion of the delegation's composition, the MFGB struck a distinctly sour note by carrying a resolution that there should be no representatives from the socialist societies. The ILP was incensed by this manoeuvre and the breach between the factions now seemed so deep as to be irreconcilable. At this stage the conference adjourned for ten days and that period saw a determined attempt not only to exclude the anti-war socialist representatives, but even to reverse the original decision. When the conference reassembled on 21 August, both decisions were indeed confirmed, but now the majority in favour of the Stockholm Conference was a mere 3,000: 1,234,000 in favour, 1,231,000 against. In view of this and together with the government's refusal to grant passports and travel facilities, the project died and the Labour Party now seemed to be at the very nadir of its fortunes.

Yet already events were in motion which were to reunify the factions and revive the organisation. The key figure in this process was Arthur Henderson. His position in the coalition government had become distinctly shaky as a result of his open conversion to the idea of a negotiated peace which Lloyd George, committed as he now was to unconditional surrender, regarded with considerable disfavour. He later wrote of Henderson's conduct: 'He had more than a touch of the revolutionary malaria. His temperature was high and his mood refractory.' The deteriorating relationship was highlighted by the famous 'doormat' incident of 1 August when Henderson was kept waiting outside the war cabinet's room for a considerable time while the other four members discussed his behaviour. However, this did not lead to an immediate show-down. Henderson chose to minimise what was undoubtedly a highly humiliating experience, while Lloyd George for his part was not anxious as yet to push matters to extremes. He seems to have hoped that Henderson would see sense before the Labour conference on 10 August, and in fact Henderson himself somehow gave the prime minister the idea that he was going to speak against the Stockholm project. Further, Lloyd George had some hopes that the conference would solve the problem for him by throwing out Henderson's recommendation if he decided to persist with it. However, such calculations were set at naught by the outcome, and on the day after, 11 August, Henderson resigned from the cabinet. He may well have been at this time in a somewhat confused, perhaps emotional, state and certainly his letter of resignation drew attention to the problem of divided loyalties which had always worried him since he had first taken office under Asquith. But on two points at any rate he seems to have been clear enough: the need to reconcile the party's differences and, perhaps more important for the future, the need for complete independence. A. J. P. Taylor in *English History, 1914–45* puts the point crisply, 'From this moment Lib–Lab was dead.'

Already indeed the division over foreign policy and the war was settling itself. Henderson had moved to a position very close to that of MacDonald, Snowden and the ILP and his prestige was such that many more in the party hastened to follow. The votes at the August conference—even the second one—showed that this was no longer the position of an unpopular minority. But further action was necessary before the matter was entirely resolved. Accordingly on 28–29 December 1917, yet another special conference was held and the delegates were presented with a *Memorandum on War Aims* previously drafted by Henderson, Webb and MacDonald. It proved in substance to be the ILP/UDC plan for a better world: territorial readjustments to be made on the basis of people's wishes (to be ascertained by plebiscite); no imperialist annexations; armaments to be limited and compulsory military service to be dropped; the democratisation of all countries; cooperation in the solution of post-war economic problems; finally, the establishment of an international association of states with effective machinery for the maintenance of peace. The memorandum had already been accepted by the National Executive and the TUC Parliamentary Committee, and it was now confirmed by the conference. This marked a real reconciliation and only a comparatively small number of extremists on both wings were out of step. Still, Henderson was not fully satisfied. This newly recovered unity might still prove frail and, in the circumstances, he decided that only a thorough overhaul of the party's organisation coupled with a re-examination of its aims and philosophy would ensure its survival and make it into a truly national party. Accordingly, soon after resuming the Labour leadership in 1917 he relinquished it again to Willie Adamson and together with Sidney Webb concentrated on these fundamental problems in his capacity as party secretary.

Basically, Henderson's proposals for a new party constitution sought to solve two problems: the shortcomings of the local organisation and the shortage of money. Something has already been said about the heterogeneous nature of the Labour organisations in the country and as time went on the structure had become even more diversified. By 1917, there were at least seven different types of local organisation of which the trades councils were still by far the most numerous. Then, although the number of local Labour groups grew steadily throughout the war, the network did not cover the whole country, in particular being virtually non-existent in large parts of southern England. Finally it was still impossible for an individual to become a member of the Labour Party in the way that he could join the Conservative or Liberal parties. Membership could only be secured through an affiliated society, such as a trade union or one of the socialist societies. Henderson concluded that the only sensible answer was the establishment of a system of local Labour parties covering the whole country and open to individuals to join. As for the financial problem, there seemed equally only one answer: the big trade unions must somehow be persuaded to make more generous contributions. Henderson was, however, fully aware that his intentions were likely to meet with quite strong opposition from within the party. It seemed, for example, fairly certain that neither the ILP nor the trades councils would take kindly to proposals which were designed to reduce their local significance in the labour movement. Actually as things turned out their opposition was not so much of a problem. The ILP, although uneasy, calculated that the new local parties far from drawing off their adherents would in fact stimulate more interest and participation in their branches. Furthermore, MacDonald was very much behind Henderson, and his influence counted for a good deal throughout the ILP. In the event its attitude varied considerably from district to district and in some areas there was prolonged hostility between the ILP and the local Labour party. As for the trades councils, although numerous, their opposition could generally be discounted for they lacked financial resources and were none too highly regarded by the parent trade unions who looked on them as bolt-holes for extreme left wing trouble-makers. But the key to the situation was held by the trade unions, for they were being asked to foot the bill. In spite of the reconciliation on the issue of war aims, there were still influential people in the movement who nursed a residue of bitterness over the ILP's early wartime activities. Furthermore, it was suggested again at this time that the unions might break away from the socialist societies and form a new purely working-class party uninfluenced by dangerous middle-class intellectuals. That the trade unions accepted Henderson's plans was due in part to a number of factors: the personal influence of men such as Smillie and J. W. Ogden of the cotton workers; the marked leftward drift of the rank and file during the war; and perhaps most of all, the fact that Henderson's scheme, by its provisions for the elections to the executive, virtually handed over control of the new party machinery to the unions.

The proposed draft of the new constitution was presented to the annual conference in January 1918 and after an adjournment during which steps were necessary to kill the idea of a purely trade union party, it was approved in February with comparatively little amendment. On the vital issues of membership and finance, the former was now open to individuals through local Labour parties to be organised in every constituency as well as through the affiliated societies, while in the latter case, affiliation fees were now doubled to 2d per member per annum with a minimum of 30 shillings. The new local organisations were to charge a minimum subscription of 1 shilling for a man and 6d for a woman and an additional 2d per member was to be levied for the central body. Also a new rate was fixed for the central party's contributions to the cost of local Parliamentary elections. Previously it had been 25 per cent of the returning officer's net expenses, now for every 1,000 electors it was to be £1 in a borough and 35 shillings in a county constituency. The party conference, meeting annually, was to be composed of delegates from the trade unions and affiliated societies on the basis of one representative for every 1,000 fully paid-up members, and from the local parties with one delegate from each constituency. The conference was recognised as the supreme policy making body, but electoral programmes were largely to be drawn up jointly by the PLP and the NEC with the latter having the final say in the case of any dispute. The executive, which was thus the key body, was to be composed of 23 members: 13 representatives from the affiliated societies, 5 from local Labour parties, 4 from the separate women's organisation, and the treasurer. Representatives on the committee were to be elected by the entire annual conference and this, since they were by far the largest element, gave the trade unions the control of the party machine.

But, there was much more to Henderson and Webb's reorganisation than a mere overhaul of the party machinery. Their constitution also had much to say on aims and objectives. The previous constitution had remained studiously vague on this subject, well aware of the deep differences between the socialist enthusiasts of the ILP and the more cautiously inclined union leaders. Now, in view of changes in the trade union movement, Henderson and Webb decided that they could write in a definite commitment to socialism, which was essential to the party's future coherence. Hence, the famous declaration of Clause Four which stated that the Labour Party existed 'To secure for the producers by hand and brain the full fruits of their industry, and the most equitable distribution thereof that may be possible on the basis of the common ownership of the means of production and the best obtainable system of popular administration and control of each industry and service.' The formulation of a detailed policy on this basis was not long delayed. In June 1918 the first annual conference under the new constitution was invited to consider a document drafted by Sidney Webb called *Labour and the New Social Order*, which set out a fairly moderate socialist programme. In the course of the debate a whole series of resolutions based on the draft was discussed and as a result certain amendments were made, although in general the proposals were well received. Some of the ILP, including Snowden, felt that the programme did not go sufficiently leftwards, but the only really discordant note was struck by the BSP which demanded a full-blooded Marxism quite out of touch with the thinking of the majority. The main features may be summmarised conveniently under four heads. First, it demanded the universal enforcement of a national minimum wage together with the concept of full employment, to be maintained if necessary by public works. Secondly, the principle of democratic control of industry was enunciated. Here there was no concession to the extreme views of the syndicalists or Guild Socialists, but what was intended was the public ownership of industry, under Parliamentary supervision, with the emphasis on certain key sectors such as land, fuel, power and transport. Thirdly, there was to be a revolution in national finance, and the redistribution of wealth through taxation, so tentatively begun in Lloyd George's 'People's Budget' of 1909, was to be extended. Finally, money from public funds was to be spent on improving cultural and educational facilities and to provide, in education in particular, real equality of opportunity.

The long-term significance of these changes has been fully appreciated by subsequent historians. In the short run it gave Labour a base from which it could make its first real attempt for power in the post-war period. In the longer run, in G. D. H. Cole's words, 'it charted the course on which the Labour Party has been set ever since'—a statement which remains valid at least until 1950 and maybe even beyond.

Not all contemporary observers were so appreciative, although some seem to have had an inkling of how things might develop. Thus, reporting to President Wilson in January 1918, the American ambassador in London, W. H. Page, commented: 'The Labour Party is already playing for supremacy.' On the other hand, so astute a politician as Lloyd George does not appear to have realised what had happened. The reason was simple. Although Henderson and Labour had in effect broken with Lloyd George, the exigencies of the national emergency caused them to refrain from 'rocking the boat' too obviously. In his letter of resignation, Henderson had underlined this by declaring: 'I continue to share your desire that the war should be carried to a successful conclusion and trust that in a non-government capacity I may be able to render some little assistance to this end.' Accordingly, Labour ministers continued in the coalition—George Barnes replacing Henderson in the war cabinet—and when this decision was challenged by the left at the January 1918 conference, Henderson argued firmly against any further action which might embarrass the government. He carried the day easily by 1,885,000 to 722,000, but it was noticeable that the minority was a fairly substantial one. One other event at this conference may also have helped to blind Lloyd George to the significance of the path Labour was taking. By the beginning of the year, the manpower question was once more so acute that a further extension of conscription was necessary, which in practice meant more 'combing out' of the factories. If recent experience was anything to go by, the approval of the Labour movement must be sought in advance, otherwise there might well be further serious industrial trouble. So Lloyd George asked for and gained permission to address the annual conference on 5 January. He seems to have made quite an impression. He expressed his aims in a way most likely to appeal to the majority now agreed on a 'just peace'; as he later put it in his memoirs: 'I made it clear that our object in the War was to defend the violated public law of Europe, to vindicate Treaty obligations and to secure the restoration of Belgium.' Admittedly some Labour men drew unfavourable comparisons with President Wilson's Fourteen Points issued three days later, but even they could hardly deny that there was much in common between the two. On 18 January Lloyd George addressed the conference once more, stressing the critical manpower situation, and the delegates gave him the go-ahead on the extension of conscription. With this important success to his credit, Lloyd George could well be excused for thinking that he still had Labour in his pocket.

However, we can see in retrospect the inevitability of the process, the logic of the events which followed and made the break between Labour and Lloyd George complete. Predictably it was the left wing which led the agitation for as early an end as possible to the coalition arrangement. Indeed, on the industrial front, the shop stewards' movement was all set to frustrate the national leaders' endorsement of Lloyd George's conscription measure until the rapid German gains of March brought all but a handful to their senses. But once the immediate crisis was over there was another outbreak of industrial unrest in the summer. This time, although the unofficial agitators in the country did much of the initial pushing, it was significant that the official leadership of the trade unions was prepared to take up some of the grievances. In June the government introduced a scheme which was intended to establish industrial conscription, whereupon the unions protested bitterly and the matter was dropped. In the following month there was a wave of unofficial strikes beginning in Coventry and rapidly spreading to Birmingham and other parts of the midlands, mainly over the old issues of dilution and attempts by the employers to restrict mobility. Other groups which turned to strike action included the Lancashire textile workers and, perhaps most alarming of all, the London police, who demanded the recognition of their union. In the political sphere the left-wing element voiced two demands: strongly critical of the continued presence of Labour ministers in the government, they continued to press for their withdrawal; in addition they wanted an end to the electoral truce. In fact, in the spring of 1918 this truce was all but breached, for in April an ILP candidate stood in a by-election at Keighley, polling quite respectably, and in the following month the miners' candidate at Wansbeck very nearly defeated the official coalitionist. In June, at the annual conference of the newly reconstituted party, Bob Smillie and Sylvia Pankhurst of the BSP spoke strongly in favour of both ending the truce and withdrawing the ministers, and the former was agreed though the majority felt the national situation was still too critical to go any further. The final step was delayed until the very end of the war, but even so relations between the labour movement and the government were further strained by an episode in August. Then a joint TUC and Labour delegation led by Henderson had been on the point of departing to attend an international socialist meeting in Switzerland. The meeting was to be attended by members from the enemy countries and the discussion was to centre on the question of war aims already accepted by the Allied Labour movements. The government, however, refused to issue passports and this caused ill feeling which was loudly expressed at the TUC's Jubilee meeting in September and at several other conferences. With the announcement of the Armistice on 11 November, the Labour Party could now take decisive action without being accused of upsetting the national interest. At an emergency conference on 14 November, Clynes, backed by the majority of the PLP, felt that Labour should continue in the coalition with Lloyd George. His main argument was that only in this way could Labour influence the peacemaking on the lines it had already decided. According to Beatrice Webb, he also 'openly threatens every Labour member who refuses the coalition ticket with annihilation.' Speaking against were Smillie, J. H. Thomas (of the National Union of Railwaymen) and Bernard Shaw who concluded with his famous exhortation, 'Mr Clynes has come from Mr Lloyd George and done the best he can. I ask you to send Mr Clynes back to him with the message "Nothing doing!"' The result was, again in Beatrice Webb's words, 'a foregone conclusion': 2,117,000 backed the motion to withdraw from the government, while 810,000 were against. The vote produced another split in the party, though it turned out to be of minor significance. Clynes, who had contested sincerely for what he believed was right, now loyally accepted the majority decision, but four ministers—Barnes, Roberts, James Parker and G. J. Wardle—decided to stay on. This 'National' Labour group was too small to wield any real influence in the peacetime government although Barnes himself retained a seat in the new cabinet. A handful of candidates stood for election in 1918 of whom only four were elected. For the movement as a whole the decision proclaimed clearly Labour's intention to become a truly independent and national organisation like the other two great political parties.

# Part VIII

## Labour and the Post-War World 1918–24

### [22] Disappointment and Disillusion 1918–21

With the end of the war and Lloyd George's decision to continue with his coalition government into peace time, a general election was almost the first priority. Those who have argued then and since that it was held with almost indecent haste, and in a sense paralleled the 'khaki election' of 1900—polling day, fixed for 14 December, was just over a month from the Armistice—are scarcely justified. An election was very much overdue and, more important, only a fresh Parliament with a new mandate from the people could honestly tackle the problem of peace abroad and a return to normality at home. The Labour Party welcomed the struggle, with the majority of their leaders and rank and file confident that now was the time to strike out on an independent line. Certainly there seemed much to be hopeful about: there was a new organisation and a new doctrine; the party was now publicly reunited following the embarrassing war-time splits; the faint hearts like Barnes who preferred to stay with Lloyd George, had either severed their connection or had been driven out. The reality was however to prove rather different.

In its election campaign the party had, of course, following Clause Four, laid stress on the importance of nationalisation and democratic control of industry, specifying in the first instance the mines, railways, shipping, armaments and electric power. There was also a demand for a speedy repeal of that legislation, particularly the Defence of the Realm Act and conscription, which had borne most hardly on the working class. In foreign affairs, the main point was the necessity for a fair peace on lines already laid down by the ILP/UDC pressure group and accepted by the party as a whole. As for the Empire, it was urged that now was the time to grant independence to Ireland and India. Unfortunately, admirable and clear as this programme might seem, it made little impact on the general run of electors. Basically the contest boiled down to a vote of confidence (or the reverse) in Lloyd George. He was 'the man who won the war', now could he 'win the peace'? Apart from this, the twin issues which aroused most fervour were 'making Germany pay' and a rather vague, ill-defined fear of the 'perils of Bolshevism'. Both of these worked to Labour's disadvantage, since in the minds of many it was, thanks mainly to the war-time activities of the ILP, linked indissolubly with pacifism and Bolshevism. There was also a good deal of misrepresentation of Labour's viewpoint which in retrospect seems incredibly ludicrous. Thus, Lloyd George in his closing speech of the campaign on 13 December, accused Labour of 'being run by the extreme pacifist Bolshevist group' and he warned his audience: 'look at what has happened in Russia!' Then, in one of its reports of the campaign, the respected *Fortnightly Review* committed itself to the absurd statement that for MacDonald 'the Red Flag is the only flag which stirs his emotions and the European revolution will not, if he can help it, be confined to the continent.' All of this, and much more besides, had its effect and Labour went back to Westminster only some 59 strong compared to the big battalions of the Coalition, estimates of whose numbers are imprecise but vary between 470 and 480. Admittedly the picture was not all black. The Labour members might be swamped but perceptive observers would have noticed that there was still a marked improvement on the previous general election results. In December 1910, they had returned 42 MPs (reduced by unfavourable by-elections to 39 at the time of the 1918 dissolution) on a vote of under 400,000 or just over 7 per cent; now they had increased their numbers by 17 and polled well over 2 million or 22 per cent of the vote. However, it has to be remembered that this trebling of their percentage was achieved mainly by running many more candidates, six times the number in 1910. But the real setbacks in 1918 were not immediately obvious although they eventually became crystal clear: the failure of the party's leadership and the development in Parliament of a climate of opinion hostile to its philosophy.

When all the dust and tumult had settled and the new MPs assembled at Westminster, they found that almost all the capable and experienced leaders had lost their seats. MacDonald at Leicester and Snowden at Blackburn had gone down in a patriotic reaction against their alleged past 'treacheries' and Arthur Henderson, following the loss of his Barnard Castle seat due to redistribution, had failed in an attempt to win East Ham. The Labour group was, almost to a man, composed of trade unionists, honest and conscientious enough, but with no spark, a solid body but one which had no head. When they met to choose the chairman, they re-elected Willie Adamson, whom Beatrice Webb cruelly but correctly described as 'dull-witted'. Later, in 1925, the *Book of the Labour Party*, a semi-official publication, commented in a similar vein on Adamson's abilities, or rather, the lack of them: 'It is generally agreed now that the first choice of a Parliamentary leader was not a wise one.' However, the reasons for the choice are not difficult to find. In the first place, the miners, with twenty-five MPs, were far and away the largest group in the PLP and hence were bound to dominate the proceedings, so much so that MacDonald, rather tactlessly and contemptuously, referred to Labour as merely 'a party of checkweighmen'. The other point is that there were, in fact, two alternative and more able candidates in Clynes and J. H. Thomas, but support for them was so evenly divided that Adamson was accepted as a compromise. Clynes did secure election as deputy chairman and his experience proved useful though he contributed nothing startling. Even the return of Henderson at a by-election at Widnes in August 1919 brought little improvement, for he was still immersed in the problems of building the new organisation and hence gave comparatively little attention to the affairs of the PLP.

The electoral disappointment and the inadequacies of its leadership were not the only set-backs experienced in this period. Labour was now to find the going harder due to a marked change of opinion reflected in the press, in Parliamentary and official circles. Now that the war was over the collectivist ideal became less acceptable and not only was there increasing resistance to the extension of government control of industry and the economy, but also a feeling that the state should speedily divest itself of the responsibilities it had undertaken in the preceding four years. On the very day after the Armistice, Sir John Walton, a Liberal MP, gave voice to this in the Commons when he launched an attack on the activities of civil servants, claiming that 'every trade and industry they have touched, they have hampered and injured.' Predictably the call was echoed by the Federation of British Industries which in the course of 1919 produced a report attacking nationalisation, arguing in particular that 'centralised management by a Government Department is fatal to commercial enterprise and efficiency.' The Lloyd George government in general was anxious to meet its critics on this score and get back to 'the good old days' of pre-1914 as far as possible. So, additional government departments such as the ministry of food were wound up; the controls over industry, particularly the railways and mines, were to be relinquished; plans which had already been drawn up for rationalising the electricity supply industry and bringing it under public control were abandoned. Admittedly Lloyd George was not entirely consistent and circumstances compelled him to further the collectivist cause in two instances. The first was Dr Christopher Addison's Housing Act of 1919 which established a scheme for local authority subsidised housing. After all, one of the planks in Lloyd George's electoral platform had been 'Homes Fit For Heroes' and, cynical opportunist as he has been judged, he apparently decided that this was a promise which could not be shirked. The other issue where an extension of government activity was found necessary was unemployment which began to rise ominously after the short-lived post-war boom came to an end in the spring of 1920. The outcome was the Unemployment Insurance Act by which the government extended the limited scheme in the 1911 Act to cover the whole working class, and furthermore allowed 'uncovenanted benefit'—that is, benefits not covered by the recipient's previous payment. This was the origin of the infamous 'dole'.

But legislation such as this, important as it was, could not reverse the general movement away from collectivism which received further stimulus from an 'anti-waste' campaign against government spending, launched early in 1920 in the newspapers of Lord Rothermere. Rothermere received support from the demagogue, Horatio Bottomley, who successfully ran a number of 'anti-waste' candidates in by-elections. While the movement had no immediate effect, petering out in the early months of 1921, the government could not afford to ignore it entirely and, as the economic difficulties increased, the possibilities of a retrenchment in public spending were seriously considered. The Labour MPs, heavily outnumbered, could do nothing to check this trend which reached its climax with the so-called 'Geddes Axe' in 1922. A special committee set up under Sir Eric Geddes, a member of the cabinet, recommended a series of drastic cuts in expenditure, including £18½ million on education, £2½ million on health, and £3,300,000 on war pensions. Labour members were bitterly resentful, and, according to *The Economist* (February 1922) queried the need for such action 'whilst the rich betake themselves to St Moritz and the ladies of Mayfair spend extravagantly on dresses.' This increasing sense of frustration had important political effects. Initially it led to fierce criticism of the PLP, which was openly expressed at party conferences, and it also led to a questioning of the fundamental effectiveness of political action and a swing over to the belief that Labour's best chance of achieving its aims was through militant trade unionism.

The critics of the PLP launched their attack within a mere six months of the new Parliament's assembly. At the 1919 party conference, they were led by Herbert Morrison, then secretary of the London Labour Party, who called the PLP report 'an insult to the energy, the intelligence and the vigour of the whole Labour movement of the country.' He bluntly declared that 'the party has been a failure in the present Parliament' and demanded much more in the way of 'straightforward and energetic politics' for the future. He received a good deal of vocal support. One complainant, for example, underlined his criticisms of inactivity by claiming that the average number of questions put by each Labour MP was only $1\frac{1}{2}$ per week. The attack was held off and the PLP report accepted but the following year's conference saw the same issue develop into a full scale row. On this occasion the chief spokesman was Emanuel Shinwell, representing the ILP, who pushed the argument a stage further by claiming that not only was the PLP ineffective, but also 'they were a law unto themselves.' The remedy for this, he said, was for the party outside Parliament to exert more control over its MPs. Shinwell was soon followed by others including Morrison, who this time chose to make a personal attack on Clynes, particularly for the latter's failure to make a 'fighting speech against capitalism'. Clynes himself and Sexton reacted strongly, defending their record and bluntly rejecting all talk of 'control' of MPs. Clynes told Shinwell that he did not know what he was talking about and argued that while there must obviously be close harmony between the PLP and the NEC, the latter 'had no authority over the Parliamentary Party'. None of this bitter wrangling could do the slightest good: any attempt to subject the PLP to closer outside control would obviously have led to lack of flexibility and an even less effective performance. Furthermore, no amount of ranting by the left could alter the fundamental political imbalance which, for the time being, left Labour in a hopeless minority in the Commons.

The idea of direct action was not new. It was really nothing more than a continuation of pre-1914 syndicalism and the war-time shop stewards' movement, with the significant difference that this time the official leaders, or at least some of the official leaders, of the trade unions were now involved. Influential personalities like Smillie and Frank Hodges of the miners and Robert Williams of the National Transport Workers' Federation were now heard saying that this was the only path Labour could follow. In addition powerful support came from George Lansbury in the columns of the *Daily Herald* where, at this time, he was consistently preaching the rottenness of the capitalist system and the need to overthrow it as quickly as possible. There was also the feeling that not only was revolutionary industrial action likely to be more effective, but it was necessary to keep the movement's ideals pure and uncorrupted. This was the view of a contributor to the shop stewards' journal *Solidarity* in March 1921: 'Imagine a Labour majority, a Labour government composed of the present crowd of reactionaries, swindlers, and traitors. Imagine the patronage that will be in the possession of this evil crew—the number of jobs they will be able to give to their friends—the bribery and corruption that will be brought into the Labour Movement.' Even though the leaders of the PLP and some distinguished union leaders like Thomas were against direct action, in the circumstances of 1919 their views were largely ignored. As a whole the British trade union movement was both willing and able to follow the extremists' line.

In the first place trade union power had been increased significantly by three developments: a large and rapid rise in membership; a significant movement towards larger units; and the establishment of machinery for coordinating joint action. The increase in numbers was almost entirely due to the expansion of the labour force made necessary by the war but the impetus this provided carried on beyond the cessation of hostilities. In 1914 the number of trade unionists was 4,145,000, of whom some 2,682,357 were in organisations affiliated to the TUC. In 1919 the total numbers had almost doubled to 7,926,000 and the proportion affiliated had also increased significantly to 6,505,482. Admittedly by 1920 there was a slight decline for, while the total number rose to well over the 8 million mark, the affiliated figure was reduced by something under 100,000, but in general, the figures represent a very impressive rate of growth. Numbers, however, in spite of Napoleon's famous remark, are not everything. Organisation is of importance too and some at least of the union leaders of the period showed themselves aware of this. In particular there were moves to make bargaining and industrial action in some industries more effective by carrying through amalgamations or mergers of existing unions. This, in a very real sense, was in imitation of similar trends on the other side of industry and, as in the case of the employers, the origins are to be found in the pre-war period. The Transport Workers' Federation had come together in 1911 and the NUR had united most of the railway-

men's unions in 1913. Union leaders who had urged this action had
however run up against a serious obstacle, for the 1876 Trade Union
Act specifically prevented such mergers unless there was a majority in a
poll of at least two-thirds of the membership. In 1917 the procedure was
greatly simplified when John Hodge, then minister of labour, used his
powers to carry an amending act. Not surprisingly, his union, the steel-
workers, was almost the first to take advantage of the new situation and
the outcome was the foundation of a new body covering the iron and
steel industry, known as the British Iron, Steel, Allied and Kindred
Trades Association (BISAKTA). After the war in 1920 the Amalgamated
Engineering Union was established when the ASE absorbed a number
of smaller unions in the trade. A year later Ernest Bevin and Harry
Gosling's efforts to bring together the road transport industry's and the
docks' labour force came to fruition in the Transport and General
Workers' Union. Apart from these mergers there was a good deal of
thought given to the problem of inter-union coordination. Again, much
of the stimulus came from the pre-war period, when the influential
syndicalist groups were working to establish machinery for an effective
general strike. In January 1914, their efforts led to the formation of the
so-called 'Triple Alliance' of the miners', railwaymen's and transport
workers' unions. The parties declared their intention to back each
other's industrial actions and a strike was in fact fixed for the autumn.
The war intervened and with the declaration of the industrial truce, the
Alliance seemed to have died a natural death, until, in February 1919,
it was revived with consequences we shall examine shortly. Otherwise,
the attempts to improve inter-union cooperation concentrated on
strengthening the TUC. It was becoming increasingly clear to many
union leaders that the Parliamentary Committee was no longer adequate
for the purpose of providing continuity between the movement's annual
congresses. The spokesmen for this group were Gosling and Bevin. The
former had voiced his thoughts as early as the 1917 congress where he
seems to have led a movement to secure wider powers and discretion
for the Parliamentary Committee. Initially this had no results, but a
seed had been sown and it matured with surprising rapidity, for at the
1919 congress a plan was produced to replace the Parliamentary
Committee with what Bevin called a 'General Council'. This was to
'develop the industrial side of the movement as against the "deputising"
or "political" conception'. A special congress, summoned for December,
accepted the idea and the first half of 1920 saw the working out of the
details ready for the annual congress's approval. The following year the

new council, composed of thirty representatives, took up its duties. In particular it was to 'coordinate industrial action', prevent inter-union disputes and generally give what assistance it could to unions in organising their members. At last, it seemed the British trade union movement had a proper head, or, as C. L. Mowat felicitously put it, 'a sort of general staff'.

These developments in themselves go some way towards explaining the leftward shift in trade unionism and the increased willingness to consider militant action. It was all very well for Bevin to declare, apropos of the new body, that 'strikes will be less because of the power of our new organisation', but the working class and its leaders were naturally conscious of their increased strength and hence more inclined to flex their muscles and wave the big stick. The war also played its part in this process in two apparently opposed ways. On the one hand, the status of the movement had been enormously increased by open and continued evidence of the government's need to come to terms with it if the war effort were to be sustained. On the other hand, the 'unofficial' movement, led by the shop stewards, had seemed to show clearly enough that much might be achieved by militancy. Then, of course, the Russian revolution was a tremendously potent factor as an example of what could allegedly be done by determined working-class action and the new Soviet state which was slowly emerging was regarded very much as a 'workers' Mecca'. But, if all these factors seem rather indeterminate, it should be remembered that there were more solid reasons in the immediate post-war world for the adoption of a militant line. As usual, the movement's fears centred on wages and unemployment. As we have seen, wage rates had risen on the whole somewhat ahead of prices during the war and the unions were concerned to maintain the real gains that had been made, particularly as there were ominous signs that these might quickly be eroded in the post-war boom. True, wages continued to rise but now they were in many cases lagging behind prices; food prices, for example, increased by over 25 per cent in the period January 1919–November 1920. The fear of unemployment was equally natural enough as it was believed that mass demobilisation —which everyone wanted of course—would flood the labour market before industry had re-orientated itself sufficiently to absorb the homecoming men. Consequently there was a strong feeling that the new found power of the trade unions should be used to secure increased wages to match the cost of living and a reduction of hours so that the work available might be spread among more people. On the extreme left there was much wild talk of revolution and, although this was not typical, the moderate majority were prepared to back action to secure not only an amelioration of conditions but also a more fundamental reform of the whole economic system. That this was indeed the case was shown by a memorandum drawn up by Arthur Henderson and G. D. H. Cole in March 1919 and presented to a National Industrial Conference: 'The extent to which workers are challenging the whole system of industrial organisation is very much greater today than ever before, and unrest proceeds not only from immediate and special grievances but also, to an increasing extent, from a desire to substitute a democratic system of public ownership and production for use with an increasing element of control by the organised workers themselves for the existing capitalist organisation of industry.'

The attempt to implement this policy of direct action lasted on and off for just over two years, from January 1919–April 1921, and, while the details belong strictly to the history of the trade union movement rather than that of the Labour Party, a full understanding of the latter is impossible without some survey of the main features. Had it succeeded, the proponents of revolution on the left would almost certainly have got their way and the Labour Party would have been a minor irrelevance. As it was, its failure went far towards convincing the working-class movement that the only possible method of attaining any of its long-term aims was by orthodox political means through the Labour Party in Parliament. The General Strike of 1926, so menacing at the time, in retrospect appears almost a temporary aberration by the union leadership. It merely underlined the basic good sense of the decision taken in 1921. As one of the TUC general council put it: 'Never again!'

Typically it was 'red Clydeside' which showed the way. In January 1919, the local shop stewards' movement, led by Gallacher, Shinwell and Kirkwood, this time backed by the official trade union organisation, called for a general strike to impose a 40-hour week to absorb the unemployment the end of the war was expected to cause. On 27 January, industry in the west of Scotland came almost to a complete standstill. A mass meeting of 30,000 strikers converged on the city hall to run up the red flag, thus beginning a week of high drama. The demonstrations were renewed on 29 and 31 January, and on the latter occasion while the leaders were in the city hall serious violence broke out, probably partly due to a precipitate attempt by the police to break up the crowd. This so-called 'battle of George Square' led the government, over-reacting from fear of revolution, to order what was in effect a military occupation of the city, even to the extent of leaguering tanks in the market. The leaders were arrested and two months later stood trial in Edinburgh, two of them, Gallacher and Shinwell, drawing short prison sentences as a result.

Clydeside had shown the way but not the method. Indeed the episode so thoroughly discredited the revolutionaries that serious talk of revolution in the labour movement died away almost to nothing. Instead the union leaders decided rather to lean on the government by the threat of strike action. In particular with the reconstitution of the Triple Alliance in February 1919 there was the ultimate sanction of a general strike.

At first the policy worked and achieved some remarkable successes. The miners were the first off the mark. In January 1919 their conference accepted a programme demanding a 30 per cent increase in wages, a 6-hour day and the nationalisation of the mines, indicating in addition, by a majority of 6 to 1 in a ballot, that they would take strike action if the claim was rejected. Lloyd George showed himself apparently willing to compromise, and on the understanding that the strike threat was withdrawn, he offered to set up a government commission to consider the demands. The upshot was the Sankey Commission, a peculiarly disparate body of three mine-owners, three other industrialists, three miners' leaders (Smillie, Frank Hodges and Herbert Smith) and three economists, all of whom were Labour sympathisers. The whole body was to meet under the chairmanship of a distinguished judge, Sir John Sankey. This composition alone was enough to ensure that no real agreement was possible. No less than four reports were finally issued in June and on nationalisation the division was particularly obvious, though Sankey himself joined with the miners and the economists, declaring in favour of 'the principle of state ownership of the coal mines.' But the obvious division of opinion gave Lloyd George the excuse to declare on 18 August against the idea of nationalisation, though he said he was willing to legislate on a number of minor reforms. Now, suddenly and too late, the miners woke up to the significance of Lloyd George's strategy. All along he had merely played for time, gambling on the almost cast-iron certainty that the longer he delayed, the less justification they would have for striking and the less chance of their colleagues in the Triple Alliance supporting them. No wonder that Vernon Hartshorn commented bitterly that they had been 'deceived, betrayed, duped'. In the circumstances all that could be done was to mount a singularly futile campaign on the slogan 'The Mines for the Nation'.

While the miners were rebuffed after the initial success, their colleagues in the NUR did rather better. On 26 September 1919 they declared a strike against the 'standardisation' of their wages—a euphemism for cuts of 11 shillings and more per week. The government attempted to depict the men as irresponsible anarchists blackmailing the community, but the union's publicity department, cleverly masterminded by J. H. Thomas, was more than equal to this misrepresentation. The strike was 100 per cent effective and at the end of a week Lloyd George personally intervened and settled the matter virtually on the men's terms.

The success of the NUR, which was on a purely industrial matter, was followed by an apparently greater political triumph for the trade unions on the issue of the government's Russian policy in the spring and summer of 1920. Inevitably, the labour movement had been opposed to Lloyd George's cabinet's decision to intervene in the Russian civil war and, perhaps equally inevitably, when the PLP showed itself unable to check this, there were going to be demands for direct action. The party conference of June 1919 approved by a 2 to 1 majority Herbert Morrison's suggestion that the government's policy 'should be resisted with the full political and industrial power of the whole trade union movement.' This stirring resolution however produced nothing immediate nor very effective, apart from the establishment of a 'Hands Off Russia' Committee in November. In a sense, the labour movement was knocking on an already half-open door, for the cabinet was none too happy about the episode in spite of Churchill's dramatic warnings about the perils of Bolshevism. Accordingly steps were taken to wind up the whole sorry business by withdrawing the troops previously sent and preventing the dispatch of further munitions to the White Russian counter-revolutionaries. There the matter would probably have ended, had it not been for the Polish offensive against Russia the following year. The Poles were getting some of their munitions from Britain and, as this became known, there was a further reaction from Labour. On 10 May 1920, the movement's dissatisfaction came to a head when the London dockers took action to prevent munitions leaving for Poland on a vessel called the *Jolly George*. At first the government did nothing but later in the summer the Poles were driven out of the Ukraine and forced back to Warsaw itself, whereupon Lloyd George, pushed by Churchill and the French, seemed on the point of further action. Immediate steps were now taken by Labour to put pressure on the government in the country. On 4 August, Henderson issued instructions to the local Labour parties and affiliated societies to mount citizen demonstrations against government policy. Five days later, on 9 August, a joint meeting of the TUC Parliamentary Committee, the NEC and the PLP agreed on a motion which declared the war 'a crime against humanity' and threatened to use 'the whole industrial power of the organised workers' if the government persisted with its apparent intention to intervene. A council of action was formed to put the threat into effect, though at the same time it was decided to send a deputation led by Bevin to meet Lloyd George on the following day. There are two conflicting versions of this encounter. According to one, the prime minister was quite obdurate and made it clear that he was set on his course of action; but the second account depicts him in a much more conciliatory mood, declaring his fundamental agreement with Labour's views and claiming that it was not his fault but rather that of headstrong colleagues who needed considerable restraint. But in any event, he seems to have given no hard and fast assurances and so, on 13 August, a Labour special conference called on the council of action to demand three specific guarantees: that no British forces should support the Poles or the Whites; the withdrawal of all British naval units operating against Russia; the recognition of the Soviet government together with the establishment of trade and commercial links. The sanction of industrial action was further stressed if satisfaction were not obtained. As it turned out, the government decided not to persist with its interventionist policy but it is hard to gauge exactly what influence Labour had in bringing about this conclusion. The fact that Labour was in such a determined mood may perhaps have slowed Lloyd George down, or, as he himself claimed, have been used to convince recalcitrant colleagues of the unwisdom of their actions. On the other hand, the ultimate outcome—the battle of the Vistula on 14 August and the Polish recovery—meant that the government need no longer contemplate action anyway. Finally, as to the question of recognition, Lloyd George ignored Labour's demands, although he was alive to the possibility of normal economic relations and pressed this policy unsuccessfully at the Genoa international conference of April 1922.

In retrospect it is clear that the Russian episode was the peak of the direct action campaign. The labour movement itself was beginning to realise the limitations during the latter part of 1920 when action over the issue of unemployment was contemplated. The post-war boom proved so short-lived that before even the end of that year unemployment levels had begun to soar alarmingly: 691,103 in December, 1,355,206 in March 1921 and thence to a peak of 2,171,288 in June. One can see how apt was the description of 1921 as 'one of the worst years of depression since the industrial revolution'. At first there was a good deal of direct action which was quite spontaneous and unorganised. In October of 1920 a crowd of unemployed gathered in Whitehall to demonstrate in support of a deputation of Labour mayors to the government. The gathering was broken up by the police and this set the pattern for the winter of 1920–21 which saw a good deal of violence in London and the major provincial centres. At the turn of the year the whole question of unemployment was taken up by both the Labour Party and the TUC. A special conference in January approved a programme which included government credits to stimulate public works' schemes and reasonable maintenance for the unemployed, following which the delegates adjourned for a month to give the trade unions time to take 'any further steps that may be necessary to secure the adoption of the recommendation.' But when the conference reassembled, all talk of strike action was now discounted and instead it was decided to mount a political campaign in preparation for the next general election.

The fact of the matter was—as the left wing, particularly the newly formed Communist Party, was only too ready to point out—that the union leadership by and large was not prepared to countenance revolutionary action. Furthermore, the advocates of caution seemed even more justified when the miners, now the most militant group, in a burst of irritation, first attempted to force the rest of the Triple Alliance into a general strike, and then, having failed in this, persisted on their own to defeat and humiliation. They had good reason to be bitter about the government's double-cross on the Sankey Report but, much as one sympathises with their predicament, their subsequent action goes some way to justifying Birkenhead's oft-quoted remark that they were only a degree or so less stupid than the mine-owners. It seems, for example, quite unbelievable that men of the calibre of Smillie, who had spent a lifetime's work in the cause of Labour in general and the miners in particular, should now jeopardise all past gains in a moment of madness. But increasingly the tune was being called by inflexible extremists like Herbert Smith and A. J. Cook, and it was now not merely the issue of nationalisation at stake, but the more fundamental matters of wages and hours. Throughout 1920 the tension rose, reaching a climax in the autumn when the miners called a strike in support of their claims on 16 October. Not only was the stoppage complete but the miners also seemed to have the support of the other two elements of the Triple Alliance for, despite J. H. Thomas's predilections for a compromise, the NUR decided to follow the miners and the transport workers seemed set on the same course. Typically Lloyd George's reaction was to use the stick and the carrot, with the underlying and perhaps most important intention of simply buying time. The Emergency Powers Act revived the government's war-time powers under DORA and at the same time negotiations with the miners granted them an increase in shift earnings. This settlement was only to last until 31 March 1921, but further complications soon developed. The miners made it clear they wanted a national wage structure, in place of previous local agreements, and the new deal was intended to consolidate the war-time gains. Unfortunately, by now not only was the general economic recession well under way but the coal industry was in special difficulties as its European export markets were being eroded by the revival of continental pits, previously out of action due to the war, and by the payment of German reparations in coal as well as other goods. In the circumstances the government sought to wash its hands of the whole affair as quickly as possible. It announced that decontrol (i.e. handing back full control of the pits to the former owners) would take place almost immediately. At the same time the owners made it clear that they intended to solve their problems entirely at the men's expense by instituting hefty wage cuts, in some cases as much as 50 per cent. The crisis now had something of the inevitability of a Greek tragedy: on 31 March, decontrol became official; on the following day, the owners declared a lock-out when the miners refused their terms. Everything now depended on whether the Triple Alliance would be effective: with a near-general strike, the miners might well get their way; without it their chances, given the prevailing economic conditions, were slim. Their leaders seem to have assumed right from the start that their colleagues in the Alliance were wholeheartedly behind them and at first this did seem to be the case. On 8 April the leaders met and issued strike notices for midnight on 12 April, although a last-minute attempt by the government to re-start negotiations meant the date being postponed to 15 April. It was at this stage that serious divisions began to appear in the unions' ranks. Thomas all along had wanted a more flexible approach towards the negotiations and now he was joined by Bevin. For a brief moment it seemed as if the miners might prove amenable to such suggestions, particularly when their secretary, Frank

Hodges, intimated to a group of MPs that he himself was in favour of renewed negotiations on the basis of a 'national wages pool' as a means of equalising rates of pay between the more prosperous and the poorer coal-fields. Unfortunately the miners' executive turned down the idea, albeit by only one vote, and determined to go ahead. At this stage the fragile unity of the Triple Alliance disintegrated completely. Thomas and Bevin rejected Herbert Smith's angry demands for solidarity— 'Get on t'field,' he is supposed to have said, 'that's t'place!' They pointed out that they could not possibly now commit their members to the support of what seemed totally unreasonable action. Thus, on Friday, 15 April—'Black Friday' as it has become known in Labour mythology —the miners went on strike alone, quite inflexible in their bitter determination. Inevitably they were beaten, although they hung on until June before they were forced back to work on even worse terms than those originally offered by the owners. 'Black Friday', for the time being at any rate, marked the end of direct action. The blow to the trade union movement's prestige, the weakening of its power due to the economic recession, together with the crumbling of Lloyd George's position bringing with it an early general election, all combined to turn Labour back to politics. This change of tactics was to coincide with a remarkable revival in the party's fortunes.

## [23] The Conditions for Revival

The ultimately disastrous concentration on 'direct action' had tended to divert attention from the fact that there had been real progress since the general election of 1918. This is to be seen most clearly in the party's performance in by-elections. Admittedly in the period up to April 1921 only a comparatively small number of seats was gained, but in most of those contested Labour's share of the vote went up, in some cases very substantially. Even more hopeful was the evidence that at last Labour was beginning to make some appeal in parts of the country outside the industrialised urban areas where hitherto its strength had been concentrated. In fact, the stage was already being set for the apparently dramatic changes of 1922–4.

In the first place, the electoral changes of the 1918 Representation of the People Act were likely to be of considerable advantage to Labour. This measure, by granting manhood suffrage, brought on to the register a substantial number of working-class males, most of whom were likely to vote for the party. Secondly, although the trade union movement had taken a hammering as a result of the post-war slump, it still retained a significant proportion of the new members picked up since 1914. Thus, while there was a marked decline from the peak period at the end of the war, there were still over 5 million trade unionists affiliated to the TUC in 1921 and, although there were further losses in 1922–3, the numbers remained well over the 4 million mark. Moreover, with the advent of the general council, the organisation was significantly improved and there also emerged a new, astute and more politically conscious leadership, typified by men like Thomas and Bevin. Steps were also taken in this period to improve the coordination between the TUC and the party by promoting a new National Joint Council (later renamed the National Council of Labour) in place of the old Joint Board. The unions agreed to make a higher financial contribution and joined with the party in an important venture which improved the movement's publicity by acquiring an interest in the *Daily Herald*. For some years now, George Lansbury had run the paper more or less as a private venture and while he had been successful in building up a sizeable circulation of some 330,000, it was now in serious financial difficulties due to an advertising boycott. The TUC/Labour Party decision saved the paper's existence and ensured the movement a consistent and widely read outlet for its views. Thus despite the setbacks, the trade union movement was fundamentally stronger and once it had abandoned its penchant for direct action Labour's political fortunes were likely to improve.

Another important factor in the revival was the success of the reorganisation of the party machine, which had been progressing quietly but effectively in the immediate post-war period. The Coupon election had come too early to be a test of Henderson's work. The local parties were still in a state of disarray and indeed did not exist in many constituencies. But within a matter of three or four years all this was changed. By 1924 the number of divisional and local parties in existence was nearly 3,000 and only three constituencies were not covered. Whereas in 1918 Labour thought it worthwhile to contest some 380 seats, in 1922 this had risen to 411, and the number increased again, though only marginally, the following year. At the same time there was a rapid expansion of the separate women's sections — 150,000 members by 1923 — and in 1922 steps were taken to develop a youth organisation. In only one respect was Henderson's work rather less than successful:

his hopes of absorbing the Cooperative party into the Labour machine. The Cooperative movement, while in broad sympathy with the Labour cause, had as far as possible kept clear of active involvement in party politics. In 1917, the annual conference had decided the time had come to take overt political action and a joint committee of the Cooperators, the NEC and the TUC Parliamentary Committee was formed in January of 1918. The same year however the Cooperative conference demanded that all Parliamentary candidates stand as independents and not as Coop and Labour. Henderson seems to have had some worries as to possible duplication of working-class candidatures and the consequent splitting of the vote. But all the attempts to secure, at the very least, an electoral understanding were doomed to failure when the Cooperative conference of 1921 once more rejected the possibility of a tie-up. Even so this set-back was more apparent than real. The new Cooperative party had put up a number of candidates at the 1918 election, securing the return of one of them, A. E. Waterson, at Kettering. Waterson promptly declared his adhesion to Labour and this set a precedent which was followed by later successful Cooperative candidates.

There was however another sense in which Henderson's work materially strengthened the Labour Party in the immediate post-war years. In 1918 when he and Webb produced their master plan, their aim was not merely to improve the local machinery but also to weld the party into a more coherent unit on the basis of a moderate socialist programme. The main danger came from certain irreconcilable elements on the extreme left, notably the Marxist BSP. In the course of 1920–1 these groups came together to form the Communist Party of Great Britain with the avowed aim of taking over the Labour Party and using it as an instrument of revolution. Henderson was only too well aware of the Communists' intentions and used his influence to the utmost to block their attempts to secure affiliation. His task was not an easy one for the Communists had a number of sympathisers and supporters throughout the labour movement: prominent trade unionists such as A. J. Cook of the miners, and Harry Pollitt of the boilermakers were Communist Party members; the miners' union as a whole was much impressed by the support organised by the Communists in the 1921 strike; there was a strong cell of Communists in the influential London Trades Council; it was also confidently claimed that by 1921 some 5,000 members of the ILP had been converted to the cause. For a time, they even had the support of George Lansbury in the *Daily Herald* still advocating the idea of direct action. But his basic Christian kind-heartedness triumphed in the end. When he realised that the Communists actually meant all they said about violent and bloody revolution, he changed tack, calling for united action 'to prove that Parliamentary methods are a more excellent machinery for accomplishing social salvation than the dictatorship of the proletariat.'

The Communists, in fact, made no less than four separate attempts to secure affiliation between August 1920 and the summer of 1923, only to be rejected on each occasion. The first application delivered to the NEC on 10 August 1920 touched off a prolonged correspondence between the leaders and Henderson. Basically his objection was that there were fundamental and insuperable differences between the two parties. When the Communists argued that this was not so and they were merely claiming the same latitude enjoyed by the ILP during the war, Henderson neatly riposted by drawing attention to the public statements of Arthur McManus, the Communist chairman, that the two parties were irreconcilable. Then, the Communists took their case to the party annual conferences in 1921 and 1922 only to see it overwhelmingly rejected in spite of the persuasive arguments of their friends. On the second occasion an amendment to the rules was carried to prevent Communists from being adopted either as delegates to the conference or as Labour candidates. This proved to be a tactical error as some trade unions resented what they regarded as an infringement on their right to choose delegates, and individuals could exploit this to creep in until the 1924 conference stopped up the loophole completely. The Communists' final attempt in this period was in 1923, when once more they were rejected by the NEC, a decision confirmed overwhelmingly by conference.

The Communist failure to secure affiliation was due as much as anything to their own political ineptitude. They refused to make any compromise, and even publicly proclaimed their ultimate aim of suborning the party. Thus their first application talked openly of revolution and declared that any Communist elected an MP would be responsible only to the Communist Party and not to Labour or to his constituents. In addition their spokesmen publicly proclaimed their acceptance of Lenin's outrageous advice 'to support Henderson . . . in the same way as a rope supports one who is hanged'. Article after article in their journal *The Communist* at this time argued the need to help Labour as a prelude to destroying it, or converting it into an instrument of revolution. There was even the speaker at the party's 1922 conference who outdid Lenin, by declaring that he would take the Labour leaders by the hand 'as a preliminary to taking them by the throat'. This honesty was scarcely practical politics and it stirred resentment amongst some who might otherwise have been duped by appeals for a united front. There were other ways too in which the Communists did themselves no good with the labour movement as a whole. Their open adhesion to the Moscow line caused many to agree with Frank Hodges' description of them as 'intellectual slaves . . . taking orders from the Asiatic mind'. Finally there was the ill-judged attack on the Labour leadership, not only Henderson but also MacDonald and Thomas. MacDonald, for example, suffered their attentions when he stood at the East Woolwich by-election following Will Crooks' death in March 1921. Much mud was slung in this celebrated contest, particularly at Mac-Donald's war record, and the Communists gleefully joined in, calling him 'a broken-down political hack' and claiming that he and the Labour Party were amongst the 'forces of capitalism'. At the end, they openly boasted that their campaign had cost him the election and since he was only defeated by 638 in a total poll of 27,000, this may well have been the decisive factor. For his part, Thomas was freely reviled as a traitor for his contribution to the collapse of the Triple Alliance on 'Black Friday' and the abuse became so virulent that he judged it expedient to sue for libel, being awarded as a result damages to the tune of £2,000. Such attacks as these were counter-productive. Far from discrediting the victims, they brought them much sympathy and a growing determination in the labour movement to keep the Communists out at all costs. But even had their tactics been less politically maladroit, it seems unlikely that they would have succeeded in their permeation plans. Fundamentally, there was the difference between their revolutionary ideal and the democratic methods acceptable to the British labour movement. On this there could be no compromise; as Henderson put it to the 1921 Labour conference, there was 'not a particle of evidence of an intention to accept and honourably abide by either the constitution or the decisions of this conference'. As to their extravagant claims that Communist support could swing elections in Labour's favour, Henderson well knew that their oft publicised pro-Moscow revolutionary line was an electoral liability that Labour could not afford to carry. Without these wild men of the left, the party was more coherent and uniform, with a better chance of winning the electoral support it needed outside the working class. Once they had decided to go out in 1920, Henderson was determined that they should stay out.

But not only was Labour growing appreciably stronger in itself in these years, it was also materially assisted by developments in the other two parties. In the first instance there was the rapid and continuing decline of the Liberals. The question as to when this decline began, what caused it and whether or not it was inevitable have recently been a matter of some controversy between modern historians. The details are not really relevant to a study of the Labour Party, and suffice it to say that by the middle years of the war the Liberals were clearly dividing into followers of Lloyd George and those of Asquith, and Lloyd George's decision to continue with the coalition arrangement after the war perpetuated the split. The 'Coupon' election revealed how weak the party was: 136 Liberals were returned as Coalitionists but it was significant that many of their seats were held by courtesy of the Unionists and several were in industrial areas where electoral support was being rapidly eroded by Labour. The followers of Asquith were now reduced to a mere 26 members, their leader and most of his prominent adherents failing to secure re-election. Furthermore, the changes that had taken place in Ireland during the war were a serious loss to Liberalism. Before 1914, the party could usually count on the support of the 80 or so Nationalist MPs, but now, with the rise of Sinn Fein, the party of Parnell and Redmond had virtually been wiped out. Thus in 1918 there was something of a political vacuum on the left of British politics, and although Labour had only 59 MPs in the new House of Commons, they were in effect already the official opposition.

The decline of the Liberal Party not only gave Labour its opportunity to become the second party in the state, it also brought over many middle-class Liberals who were thoroughly disgusted with their party's pre-war record in the field of foreign policy and felt that Labour's internationalist approach provided a better hope for the future. This process can be traced back as far as 1911 when at least one Radical MP, C. P. Trevelyan, expressed himself in opposition to the tone of Lloyd George's Mansion House Speech during the Agadir crisis. Then, soon after the outbreak of the war in 1914, he and others together with MacDonald had been instrumental in forming the UDC which had gradually aligned itself with the ILP. During the war itself, the erosion of traditional Liberal rights by such measures as conscription brought many more in the party closer to the UDC position, while stopping short of actually joining it. But the transference of a significant section of the party to Labour on these and related issues was not inevitable. As late as 1917 there was still a good deal of support for Asquith and one

MP, R. C. Lambert, wrote at this time: 'Liberalism is not dead. It will revive with renewed strength now that the world has seen what militarism really means.' But soon, even before the end of the fighting, there were signs that disenchantment was setting in. This first became obvious in certain influential sections of the Liberal press. H. W. Massingham in the radical periodical *The Nation* in October 1917 had published an article in which Labour was described as 'the one quarter from which a really fresh and hopeful development can come.' In December the paper went even further, arguing 'it is not to the existing Liberal Party that the younger and finer spirits look for the Risorgimento of British democracy. On the contrary they are beginning to flock to the banners of Labour.' Finally, in December 1918, at the time of the general election, Massingham openly declared for Labour as 'the one powerful integral force in our politics outside Mr George's compact'. More surprisingly, C. P. Scott, Liberalism's anchorman in the north-west, had shown signs of moving the *Manchester Guardian* leftwards, indicating particular approval in December 1917 of Labour's 'masterly statement of war aims and peace policy'. Inside Parliament the pace was a little slower but the movement was beginning to take shape early in 1918. In March a large number of Liberal MPs met to hear a Labour spokesman expound his party's cause and this was followed by the formation of a 'radical committee' with some MPs already talking of the importance of close cooperation. But the really dramatic abandonment of the Liberal ship did not come until after 1918, when it became increasingly obvious to the radicals that Liberalism had nothing to offer. The leadership was feeble in the extreme. Although Asquith got back into the Commons at the Paisley by-election, he was by now a mere shadow of a once great politician, lacking both energy and decisiveness, and, for all the talk of finding a replacement, there was in fact no possible alternative. Perhaps even more important was the dearth of Liberal thinking on policy. It was now not just a case of dissatisfaction with the party's foreign policy, but of deciding what exactly Liberalism meant in domestic terms now that the great issues of the past—Home Rule, free trade, disestablishment, temperance reform, non-sectarian education—seemed to be dead or dying. Attempts to update the party programme with demands for economic and social reform, including amongst other things measures of nationalisation, foundered on the rock of Asquith's instinctive commitment to laisser-faire. As a result, men like Chiozza Money and Christopher Addison, who regretted the post-war retreat from collectivism, now followed those like Trevelyan who had joined Labour on the issue of foreign policy. In short, from 1918 onwards an increasing number of Liberals were for one reason or another disillusioned with their party and were joining the ranks of Labour. Nor was it only the comparative unknowns like Trevelyan, Wedgwood Benn and Arthur Ponsonby. By 1922 it was clear that Labour had landed one of the 'big fish' in the person of Haldane.

It would appear that both Asquith and Lloyd George were aware to some degree at least of the damage that Liberalism was suffering. Both moreover came up with the same solution to the problem—a belated revival of Lib–Labism. Asquith expressed this in a speech at the National Liberal Club in March 1920 in which he claimed to be 'a Labour member in quite as full and . . . true sense as any man who, representing a great trade union . . . comes to the House of Commons with a Labour mandate.' Putting this philosophy into practice meant, in the first instance, Asquithians agreeing to stand aside in by-elections to give Labour candidates a better chance. On the Labour side it seems that Henderson and Clynes gave the idea some consideration but that was as far as they were prepared to go. Their decision was probably a combination of shrewd calculation that Asquith had nothing to offer and a realisation that there was a strong feeling in the Labour ranks against it. On the other hand such considerations did not apply quite so much in the case of Lloyd George. He after all had always been much more of a radical than Asquith and from the early months of 1922, when he began to run into serious difficulties with his Conservative partners in the coalition, there was a possibility that he might try and resume his political career on the left. Certainly there were some amongst the Labour leadership who gave serious thought to such a possibility. At this time, it seems that Thomas, Stephen Walsh and Hartshorn were in communication with him, though what sort of arrangement they were seeking is not entirely clear. Furthermore, when the coalition fell and Labour turned the main weight of its opposition on to the Conservatives, in theory Lloyd George's chances of winning its support looked better. There were indeed rumours in some circles that Labour was seriously negotiating with him. But these were idle talk for there were far too many powerful influences in the party opposed to the idea. MacDonald, now on the brink of returning to the leadership, was determined not to be cheated out of what he regarded as his due. Henderson was also hostile and Clynes, in a speech made shortly after the coalition's fall, went so far as to describe Lloyd George as 'a comic turn . . . [a] mountain of froth'. Among the rank and file, it goes without saying that the left wing felt even more strongly, being quite unable to stomach his too recent association with the Conservatives. The Clydesiders in the 1922 Parliament were particularly virulent in their criticisms. What probably ruined his chances in the last resort was the 1922 election when a large number of his followers lost their seats and many of those who were successful were returned on very slender majorities. Nonetheless he persisted in his attempts to build a new radical party which was to unite both factions of the Liberals together with the more moderate Labour men. The project was launched in a major speech to the Manchester Liberal Party on 29 April 1923. It brought no response from Labour, merely underlining the fact that Lib–Labism was dead and attempts to revive it were doomed.

The contribution of the Conservatives to the rise of Labour is less apparent but according to one recent study it was highly significant. Maurice Cowling in *The Impact of Labour, 1920–24* argues that in this period the Conservative leadership took a conscious decision 'to make Labour the chief party of opposition'. Clearly this interpretation is somewhat at variance with the conventional one which regards the Conservative Party as simply motivated by a desire to check Labour's advance and trample it in the dust at every conceivable opportunity. Cowling's argument begins with the premise that the really important decisions resulted from manoeuvres in the field of 'high politics' which he defines as the activities of some fifty or sixty leading politicians in Parliament. In the four or five years following the end of the war, these men were mainly concerned with the problem of resistance to the threat to the existing social order posed by the rise of Labour. At first it was believed that the coalition arrangement with Lloyd George was the best solution but, as time went on, many of the second rank Conservative leaders, Stanley Baldwin amongst them, began to have serious misgivings. Moreover their doubts were shared by Bonar Law, who gave up the party leadership to Austen Chamberlain in March 1921, by many backbenchers and finally by the influential party manager, Sir George Younger. Apart from specific complaints that the coalition had done nothing to implement certain cherished Conservative legislative proposals, the main criticism was the style and tone adopted by Lloyd George. It was increasingly felt that the prime minister's dynamism, far from resolving class conflicts was rather stirring up a good deal of dangerous working-class hostility. Not only was this illustrated by trouble in the industrial field, but also the Labour advance in by-elections in the period 1919–21. In short, Lloyd George was not proving to be a very effective resistance leader. Accordingly, prompted by its second rank leaders and totally ignoring the advice of Austen Chamberlain, the Conservative Party ditched Lloyd George and then, under the leadership of Law and Baldwin, set out to promote itself as the 'party of resistance'. The process took some time and there were serious setbacks, but by the general election of 1924 it was complete and the Conservatives held the ground they have occupied since.

This success inevitably squeezed the Liberal Party which, by 1924, had virtually ceased to be a going concern. But what is important is the evidence that the destruction of the Liberal Party and its replacement by Labour was deliberate policy on the part of the Conservative leadership. It may well be that originally Baldwin hoped that the Liberals might survive as a safe alternative, but the 1922 election revealed their weakness and basic inability to perform this role. So, from then onwards, Baldwin devoted a significant part of his time and energy to securing what Leo Amery was to call 'the right solution', that is 'for the Liberal Party to disappear by one section of it gradually joining with and diluting the Labour Party and the other section coming into line with us.' (Letter to Geoffrey Dawson, 9 January 1924.) For example, Baldwin's much debated decision to go to the country on the issue of Protection in the autumn of 1923 may well have been influenced by the calculation that it would force the Liberals into an election they were scarcely ready to face. Again, following the equivocal result of that election, he stoutly refused all suggestions of a coalition with Asquith, believing that the alternative of a Labour government with the support of the Liberals would have a devastating effect by compelling their supporters to make a clear choice between Conservative and Labour. As for Labour itself, the Conservative leaders had clearly come to the conclusion that alarmists like Austen Chamberlain were not to be believed and that it posed no real threat, particularly if it were accepted into the existing system. Labour's leaders, both in Parliament and the unions, were reasonable men at heart and, in Baldwin's view, the party's policy could not be described as 'robbery'; it was 'genuinely for the uplifting of the masses of this country'. A cynic might add that the Conservatives could also have been consciously motivated by a belief that they could more easily beat the Labour Party in an electoral straight fight.

In his conclusion, Cowling points to the fact that his interpretation provides a more convincing explanation of certain other questions. In particular he instances the attitude of some Conservatives like Neville

Chamberlain and Edward Wood, who evinced a far greater dislike of
the Liberals than Labour, and, of course, the growing understanding
between Baldwin and MacDonald. At the very least one must allow a
good deal of weight to this argument, particularly as it is presented with
massively detailed documentation, but there must be some reservations.
The first is that while this may have been deliberate policy by the
Conservative leaders it was not necessarily appreciated by their followers either in Parliament or the country, and, to be fair, Cowling
makes this distinction very clearly. But of more fundamental importance
is the implied suggestion that, given the importance of high politics,
this was a central factor, possibly the decisive one, in Labour's emergence. It still needs to be demonstrated more convincingly whether the
world of high politics is so important, and one is left with the impression
that Labour would have advanced in these years whatever the Conservatives decided to do.

## [24] Into Office 1922–4

Even allowing for the cumulative effect of the developments discussed
above, the Labour Party still had one considerable barrier to overcome,
and that was to convince the country that it could mount an alternative
government. It was all very well to declare, as one Labour MP had in
1919, that 'the workers were the governing party' and were just as
capable of running the country as the upper class, but there were still
many who doubted this claim. Even amongst the working class itself
there was still a good deal of what has been called the 'politics of
deference' which led, and still leads, a significant minority to give its
electoral support to the Conservative or Liberal Parties. Labour
leaders were well aware of this, but in the early 1920s they were more
concerned to win over sections of the middle class by assuring them that
their interests would be safe under a Labour government. Only by thus
broadening its base, it was argued, could the party continue to make its
way.

It was of course particularly difficult to assert the responsible and
non-revolutionary character of Labour in the wake of almost two years
direct action and rumours of a possible tie-up with the new Communist
party. However, Clynes, who had replaced the ineffective Adamson as
PLP leader in 1921, did his best. One of his arguments was to try and

reverse the usual criticism of Labour as being entirely class based. Rather, he said, this was the flaw of the coalition government and Labour for its part was 'not a detached section of the nation [but] came near being the country itself.' (Speech to the Imperial Commercial Association luncheon, 24 January 1922.) At the same time, while he and his colleagues continued to deplore the high rate of unemployment, they were careful to lay the blame on the government and not on the capitalist system which they said Labour had no intention of destroying. Later, in the course of April 1922, Clynes, in outlining Labour's alternative policies, claimed (not altogether convincingly) that proposals embodying the capital levy and nationalisation were not socialist dogma but plain common sense. Yet another approach was to stress Labour's high-mindedness and moral superiority—that the party was, again in Clynes's words, for 'the value of life as against property'.

This campaign for wider support came to a head in the general election of 1922 and the results indicate that it had little obvious effect. While the party more than doubled its pre-dissolution total by returning 142 MPs, it was significant that most of the additional seats were won in the traditional urban and industrial areas. 'Deference' might have taken a further and long overdue knock, but the middle class were still not much impressed by Labour's claims. The party lacked leadership. Clynes had done well in his own way but he lacked stature and inspiration. What was needed now was a personality who could project himself more effectively and who would be recognised by the country as a whole. The only man who could fill this gap was Ramsay MacDonald and, on the morrow of the election, the PLP elevated him to the leadership.

It had been a long haul back for MacDonald, to what he undoubtedly regarded as his rightful place in the movement. His pacifism in the war had reduced his influence and then brought about his defeat in the 1918 election. According to Snowden, even before his belated return to Parliament in 1922, there had been a move to ease him into the counsels of the leadership by creating him 'General Adviser to the Party on the best method of making itself more efficient'. Not unnaturally this had been rejected though it appears to have provoked much heated discussion. Now things were to be different. On 21 November, a week after the election, the PLP met at Westminster under Clynes' chairmanship. He had been re-elected leader at the close of the previous session and he and his supporters were rather surprised when demands for a fresh election were voiced and carried. In the contest that followed between himself and MacDonald, the latter was voted in by a majority which varies according to a number of accounts but which was certainly less than six: 61 votes to 56 being the figures most usually accepted. Surprised Clynes may have been but, by his own account, he was not over-concerned at the time, though later he experienced some annoyance when he discovered 'the complicated schemes and plans for my defeat'. Anyway, the pill, such as it was, was sugared acceptably enough when MacDonald urged he be elected deputy leader and this was done.

Two factors seem to have ensured MacDonald's success. In the first instance he had a highly organised pressure group, the Glasgow ILP, working for him. Fenner Brockway later wrote that 'the extraordinary loyalty of Glasgow to MacDonald . . . was responsible for his election.' The hard work of John Wheatley over the years finally paid off handsome dividends in 1922: 10 of the 15 Glasgow city seats were carried by the ILP and taking the west of Scotland as a whole, 21 out of 29 seats were held. All these MPs, in David Kirkwood's phrase, were 'Ramsay MacDonald's men' and were bound to have a considerable effect not only on the ILP but the Labour Party as a whole. For Wheatley, Kirkwood and the rest, he was the true man of the left. They remembered his opposition to the war, when Glasgow had been the only place where his ideas were sure of a fair hearing; they had read his regular articles in *Forward* in which he had preached the cause of socialism; perhaps also they had, like Kirkwood, been more than a little bewitched by 'a magnificent presence, a full resonant voice and a splendid dignity'. But the enthusiastic support of the Clydeside pressure group would not have been enough but for the fact that, following the 1922 election, the party had now been transformed from an almost purely trade union group into one in which the union element was proportionately (though not numerically) considerably less. While the overall numbers of trade unionist members among the 142 MPs had risen, there were now 32 ILP men and 19 sponsored by local parties, the latter figure including many ex-Liberals like Trevelyan and Ponsonby who had worked with MacDonald in the UDC. Moreover, when it came to the vote, not all of the trade union MPs could bring themselves to vote for Clynes as they had been rather upset by his apparently easy acquiescence in the Speaker's ruling that the Labour Party could not occupy the major part of the opposition front bench in the Commons. Finally, it would appear that some of Clynes' supporters failed to turn up at the meeting. Most accounts agree that about twenty of the party's MPs were absent from Westminster, many of whom were trade union officials away on union business.

MacDonald's own behaviour throughout the whole proceedings was curiously ambivalent, combined with some rather unpleasant histrionics. According to Kirkwood, he had 'let it be known that he was not going forward to the election of leader. There was a rumour that he did not feel well enough.' Snowden, on the other hand, tells a rather different story: 'It had come to my knowledge that Mr MacDonald had been actively canvassing among his friends for support and he had been especially concerned to get the support of the new Scottish members.' Further, during the actual process of the election he had apparently maintained a pose of disinterest and languor but, when the vote was clear there was a dramatic change in his demeanour. 'The result acted like magic,' Kirkwood wrote later. 'He sat up at once. All the lassitude and illness disappeared.' It was this sort of performance which caused some to feel uneasy and even Wheatley had misgivings, if Kirkwood is to be believed. Snowden, looking back later, was critical of Mac-Donald's 'passion for intrigue and compromise and his desire to be regarded as a "gentleman" by the other two parties.' J. H. Thomas too expressed his regret, though for rather different reasons, feeling that the whole affair had been an unmerited slight on Clynes. The question as to whether Labour made the right choice in 1922 is more than merely academic in view of MacDonald's later career and his ultimate 'betrayal' of the cause. Some of his critics subsequently claimed, rather unconvincingly, that they had seen all this coming long before it happened. In most cases this was only with the benefit of hindsight. Very few people at the time had misgivings in the same way as Beatrice Webb who, in her diary, had questioned the sincerity of MacDonald's commitment to socialism as far back as 1912. She had also recorded an alleged conversation with him in 1920 in which, speaking of the party 'with angry contempt—he thought it might be better to make a new combination and "smash" the present Labour Party.' In fact, for all his undoubted faults—his conceit, his tendency to intrigue, his penchant for rather involved oratory—he was the only truly national figure Labour had with the necessary Parliamentary ability and the confidence of both trade union and socialist factions. Most would have agreed with Arthur Henderson who, according to his biographer felt 'MacDonald was the indispensable leader'.

The party that MacDonald now led was clearly in the position of second party in the state. The Liberals were still divided and while the

Asquithians had gained significantly, their rivals had taken a terrible hammering, losing over eighty seats with only Lloyd George amongst the leaders securing re-election. Both factions had done particularly badly when challenged by Labour in areas such as Wales, Scotland and the West Riding, previously regarded as Liberal strongholds. And even if the two groups were counted together, there were still only 117 Liberal MPs compared with 142 Labour, although their total vote of just over 4 million was not all that short of Labour's 4,241,383. Only one flaw marred this otherwise encouraging situation for Labour and, in its way, it was a minor tragedy: Arthur Henderson, whose hard work had done so much to make this success possible, failed to secure election.

When MacDonald began to exercise his powers in the new Parliament, the essential moderation of his policies soon became clear. He had always believed in the evolutionary nature of socialism, declaring on one occasion that the true socialist 'rejects everything of the nature of violent breaks and brand new systems.' Moreover, from a tactical point of view it made sense to sit and wait for the natural course of events to take Labour into power. Nor was he alone in this attitude: in 1923, Sidney Webb, speaking at the party conference, produced his spurious statistical argument that 'from the rising curve of Labour votes, it might be computed that the party would obtain a clear majority . . . somewhere about 1926.' The trouble was that the left wing did not see it this way at all and soon gave notice of its intention of stirring things up, whether MacDonald liked it or not. On the very day of his election as leader, the Glasgow ILP sent him a congratulatory telegram which closed with the ominous words, 'Labour can have no truck with tranquillity'. Moreover, the ILP, as always the standard-bearer of socialism, had at this time experienced something in the nature of a major revival: new leaders, in the shape of Clifford Allen, Fenner Brockway and Clement Attlee; an improved organisation with more money, more members and more branches; a revamped press with the *Labour Leader* becoming the *New Leader* under the capable editorship of H. N. Brailsford. In Parliament, its MPs, with the Clydesiders well to the fore, evinced a burning desire to fight the class war as fiercely as possible. Thus Kirkwood, in the debate on the King's speech in November 1922, complained of the government's incompetence and its failure to do anything, 'while my class are outside starving' and he warned, there would be 'no tranquillity as long as there are children starving in Scotland'. The following April a debate on ex-servicemen in the civil service led to considerable rowdiness culminating in some of the Labour members singing 'The Red Flag' and compelling the House to adjourn. Finally came the famous occasion on 28 June when Maxton, beside himself with emotion at the plans to cut down on child welfare schemes, attacked the government in the strongest possible terms. 'In the interests of economy they condemned hundreds of children to death, and I call it murder.' Tory protests at this 'unparliamentary language' then precipitated a full scale row on the floor of the House which lasted over an hour and ended with Maxton and three other Clydesiders being suspended for seven weeks. MacDonald might well claim to one of his acquaintances that 'he was bringing the wild socialist labour members to heel' but incidents such as this merely illustrated his impotence to carry out the threat.

In spite of his anger and his fear that these activities would do the party's prospects harm, in fact events now began to break Labour's way as the Conservatives seemed to commit something very near to political suicide. In May 1923, Bonar Law, already seriously ill with cancer of the throat, resigned and was replaced by Stanley Baldwin as prime minister. In October, Baldwin suddenly, and apparently without much attempt either to sound out his party or convert the country, declared himself in favour of a protectionist policy as the only solution to the country's economic problems. This decision made an election almost inevitable and Baldwin duly secured the dissolution of Parliament for 16 November with polling day fixed on 6 December. In addition to its usual platform of nationalisation and social reform, Labour fought the contest on the issue of free trade, claiming that Baldwin's policy was no permanent cure for unemployment. The Liberals too stood firm on Free Trade and this in fact enabled them to secure an admittedly somewhat uneasy reunion between their two factions. The results, when declared, hardly helped to resolve the overall situation. The Conservatives, though still the largest single party with 258 seats, had lost their control of the Commons. Labour had made a further marked gain in seats, now being 191 strong, though its total vote had not gone up by much. The Liberals, as a result of their rediscovered unity and some energetic campaigning, had regained some of the ground lost over the previous decade, returning 158 members. Thus, no one had an absolute majority and it was not at all clear what would emerge from this highly equivocal situation. Baldwin decided that he was justified in carrying on but the logic of the situation pointed in an altogether different direction. The election had, after all, been fought basically on the issue of free trade or protection and the two parties standing for the former had come out on top. The only possible solution was that Labour, as the larger, should take office with Liberal support and Asquith, in spite of sustained appeals to 'save the country from the horrors of Socialism', had already judged this to be the correct line to follow. Labour's own feelings on the matter were rather mixed. There were many, at all levels in the party, who were quite opposed, arguing that to take office without real power would merely end in complete discredit. MacDonald himself was dubious. Philip Snowden records that, at a private dinner party on 11 December held at the Webbs' and also attended by Henderson, Clynes and Thomas, the leader expressed his fears on the grounds of shortage of talent and the possibly disruptive tactics of the left. But, significantly, he concluded that, despite the difficulties, Labour must take office if the opportunity arose, otherwise its pretensions would never be taken seriously. The following day, at a meeting of the NEC this view was endorsed, though with the addition of the rider that there must be no 'compromising itself with any form of coalition'.

With Labour and the Liberals having reached their respective conclusions, the fall of Baldwin and the accession of the first Labour government were inevitable. On 8 January Parliament reassembled and within a fortnight the Conservatives had been beaten on an amendment to the King's speech by the combined opposition parties. Baldwin resigned on 22 January and on the same day MacDonald was summoned to the Palace to receive the commission to form a government. In spite of the fact that this had appeared an increasingly likely possibility for some time, the final outcome took everybody by surprise, not least the Labour members themselves. The reactions varied. Clynes was quite frankly awe-struck: 'As we stood waiting for His Majesty, amid the gold and crimson of the Palace, I could not help marvelling at the strange turn of fortune's wheel, which had brought MacDonald, the starveling clerk, Thomas, the engine driver, Henderson, the foundry labourer, and Clynes, the mill hand, to this pinnacle.' Others were more light-hearted, though still clearly taken aback. Beatrice Webb has described the atmosphere of hilarity which prevailed at a luncheon party of newly installed ministers and concluded, 'Altogether we were a jolly party—all laughing at the joke of Labour in office.' But it was perhaps George V who put it best, writing in his diary on the day MacDonald kissed hands: 'Today, twenty-three years ago, dear Grandmama died. I wonder what she would have thought of a Labour government.' This simple, straightforward comment illuminates more vividly than pages of historical narrative, the achievement of the Labour Party in attaining office in less than a generation after its foundation.

PRINCIPAL EVENTS, 1914–24

1914. Initial Labour criticisms of government policy changed to support for the war by the German invasion of Belgium. Resignation of MacDonald as chairman of the PLP. Formation of the Union of Democratic Control

1915. Establishment of the Clyde Workers' Committee. Conclusion of the 'Treasury Agreements' on 'dilution' and the entry of Henderson and others into Asquith's reconstructed government. Strike of miners in South Wales. Death of Keir Hardie

1916. Passage of Conscription Acts in spite of Labour protests. Strike on Clydeside followed by the arrest and deportation of the leaders. Strike in the Sheffield engineering industry, followed by the 'trade cards' agreement which virtually gave the unions control of exemptions from military service. Labour agreed to support Lloyd George in his quest to form a new government and Henderson entered the inner war cabinet

1917. General strike in the engineering industry as a result of attempts to 'comb out' the factories. Henderson's resignation from the government over the Stockholm conference but Labour continued to support Lloyd George

1918. Henderson's new constitution and Sidney Webb's policy document both accepted by the party conference. Party decision to resume independent political action immediately after the armistice. The 'coupon' election: 59 MPs returned

1919. Industrial unrest on Clydeside culminated in the 'battle of George Square'. The reconstitution of the 'Triple Alliance'. Crisis in the coal industry: the Sankey's commission's report ignored by the government. Successful NUR strike action against an attempt to reduce railwaymen's wages. Formation of the 'hands off Russia' committee

1920. The *Jolly George* incident and threats of a general strike if the government persisted with its intervention policy in Russia

1921. 'Decontrol' of the coal industry followed by the miners' strike which the remainder of the 'Triple Alliance' refused to support ('black Friday')

1922.   General election: 142 MPs returned and MacDonald elected chairman and leader of the parliamentary party

1923.   General election: 191 MPs returned and Labour now the second strongest party

1924.   MacDonald invited to form the first Labour government after the fall of Stanley Baldwin

# Part IX
## Conclusion

The aim of this study has been to attempt to shed more light on two questions: why the Labour Party came into existence in the first place and how it came to establish itself in place of the Liberals as the alternative to the Conservatives. In a sense, the answer to the first question might simply be that the industrial revolution made its foundation inevitable. The creation of a new economic and social system which consigned a majority of the population to soulless exploitation at work and then compounded the offence by herding people together in, at the very least, drab living conditions, was bound to cause unrest and agitation which must sooner or later be expressed politically. In point of fact though, as the history of the nineteenth century shows, the process was not necessarily inevitable. Early attempts at political action such as those mounted by the Chartists were an abject failure and after that, the Victorian 'economic miracle' ensured a generation of political quiescence when the idea of 'self help' held sway generally amongst the working class. Not indeed until the 1880s are there signs of a really radical change taking place, and then a conjunction of circumstances convinced a significant and influential section of the working class that more forceful political action was both necessary and possible for the protection and advancement of their economic interests. Consequently the growth of the collective ideal and the emergence of the socialist societies struck a responsive chord. Admittedly it still took something like twenty years before the new party emerged as a coalition between the socialists and the trade unions who, after first treating the idea with considerable suspicion, were largely converted by what seemed a serious threat to their very existence. This was decisive: without the support of the unions the Labour Party as we know it could not have come into existence.

The question of the relationship of Labour with the Liberal Party is rather more complex. Until the 1880s at any rate the working class, or rather the politically aware minority of the working class, had found its natural home with the Liberals in spite of the efforts of socially conscious Conservatives like Disraeli. It is true that the relationship was rather one-sided. The Liberals were only too happy to claim working-class support, but were tardy in making any real concessions in return, in particular in the field of parliamentary representation. Nonetheless Lib–Labism was virtually unchallenged until the 1880s. The disillusion which then gradually developed was mainly due to a realisation that Liberalism had very little to offer. The much vaunted Newcastle Programme, for example, contained very little that appealed to organised labour, and there was the practical point that the Liberal Party was in the political wilderness for the last twenty years of the nineteenth century and therefore could offer nothing even had it wished. But the arrival of the Labour Party on the political scene in 1900 did not necessarily mean that the Liberals were henceforth doomed to decline. True, the 1906 election was something of a shock at the time and provoked some hysterical predictions, but careful examination of the party's history until the outbreak of the 1914–18 War makes clear the uncertain stability of the new organisation and its dubious future. It was so clearly a sectional group and equally clearly it was a client of Liberal patronage. At the grass roots its influence was restricted almost entirely to industrialised and/or urbanised regions and thus, outside London, it could command little support in England south of the Trent. Further, even in its chosen areas all was not plain sailing: the miners seemed unwilling to ratify the decision of their union to affiliate; Wales was not yet the vast 'pocket borough' it has become in latter days; Clydeside still was not 'red'. The fundamental dependence on the Liberal Party was even more striking. The electoral success of 1906 was only achieved as the result of the backstairs deal between MacDonald and Herbert Gladstone. Many Labour seats in fact were held by courtesy of the Liberals and the relative strength of the two was made abundantly plain by the unbroken run of Labour failures in three-cornered by-elections in the years immediately before 1914. Nor was the party's position in the House of Commons any more encouraging. At first its numbers were too small to make any more than a fleeting impression in the face of the big Liberal battalions returned in 1906. Then, after the two elections of 1910, it had to back the Liberals in whatever they chose to do, lest it bring about the even greater disaster of a Conservative government. The Liberals, as far as Labour was concerned, possessed the initiative all through the period 1906–14 and they even stole its thunder on the subject it claimed as its own: social reform. But perhaps the most startling evidence of Labour dependence was the Osborne Judgment which, had it not been reversed by the Liberal government, might have seen the party end almost before it had properly begun.

These early years were difficult in the extreme, for Labour was also weakened by internal feuding and doubts over the leadership. It was not surprising in the circumstances that some, the Webbs for example, came to express serious doubts as to whether the party could ever really be independent and not just exist, in Snowden's words, 'on the good-will of the Liberals in a number of constituencies'. But the next ten years were to see a rapid transformation as the Great War and its aftermath turned British politics upside down with Labour an un-doubted if not the chief beneficiary. True, the internal difficulties con-tinued: ILP pacifists clashed with patriotic trade union leaders during the war and industrial militancy both during and after the conflict made things awkward for the leadership. But in the long run none of this mattered. There was always, and continues to be, an element of shadow-boxing in the party's internal feuding and this at the time paled into insignificance as a new, more homogeneous, national organisation was welded together based on the greatly increased power of the trade union movement. Of equal importance was the final col-lapse of Liberalism, foreshadowed, some said, as early as 1910, but cer-tainly speeding up inexorably from 1916 onwards. By 1922 Labour had clearly replaced the Liberals as the second party in the state as the prelude to its assumption of the government following the election of 1923.

But one thing more needs to be said. Right from its inception and perhaps still even persisting to the present day, there has been in the labour movement a marked distrust of the concept of 'leadership'. The early pioneers felt that this was not really compatible with democracy, or rather what democracy ought to be. The result has been to play down the contribution of personalities in the emergence of the party, stressing rather the interplay of social and economic factors. This is unfortunate for it tends to obscure, to the outsider at any rate, the rich variety of the characters who played notable parts in the process. Of these, three stand out above the rest for their signal services to the cause: Hardie, MacDonald and Henderson.

In some respects, Hardie is not really an attractive figure. Even a friendly observer such as MacNeill Weir has described him as being 'downright and brutally honest' which is probably as kind a way as any of describing his lack of finesse and tact. In his dour inflexibility coupled with more than a tinge of a slightly priggish Puritanism, Hardie at times is quite repellent. Yet if he is not a man to be liked or loved, he is one to be admired and respected, if for nothing else for his passion and devotion to his cause and his ability to move others. Thus the testimony of Cunningham Graham who describes him campaigning in 1892, as 'a man in earnest . . . with aspirations and theories of a new life . . . moved by a strange inward something that makes his colour come and go, makes his hands clench, and sends you from the meeting with a choking in your throat, making the dirty streets look strangely different, and the feet step light, giving a sort of exultation.' It was this passion which also revealed itself in his emotional appeals in Parliament for the unemployed. His devotion moreover in the face of sometimes overwhelming difficulties was tremendous and secured its reward with the achievement, if only partial, of the 'great alliance' which brought the new party into existence in 1900. Of all men Keir Hardie most deserves the accolade of 'father of the Labour Party'.

With MacDonald we are dealing with a very different kind of political animal as MacNeill Weir once more makes apparent: 'Nothing could have been more definite than the contrast between . . . the pragmatical opportunism of MacDonald and the uncompromising socialism of Hardie.' Nor must we forget that in MacDonald we are dealing with the most controversial figure in the whole history of the labour movement whose fall from grace in 1931 still regrettably conceals his previous services. Certainly it is true that there were many unattractive features of his character which made themselves apparent from time to time. He seems to have been something of an intriguer, as is shown by the manoeuvres which attended his elevation to the party leadership on both occasions. He had a confidence in his abilities and his fitness for the position which bordered on arrogance and which Shinwell put down in part to his ancestry: 'The vision of his greatness was also displayed before him by his grandmother, a woman as proud as only a clanswoman who could trace pure descent from the romantic warriors of Skye could be.' His particular brand of 'evolutionary' socialism was too nebulous for some people and led to surprisingly early doubts as to the sincerity of his commitment. Shinwell thought that while he had had a difficult life 'his privations were insufficient to turn him into a revolutionary' and he seems to suggest that he had been deeply affected by hobnobbing with the Fabians 'who gave him a few entrancing glimpses of the comfortable life of the middle classes and an occasional one of the wealthy.' Shin-well also agreed with Hyndman's charge that 'personal ambition has been his one motive throughout.' But all this does not alter the fact that he performed certain essential services for the party. Thus, while subtlety and a penchant for intrigue and backstairs deals may be morally reprehensible, it was these very qualities which enabled him to conclude his electoral pact with Herbert Gladstone in 1903, without which the Labour Party might never have got off the ground. Of equal importance was his leadership in the two periods 1911–14 and after 1922. Whatever the means by which he achieved the position the fact remains that he was the only man who was acceptable to all sections of the party and, more important, was recognised as such by the outside world. It is not straining the facts too much to insist that MacDonald's leadership was one of the crucial factors which explain Labour's com-paratively rapid rise.

A much less equivocal assessment of Henderson can be made. The fact that he was known almost universally throughout the labour move-ment as 'Uncle Arthur' is indicative of the warmth and respect his character inspired in others. In complete contrast to MacDonald he tended to rate himself rather low and although holding the party leadership for some time during the First World War, he was convinced of his own unfitness for the position. His basic unselfishness in securing the return of MacDonald as soon as was humanly possible after the war, was in itself a signal contribution to the emergence of Labour. But he did more than that. Just as Joseph Chamberlain for the Liberals in the 1870s and Randolph Churchill for the Conservatives in the 1880s had created new and more efficient party machines, so Henderson did the same for the Labour Party after 1918. He took it and converted it from a largely sectional pressure group into a mass, national party that could, and did, quickly replace the Liberals.

To single out these three for special mention should not, however, be allowed to obscure the fact that there were others who contributed significantly. The journalistic talents of George Lansbury, the quiet determination of J. R. Clynes, the revivalist oratory of Philip Snowden and the intellectualising of Sidney Webb all played a part. Nor must one forget the workers at the grass roots, for this was where it all began, where elections were won and lost and where the efforts of local leaders like John Wheatley in Glasgow and Herbert Morrison in London proved crucial. It remained now to see what sort of structure would be built on the foundations these men had laid.

APPENDIX I

# List of Abbreviations

| | |
|---|---|
| ASE | Amalgamated Society of Engineers |
| ASRS | Amalgamated Society of Railway Servants |
| BSP | British Socialist Party |
| DMA | Durham Miners' Association |
| DORA | Defence of the Realm Act |
| ILP | Independent Labour Party |
| LCC | London County Council |
| LCMF | Lancashire and Cheshire Miners' Federation |
| LEA | Labour Electoral Association |
| LRC | Labour Representation Committee |
| LRL | Labour Representation League |
| LWMA | London Working-men's Association |
| MFGB | Miners' Federation of Great Britain |
| NEC | National Executive Committee of the Labour Party |
| NLF | National Liberal Federation |
| NMA | Northumberland Miners' Association |
| NUBSO | National Union of Boot and Shoe Operatives |
| NUR | National Union of Railwaymen |
| PLP | Parliamentary Labour Party |
| SDF | Social Democratic Federation |
| SWMF | South Wales Miners' Federation |
| SWRC | Scottish Workers' Representation Committee |
| TGWU | Transport and General Workers' Union |
| TUC | Trades Union Congress |
| UDC | Union of Democratic Control |
| UTFWA | United Textile Factory Workers' Association |
| YMA | Yorkshire Miners' Association |

APPENDIX II

# Labour Party membership statistics

| Date | Trade union membership | Socialist societies' membership | Number of constituency parties |
|---|---|---|---|
| 1900–1 | 353,070 | 22,861 | 7 |
| 1901–2 | 455,450 | 13,861 | 21 |
| 1902–3 | 847,315 | 13,835 | 49 |
| 1903–4 | 956,025 | 13,775 | 76 |
| 1904–5 | 855,270 | 14,730 | 73 |
| 1905–6 | 904,496 | 16,784 | 73 |
| 1906–7 | 975,182 | 20,885 | 83 |
| 1907 | 1,049,673 | 22,267 | 92 |
| 1908 | 1,127,035 | 27,465 | 133 |
| 1909 | 1,450,648 | 30,982 | 155 |
| 1910 | 1,394,403 | 31,377 | 148 |
| 1911 | 1,501,783 | 31,404 | 149 |
| 1912 | 1,858,178 | 31,237 | 146 |
| 1913 | No figures compiled due to Osborne case | 33,304 | 158 |
| 1914 | 1,572,391 | 33,230 | 179 |
| 1915 | 2,053,735 | 32,828 | 177 |
| 1916 | 2,170,782 | 42,190 | 199 |
| 1917 | 2,415,383 | 47,140 | 239 |
| 1918 | 2,960,409 | 52,720 | 389 |
| 1919 | 3,464,020 | 47,270 | 418 |
| 1920 | 4,317,537 | 42,270 | 492 |
| 1921 | 3,973,558 | 36,803 | 456 |
| 1922 | 3,279,276 | 31,760 | 482 |
| 1923 | 3,120,149 | 35,762 | 503 |

APPENDIX III

# Electoral statistics

A.  PERFORMANCE IN GENERAL ELECTIONS

| Year | Total votes | Number of candidates | MPs |
|------|-------------|----------------------|-----|
| 1900 | 63,304 | 15 | 2 |
| 1906 | 329,748 | 51 | 30 |
| 1910 (January) | 505,657 | 85 | 40 |
| 1910 (December) | 371,772 | 62 | 42 |
| 1918 | 2,385,472 | 388 | 59 |
| 1922 | 4,241,383 | 411 | 142 |
| 1923 | 4,438,508 | 422 | 191 |

B.  REGIONAL ANALYSIS OF GENERAL ELECTION RESULTS BEFORE 1914

|  | 1900 | 1906 | January 1910 | December 1910 |
|--|------|------|--------------|---------------|
| London | — | 2 | 1 | 3 |
| Southern England | — | 3 | 2 | 2 |
| Midlands | 1 | 2 | 8 | 8 |
| Northern England | — | 20 | 22 | 21 |
| Wales | 1 | 1 | 5 | 5 |
| Scotland | — | 2 | 2 | 3 |

APPENDIX IV

# Labour Party office holders

1. CHAIRMEN OF THE PARLIAMENTARY PARTY (after 1922 designated chairman and leader)

| | |
|---|---|
| 1906 | J. Keir Hardie |
| 1908 | A. Henderson |
| 1910 | G. Barnes |
| 1911 | J. Ramsay MacDonald |
| 1914 | A. Henderson |
| 1917 | W. Adamson |
| 1921 | J. R. Clynes |
| 1922 | J. Ramsay MacDonald |

2. CHIEF WHIPS IN THE HOUSE OF COMMONS

| | |
|---|---|
| 1906 | D. Shackleton<br>A. Henderson |
| 1907 | G. Roberts |
| 1914 | A. Henderson<br>F. Goldstone |
| 1916 | G. Roberts<br>J. Parker |
| 1919 | W. T. Wilson |
| 1920 | A. Henderson |

3. PARTY SECRETARIES

| | |
|---|---|
| 1900 | J. Ramsay MacDonald |
| 1912 | A. Henderson |

4. PARTY TREASURERS

| | |
|---|---|
| 1902 | F. Rogers |
| 1903 | A. Gee |
| 1904 | A. Henderson |
| 1912 | J. Ramsay MacDonald |

APPENDIX V

# Biographical notes

### Barnes, George Nicoll
1859–1940. Born in Scotland but of English parents and soon moved to England. Started work at eleven as a clerk in a jute mill. Later apprenticed as an engineer and worked in London. Became assistant secretary (1892) and later (1896) general secretary of the ASE. MP for Glasgow (Black-friars), 1906–22. Minister of pensions, 1916–17 then replaced Henderson in the war cabinet. Resigned from the Labour Party in 1918.

### Bevin, Ernest
1881–1951. Born in Somerset, orphaned and suffered great poverty in childhood. Began work as a farm boy at seven. Later moved to Bristol where he became a van driver. Active in trade union and socialist circles in Bristol and became a full-time official in the dockers' union in 1911. Largely responsible for bringing the Transport and General Workers' Union into existence in 1922. Later distinguished ministerial career in Churchill's government (1940–5) and as foreign secretary in Attlee's Labour government (1945–51).

### Blatchford, Robert Peel Glanville
1851–1943. Came from a theatrical family, and named after the Conservative prime minister. First apprenticed to a brush-maker but later was successively a soldier, clerk and journalist. Founded *Clarion* in 1891 and published *Merrie England* in 1894. Lost most of his influence when he supported the Boer War.

### Burns, John Elliot
1858–1943. Came from a very large family (sixteen surviving children) which the father seems to have deserted, leaving them in great poverty. Left school at ten and later apprenticed as an engineer. Active in trade union and SDF circles but quarrelled with the latter and became a Lib–Lab. MP for Battersea, 1892–1918 and president of the local government board, 1905–14 from which position he resigned on the outbreak of war and took no further part in public life.

### Clynes, John Robert
1869–1949. Born in Lancashire of Irish parentage. Had little formal education, beginning work in the mill at ten, but took private lessons. Active in trade union work and rose to president of the National Union of Gasworkers and General Labourers (1912–37). MP 1906–31 and 1935–45. Briefly chairman of the PLP. Held office in both MacDonald's Labour governments.

### Hardie, James Keir
1856–1915. Early childhood passed in extreme poverty. At ten, went into the pits as a 'trapper' after holding various other jobs. Became involved in

trade union organisation in the Lanarkshire coal-field and was dismissed as an agitator (1878). Then successively agent for the Lanarkshire miners and secretary of the Ayrshire miners' association. Originally a Liberal in politics but broke with them in 1888. Then moved to England where he was elected MP for West Ham (1892) and was later instrumental in forming the ILP. MP for Merthyr Tydfil, 1900–15. Chairman of the PLP 1906–8.

### Henderson, Arthur

1863–1935. Born in Scotland but family moved to north-east England when nine. Apprenticed as an iron-moulder. Active in trade union and local government affairs on Tyneside. Liberal agent for Sir Joseph Pease at Barnard Castle (1895–1903) then left the Liberals and won the seat for Labour. At various times from then on he held the positions of chief whip, parliamentary chairman, treasurer and secretary. Distinguished ministerial career took him into Lloyd George's war cabinet and he was later home secretary (1924) and foreign secretary (1929–31).

### Hyndman, Henry Mayers

1842–1921. Came from a wealthy middle-class family, and was a keen sportsman, widely travelled throughout the world. Engaged on some journalistic work (1871–80) before entering politics. Converted to Marxism and led the SDF from its foundation and also its successor the British Socialist Party. Broke his connections with it in 1916 as a result of his support for the war.

### Lansbury, George

1859–1940. Born in Suffolk but moved to the East End at an early age. Lower middle-class background, father a railway subcontractor. Spent a brief period (1884–5) in Australia and on return became a partner in his father-in-law's sawmill business in Whitechapel. Very prominent in local politics and once nick-named the 'John Bull of Poplar'. Founder (1912) and for a time (1919–23) active editor of the *Daily Herald*. MP Bow and Bromley, 1910–12 and 1922–40. Held office as first commissioner of public works, 1929–31 and led the party following the exit of MacDonald (1931–5).

### MacDonald, James Ramsay

1866–1937. Born illegitimate at Lossiemouth, Morayshire. Received a good education, continuing as a pupil teacher. Came to London where he eked out a precarious existence as a clerk and then a journalist. Marriage to Margaret Gladstone (1896) provided him with financial security. Briefly a member of the SDF but also had strong Liberal contacts which he maintained even after breaking with the party. Secretary of the Labour Representation Committee. MP 1906–18 (Leicester), 1922–9 (Aberavon), 1929–35 (Seaham Harbour). Chairman (leader) of the PLP, 1911–14 and 1922–31. Prime minister, 1924, 1929–31, 1931–5 (National Government).

### Mann, Thomas (Tom)

1856–1941. Born near Coventry. Began work in the mines at nine, later apprenticed as an engineer. Moved to London where he was active in union circles and also became a member of the SDF. First president of the dockers' union. Secretary of the ILP (1894–7). Spent some years (1902–10) in Australia and was prominent in the syndicalist movement on his return. The increasing radicalism of his later life is shown by his part in the foundation of the Communist Party in 1920.

### Morris, William

1834–96. Came from a comfortable middle-class background. Enjoyed a reputation as a poet and artist and was influential in the field of house decoration and furniture design. Became a member of the SDF but soon left to form the Socialist League. His utopian conception of Socialism was particularly well expressed in *The Dream of John Bull* (1888) and *News From Nowhere* (1891).

### Morrison, Herbert Stanley

1888–1965. Born in south London. Educated at elementary school and held a variety of jobs before becoming assistant newspaper circulation manager. Active in London politics and played an important part in establishing the London Labour Party, becoming its secretary in 1915. Leader of the LCC from 1934. MP 1923–4, 1929–31, 1935–59. Distinguished ministerial career: minister of transport, 1929–31; home secretary, 1940–5; deputy prime minister, 1945–51; foreign secretary, 1951. Created Lord Morrison of Lambeth, 1959.

### Shackleton, David James

1863–1938. Born in Accrington, the son of a watchmaker. Worked as a 'half-timer' in a weaving shed from the age of nine. Very active in trade union work. MP for Clitheroe, 1902–10. Vice-chairman of the PLP 1906–8. Chief whip, 1906. Resigned his seat in 1910 to become a civil servant, and was later involved in the administration of the 1911 National Insurance Act.

### Smillie, Robert

1857–1940. Born in Belfast, although of Scottish parentage. Orphaned at an early age and brought up by his grandmother. Ceased full-time education at nine though managed to continue on a part-time basis for three more years. Returned to Scotland where he settled in Lanarkshire and became a miner. Instrumental in organising the Scottish miners into one union. Also influential in the MFGB becoming president, 1912–21. Member of the 1919 Coal Commission. Ill-health from 1921 onwards caused a premature retirement from public life. Offered but refused a position in MacDonald's 1924 government.

### Snowden, Philip

1864–1937. Born near Keighley. Father a weaver and a strong Wesleyan. Avoided going into the mill by becoming a pupil teacher. Later was a clerk before securing entry into the civil service as an excise man. After being crippled as the result of a cycling accident in 1891, he spent more time in serious study and reading which led to his conversion to socialism.

Very active 1895–1905 in propaganda work for the ILP. MP 1906–18, 1922–31. Soon made a reputation as the party's financial expert and was chancellor of the exchequer in both MacDonald's Labour governments. Created Viscount Snowden in 1931.

### Thomas, James Henry

1874–1949. Born illegitimate and brought up by his grandmother in extreme poverty. Started work at nine and later became a railwayman. Active in ASRS affairs and also involved in local government work in Swindon. Assistant secretary of the ASRS (1910) and then of the new National Union of Railwaymen. Became secretary of NUR in 1917. MP from 1910 onwards. Colonial secretary 1924, lord privy seal 1929, dominions secretary 1930–35. Involvement in a budget leak in 1936 ended his public career.

### Thorne, William James (Will)

1857–1946. Born in Birmingham into a poor family. Father drank too much and was killed in a quarrel when Thorne was seven. Took various jobs, including navvying, until he became a gas-stoker, eventually moving to London. Joined the SDF, where it is supposed Eleanor Marx taught him to read and write. Very prominent leader of the 'new unionism'. MP for West Ham (South) 1906–45.

### Tillett, Benjamin

1860–1943. Born in Bristol into a large family. Ran away at eight and spent some time in the navy before becoming a tea-porter in the London docks. Was one of the leaders of the 1889 dock strike, and continued to play a prominent part in the affairs of the dockers' union. Member of TUC general council 1921–31. Served on the LCC. MP 1917–24 and 1929–31.

### Webb, Sidney

1859–1947. Lower middle-class background—father an accountant while mother ran a hairdressing business. Educated abroad and at the City of London college. Entered the civil service in 1878. Joined the Fabian Society in 1885 and contributed to the early tracts. Married Beatrice Potter in 1892, thus beginning a uniquely complete partnership in the field of historical literature. Largely responsible for the draft of the new party programme in 1918. MP 1922–9. President of the board of trade, 1924; dominions, then colonial secretary, 1929–31. Created Baron Passfield, 1929.

### Wheatley, John

1869–1930. Born in County Waterford but moved to Scotland (Lanarkshire) at the age of nine. Family was large and lived in very cramped and poverty-stricken conditions. Left school at eleven and joined father in the mines. Managed to set up in business in his mid-twenties and eventually established a fairly prosperous publishing concern. Soon took a leading part in west of Scotland Labour politics, sitting first on the Lanarkshire County Council and then the Glasgow City Council. MP from 1922, and minister of health in MacDonald's first government.

# Further Reading

For convenience the works below are listed in five sections. (1) General background and events until 1880. (2) 1880–1900. (3) 1900–14. (4) Local developments. (5) 1914–24.

(1) There are two very stimulating introductory essays: Asa Briggs 'The Language of Class in Early Nineteenth Century England' in *Essays in Labour History*, Volume 1 ed. A. Briggs and J. Saville (Macmillan 1960), and E. J. Hobsbawm 'Labour Traditions' in the author's own collection *Labouring Men: Studies in the History of Labour* (Weidenfeld and Nicolson, 1964).

The important aspects of the economic and social scene are dealt with in a number of books. E. J. Hobsbawm provides a crisp general survey from a left wing viewpoint in *Industry and Empire* (Weidenfeld and Nicolson, 1968; Penguin, 1969). W. Ashworth *Economic History of Modern England 1870–1939* (Methuen 1960) and J. H. Clapham *An Economic History of Modern Britain*, Volumes II and III (Cambridge University Press, 1932, 1938) are progressively more detailed. E. H. Phelps Brown has particularly useful sections on living and working conditions in *The Growth of British Industrial Relations* (Macmillan, 1959).

On intellectual cross-currents, the views of the writers of the 1820s and the theorists of the Chartist movement are summarised in G. D. H. Cole *A History of Socialist Thought* Volume I (Macmillan 1952). The competing trends of religion and secularism are examined by Edward Royle in *Radical Politics 1790–1900: Religion and Unbelief* (Longmans, 1971) while Henry Pelling considers 'Popular Attitudes to Religion' in *Popular Politics and Society in Late Victorian Britain* (Macmillan, 1969). This collection also contains an essay on social attitudes 'The Working Class and the Origins of the Welfare State' and Eric Midwinter looks at the same question from a wider view in *Victorian Social Reform* (Longmans, 1968).

The narrative of working class political activities before 1880 may be followed to some extent in two surveys by G. D. H. Cole: *British Working Class Politics, 1832–1914* (Routledge and Kegan Paul, 1941) and *A Short History of the British Working Class Movement* (Allen and Unwin, 1948). On the early 19th century there is E. P. Thompson's influential *The Making of the English Working Class* (Gollancz, 1963; Penguin, 1968) while the extensive literature on Chartism is probably best approached through

F. C. Mather's Historical Association pamphlet (General Series, Number 61). The final twenty years of the period have been well worked over recently, particularly by R. Harrison *Before the Socialists: studies in Labour and Politics, 1861–1881* (Routledge and Kegan Paul, 1965) and by a number of contributors to Briggs and Saville (above). The part played by the trade unions is covered in Henry Pelling *A History of British Trade Unionism* (Penguin, 1963, 1971) and there is a useful collection of documents in G. D. H. Cole and A. W. Filson *British Working Class Movements 1789–1875* (Macmillan, 1951).

(2) The best single volume treatment of the period 1880–1900 is Henry Pelling *The Origins of the Labour Party* (Oxford University Press, 1965). For the political framework within which new working class initiatives were being taken, reference should be made to two well tried works, R. C. K. Ensor, *England, 1870–1914* (Oxford University Press, 1936) and E. Halevy, *Imperialism and the Rise of Labour, 1895–1905* (Benn, 1961).
The activities of the separate Socialist societies are surveyed in a number of books. C. Tsuzuki considers the SDF along with the career of his subject *H. M. Hyndman and British Socialism* (Oxford University Press, 1961). John Bowle has a short section on the ideas and significance of William Morris in *Politics and Opinion in the Nineteenth Century* (Jonathan Cape, 1954) while there is a limited selection from Morris's own writings in C. Harvie, G. Martin and A. Scharf (eds) *Industrialisation and Culture 1830–1914* (Macmillan/Open University, 1970). A good deal has been written on the Fabians: M. I. Cole, *The Story of Fabian Socialism* (Heinemann, 1961) is probably the most convenient favourable account, while A. M. McBriar *Fabian Socialism and English Politics, 1884–1914* (Cambridge University Press, 1962) is rather more critical.
The vitally important subject of the ILP is best approached through a number of biographical studies: E. P. Thompson 'Homage to Tom Maguire' in Briggs and Saville (see above), L. Thompson, *The Enthusiasts: A Biography of John and Katherine Bruce Glasier* (Gollancz, 1971) and, above all, K. O. Morgan *Keir Hardie: Radical and Socialist* (Weidenfeld, 1975). This last work is the first adequate political study of the key figure in Labour's early years and brings out particularly 'the nature of Hardie's unique fusion of late nineteenth century radicalism and socialism'.
The equally essential contribution from trade unionism is well summarised in Pelling's volume on the subject (see above) but this should be supplemented by the more detailed treatment provided by H. Clegg, A Fox and A. F. Thompson *A History of British Trade Unions from 1889*, Volume 1 1889–1910 (Oxford University Press, 1964).
Finally attention may be drawn to a short collection of documents which touches not only on these years but the whole period up to 1924: G. R. Smith *The Rise of the Labour Party in Great Britain* (Edward Arnold, 1969).

(3) There is not a great deal readily available on this period. A good introduction is to be found in Henry Pelling *A Short History of the Labour Party*

(Macmillan, 1961) and the history of the LRC is treated in detail in Frank Bealey and Henry Pelling *Labour and Politics, 1900–1906* (Macmillan, 1958). Thereafter further details may be acquired by reference to the very thorough general survey E. Halevy *The Role of Democracy 1905–14* (Benn, 1961) and also to R. T. McKenzie *British Political Parties* (Heinemann, 1963).

Some specific issues have however been well documented. The conversion of the miners to Labour is the subject of R. Gregory *The Miners and British Politics, 1906–14* (Oxford University Press, 1968) and the general relationship between the party and the unions continues to receive treatment in the volumes by Pelling and Clegg, Fox and Thompson (see above).

The party's share in the formation of social policy may be gleaned from a general account, M. Bruce, *The Coming of the Welfare State* (Batsford, 1966) and, more specifically K. D. Brown *Labour and Unemployment, 1900–1914* (David and Charles, 1971). Ross McKibbin *The Evolution of the Labour Party 1910–1924* (Oxford University Press, 1974) is much concerned with the developments of organisation at local and national levels but also considers the serious problem of relations with the Liberals.

(4) While some stress has been placed on the importance of events at the local level, it remains true that this is a relatively neglected field, probably due to the difficulty in finding sufficient sources on which to base extended studies. However, Labour's progress in the individual coal fields is well documented in Bealey and Pelling and Gregory (both works see above). Scotland is reasonably well served by W. H. Marwick *A Short History of Labour in Scotland* (W. and R. Chambers, 1968) and the opening chapters of R. K. Middlemas *The Clydesiders* (Hutchinson, 1965) while for Wales there is some information in K. O. Morgan *Wales in British Politics* (University of Wales, 1970). Without doubt the most comprehensive study of a specific area so far produced is Paul Thompson *Socialists, Liberals and Labour: the struggle for London, 1885–1914* (Routledge and Kegan Paul, 1967). Other sources which are helpful in tracing events at the 'grass roots' are Henry Pelling *Social Geography of British Elections, 1885–1910* (Macmillan, 1967) and the election statistics in appendix 1 of Cole's *Working Class Politics* (see above).

(5) For the final period Pelling's *Short History of the Labour Party* (see above) remains a good introduction. The most detailed account is to be found in G. D. H. Cole *A History of the Labour Party from 1914* (Routledge and Kegan Paul, 1948) which should be supplemented by McKibbin's work (see above). There is also a good deal to be gained from reference to three general surveys of the twentieth century: W. Medlicott *Contemporary England 1914–64* (Longmans, 1967), C. L. Mowat *Britain between the Wars, 1918–40* (Methuen, 1956) and A. J. P. Taylor *English History, 1914–45* (Oxford University Press, 1965).

On the war years it is worthwhile consulting A. H. Marwick *The Deluge* (Bodley Head, 1965), particularly for the account of the 'unofficial'

Labour movement in the country. C. F. Brand looks at the party's re-actions to the conflict in *British Labour's Rise to Power* (Stanford University Press, 1941) while A. J. P. Taylor has a chapter on E. D. Morel and the UDC in *The Trouble Makers* (Hamish Hamilton, 1957).

After the war, Maurice Cowling *The Impact of Labour 1920–24* (Cambridge University Press, 1971) provides an immense amount of detail considering specifically Labour's relations with the other parties. The decline of Liberalism figures largely in the story of the rise of Labour and this may be conveniently studied in an essay in Pelling's collection *Popular Politics* (see above) and Trevor Wilson *The Downfall of the Liberal Party* (Collins, 1966). On this subject George Dangerfield *The Strange Death of Liberal England* (Constable, 1935) should also be consulted since it advances the view that the decline started before 1914. Relations with the Communists may be traced in Brand's work (see above) and in Henry Pelling *The Communist Party* (Black, 1958). L. J. MacFarlane *The British Communist Party* (MacGibbon and Kee, 1966) is an interesting account by a well-informed observer.

Good biographical studies of Labour leaders are in short supply. The most readily available, up-to-date assessment of Ramsay MacDonald is by C. L. Mowat in A. Briggs and J. Saville (eds) *Essays in Labour History, 1886–1923*, Volume II (Macmillan, 1971). But, at the time of going to press, the long-awaited publication of David Marquand's *Ramsay Macdonald* (Cape, 1977) has been announced. Otherwise the following studies may be recommended: Mary Hamilton *Arthur Henderson* (Heinemann, 1938), Colin Cross *Philip Snowden* (Barrie and Jenkins, 1966) and, although it is concerned with a trade union rather than a political leader, Alan Bullock *Life and Times of Ernest Bevin*, Volume I (Heinemann, 1960). Philip Snowden *Autobiography* (Nicholson and Watson, 1934) and Beatrice Webb *Diary 1912–24* (Longmans, 1952) reveal a good deal about their authors as well as providing interesting, if not always reliable, information. J. M. Bellamy and J. Saville, *Dictionary of Labour Biography* (Macmillan, 1972, 1974, 1977) is, as the title suggests, a valuable work of reference.

# Index